The Tabernacling
Presence of God

The Tabernacling Presence of God

—— Mission and Gospel Witness ——

SUSAN MAXWELL BOOTH

Foreword by Michael W. Goheen

WIPF & STOCK · Eugene, Oregon

THE TABERNACLING PRESENCE OF GOD
Mission and Gospel Witness

Wipf & Stock
An Imprint of Wipf and Stock Publishers
199 W. 8th Ave., Suite 3
Eugene, OR 97401

www.wipfandstock.com

ISBN 13: 978-1-4982-0014-1

Manufactured in the U.S.A.   09/04/2015

To my husband, Steve Booth
With much love and gratitude

One thing I have asked from the LORD, that I shall seek:

That I may dwell in the house of the LORD all the days of my life,

To behold the beauty of the LORD

And to meditate in His temple.

For in the day of trouble He will conceal me in His tabernacle;

In the secret place of His tent He will hide me . . .

And I will offer in His tent sacrifices with shouts of joy;

I will sing, yes, I will sing praises to the LORD . . . .

When You said, "Seek My face," my heart said to You,

"Your face, O LORD, I shall seek."

PSALM 27:4–8, NASB

Contents

Foreword

A hermeneutic that takes mission seriously as a central theme in the story of the Bible has been gaining ground in missiological circles for over a half century. But until recently it has been relatively uncommon to see biblical scholarship take seriously those insights. Many biblical scholars have gone on about their business paying little attention to the work of their missiological colleagues, and even to increasing insights of significant members of their own guild, that mission is a central category in the Bible that needs to be taken seriously if our interpretation is to be faithful.

One of the primary reasons is that there is confusion about what the word "mission" means. For centuries the word signified intentional efforts on the part of the church to spread the Christian faith among unbelievers. This might mean evangelistic efforts at home but more often it referred to cross-cultural activities that establish a witnessing presence in places where there is none. There has been movement in the middle part of the twentieth century toward a more holistic understanding of mission that moves beyond evangelism and cross-cultural missions, and includes deeds of justice and mercy. But these too remain intentional activities on the part of the church beyond its walls to spread the gospel.

Massive changes in theological reflection on mission developed in the middle part of the twentieth century and culminated in the introduction of the *missio Dei* as a framework for mission. But these developments are often relatively unknown among biblical scholars. And as long as mission means intentional efforts at spreading the Christian faith by word or deed, certainly it will not commend itself as a central rubric for interpreting Scripture especially the Old Testament. It may be a very important task for the church to engage in or a leftover relic from past colonial times. But either way it hardly merits serious consideration for biblical hermeneutics.

But a new wind is blowing. I discern four signs of hope that are leading more biblical scholars to take mission seriously. The first are changes in the global church. On the one hand, the Western church is discovering that it is right in the middle of a missional setting in its own culture. On the other hand, there has been a decisive shift of gravity in the church to the global south. Together this has led to a growing consciousness of mission that has the potential to re-open our missional categories when reading the Bible. The second is a growing convergence on a new understanding of mission that stresses that it is not first of all the intentional activities of the church to spread good news. Rather it is the identity of God's people in the story as they are called to participate in God's mission to restore the creation. This understanding of mission can more readily offer a lens to read the whole canon. The third involves various changes taking place in biblical studies from a new interest in a theological interpretation to the growing understanding from philosophical hermeneutics that our horizon shapes what we see in Scripture to hermeneutical approaches like narrative and canonical criticism that take the message of the entire canon seriously. All of these are contributing to a missional reading of Scripture. The final hopeful sign is the growing contribution of biblical scholars, many of whom are quite significant figures in biblical studies, to the conversation. As they bring their expertise to bear on the subject, and as numbers grow, it illumines various aspects of the biblical story.

And so it is a cause for joy whenever another biblical scholar tackles their work with the recognition that mission is not a subsidiary theme in Scripture but central to its story. Susan Booth's book is just such a work. She addresses a major theme in the story of the Bible—the presence of God—and shows how closely this theme is woven together with the missional calling of God's people. The importance of this theme is expressed clearly in the words of Moses to God: "If your Presence does not go with us, do not send us up from here. . . . What else will distinguish me and your people from all the other people on the face of the earth?" (Exod 33:15–17, NIV).

There are three reasons I am thankful for this book and commend it to you. First, Susan attends carefully the narrative structure of Scripture as she works through this biblical theme. She does not fall prey to the atomistic approaches to Scripture that have flourished in the wake of the Enlightenment triumph of a scientist ideal of knowledge. Treating this theme in the context of the whole canon, as she does, demonstrates its importance and close connection to mission. Second, she sets this scriptural topic in the midst of her Canadian context. As a fellow Canadian I am appreciative of her analysis of our homeland but even more thankful that she doesn't drive a wedge between what the text meant in the past and what it means today.

This is truly the only way we can attend to God's address today. Finally, with pastoral sensitivity she works out the implications of God's presence for the mission of the church today. Her study does not conform to a theory-praxis dichotomy that presents the theoretical results of scholarship leaving it for the local congregation to figure out the implications. This kind of scholarship has been debilitating to the mission of the church as scholarship follows its own self-generated agenda marginalizing the church in the process. But Susan refuses that path and grapples with the contemporary significance of this biblical theme for the church today.

We are told where universal history is headed: the new heavens and the new earth will descend from heaven to fill the earth. Then a loud voice from the throne will announce, "Look! God's dwelling place is now among people, and he will dwell with them" (Rev 21:3, NIV). The church is called to be a preview of this great day so that those outside the covenant may get a glimpse and want to be part. We are to be a contrast community that lives deeply in the presence of God in a world devoid of any knowledge of God's presence. We are to be "Zechariah 8:23 people" who live so fully in the presence of God that others are compelled to say: "Let us go with you, because we have heard that God is with you." The picture that adorns the cover this book expresses this call: a broken church that transmits the light of God's presence in the darkness of a desacralized world. My prayer is that this book will play a role in equipping the church for precisely this task.

Michael W. Goheen
Lent 2015
Vancouver, British Columbia

Acknowledgments

To my wonderful husband, Steve, thank you for being my first reader and my most ardent supporter. Thank you even more for your unflagging encouragement, enduring patience, and wise counsel every step along the way. I could never have done this without you! I am forever grateful that the Lord gave us to each other.

To my sweet sons and daughter-in-love, Caleb, Robbie, and Robyn, thank you for your support and interest and prayers. To my dad, Bob Maxwell, I can never thank you enough for all you've done and for the godly example you and Mom set by teaching us to know the Lord. To the wonderful faculty, staff, and students of the Canadian Southern Baptist Seminary and College: thank you so much for your encouragement along the way. To Bruce Ashford and Alvin Reid of Southeastern Baptist Theological Seminary, thank you for your passion for the *missio Dei* and for the gospel. To Michael Goheen, thank you for graciously agreeing to write the foreword. To Rachel Neal, thank you for your patience and graphic–design expertise in developing the figures for the appendix. To Kevin McElheran, thank you for sharing your photograph and your story.

I have constantly felt the prayers of a host of family, friends, colleagues, and students. I am especially grateful for Sherri, for Frankie and Sue Rainey, for the Thursday morning prayer group, for faithful Christine, and of course, for my immediate family. You all share in this work because of your participation in prayer.

To the One who desires to tabernacle in the midst of his people, words simply fail; eternity alone will be sufficient for appropriate praise and thanksgiving for all that you are and all you have done. Lord, fill us with your presence and power for the sake of the gospel and for your glory until that day when we see you—face to face.

— 1 —

Introduction

IN THE EARLY WEEKS of 2015, the news reports that swept the globe featured sights and sounds from a series of shaky raw videos shot from the balconies of Paris. The first video captured footage of two machine-gun-wielding terrorists on the street below, boasting that their massacre in the *Charlie Hebdo* offices had just avenged the cartoonists' blasphemy against Mohammed. A second video recorded a barrage of gun blasts as a black-clad police force stormed a kosher market, releasing terrified hostages, who then spilled onto the street across the way. Finally, a third video panned back and forth over an ocean of people inundating the boulevard beneath, one million strong, united in their stand against terrorism: "*Je suis Charlie!*" Ironically, the lyrics floating over this multitude were not in French but in English—accompanied by the familiar melody of John Lennon's song, "Imagine." The crowd below embraced the wistful ballad, some singing; some swaying; all bursting into applause as the notes faded away.

And no wonder. In a world rocked by terror in the name of religious extremism, "Imagine" seems to embody the world's yearning for peace. The song's message is simple: Imagine a world without religion or life after death, without national borders or personal property. Lennon dreamed that if the world had nothing worth slaying or dying for, then all would live in harmony. Sadly, the brilliant musician who penned "Imagine" died thirty-five years ago—gunned down on the street for no reason at all.

In some ways the West has adopted "Imagine"—one of the most popular songs of all time—as its theme song. The secularism that took root in

Europe now flourishes in North America where the fastest growing religion is the category of "No Religion." Religious affiliation and church attendance have dropped dramatically, particularly in Canada, which at one time had a higher percentage of church attendance than the United States. In the past few decades, however, Canadians have outpaced the Americans, abandoning religious services in droves. Whereas weekly worship attendance in 1950 stood at 60 percent, by 2010 it had declined to 19 percent.[1] Evidently, many have found it rather easy to imagine there is no religion.

The concept of there being a God above, however, is a bit harder to un-imagine. In spite of sundering formal ties to religious institutions, Canadians have continued to evince a strong interest in spirituality. Interestingly, the 2010 ISSP Religious Survey reports that while most Canadians believe God exists, the great majority express uncertainty about whether or not they can know for sure. Additionally, most respondents affirmed that they have their own way of connecting with God.[2] Likewise, even though most seem to live only for the present, the question of life after death remains rather difficult to erase. Canadian sociologist and researcher Reginald Bibby reports that more than 90 percent of Canadians—regardless of age—say they have wondered about life after death. Their musings on what it might actually look like are all over the map.[3]

Although Canada has not imagined away its national borders as verbalized in Lennon's poetic lyrics, the country has taken huge strides toward becoming a "multicultural mosaic." In 1971—the same year that Lennon wrote "Imagine"—Canada became the first nation to adopt an official policy of multiculturalism. As a result of Canada's immigration policies, the 2011 census data report the results of this intentional trajectory: the percentage of foreign-born population now represents one in five Canadians, "the highest proportion among the G8 countries."[4] Cultural pluralism has become a hallmark of Canadian society.

There are indications, however, that Canadian buy-in to a "mosaic" society rather than a "melting pot" has reversed in recent years.[5] While the majority of Canadians still believe that the nation has benefited from multiculturalism, they are equally divided on whether or not immigration

1. Bibby, *A New Day*, 4, 9.

2. International Social Survey Programme, "Religion III," n.p.

3. Bibby, *Beyond the Gods*, 174.

4. Statistics Canada, "2011 National Household Survey," 1.

5. According to Reimer, "Does Religion Matter," 110, support for the "mosaic" vs. "melting pot" was 50% vs. 31%, respectively, in 2005. Conseco, "Canadians Are Divided," n.p., reports that the numbers stood at 30% vs. 58% in 2012. In less than a decade, the percentages have essentially reversed.

has had a positive or negative impact.[6] Bibby marshals mounds of evidence, statistical and anecdotal, that support his argument that the "range and elasticity of Canada's mosaic is being severely tested in the case of religion."[7] Although half of Canadians fall in the middle ground that is ambivalent toward religion, the quarter that tenaciously hold on to faith meet fairly hostile criticism from the equally entrenched quarter that have rejected it outright. Canada is thus exhibiting an increasing polarization. Apparently brotherhood is easier to imagine than to achieve.

Perhaps one last reason the song "Imagine" still resonates today is that it seems to embody the philosophical trends that have developed over the past few decades. For example, as a result of multiculturalism, Canada has gradually shifted from a simple demographic pluralism to a philosophical pluralism. The relationship is fairly simple: "Pluralism establishes choices; relativism declares the choices valid."[8] In a culture steeped in philosophical pluralism, tolerance becomes the highest virtue; intolerance, the worst vice. This same time period has also witnessed the rise of postmodernism, a cultural phenomenon that embodies an intellectual mood and cultural expressions that are a radical break from the previous era of modernity.[9] In essence, postmodernism rejects the existence of a transcendent center of reality; consequently, it rejects the idea of objective truth and a unified grand narrative.[10] By imagining there is no transcendent center of reality, one is free simply to imagine his or her own truth and narrative.

In light of all the above, just imagine attempting to share the truth of the gospel in a cultural setting that is suspicious of religion, spiritually confused, pluralistic, postmodern, and increasingly polarized. It certainly presents a challenge! But if the vast majority are no longer looking to the church for answers, believers must learn to adapt their gospel witness to reach those immersed in this particular culture. Sharing one's faith is not always welcome in Canada where politeness is just as much a hallmark of the country as is diversity. Some think it is un-Canadian even to talk about religion in a pluralistic society. Not surprisingly, a recent survey of Protestant churchgoers suggests that Christians struggle more with sharing their faith than with any other aspect of discipleship.[11] Although 80 percent agreed that Christians have a responsibility to share their faith, a large majority

---

6. Conseco, "Canadians Are Divided," n.p.

7. Bibby, *Beyond the Gods*, 71.

8. Bibby, *Mosaic Madness*, 10.

9. Grenz, *A Primer on Postmodernism*, 13.

10. Ibid., 6.

11. Wilke, "Churchgoers Believe in Sharing Faith," n.p.

reported that they had not shared their faith in the last six months. Muffling one's witness is all too easy in a culture swept up in a tide of philosophical pluralism and postmodernism. There is a strong temptation to join the crowd, link arms and sway to the music, hold up a lighter and lip-sync the pensive lyrics—"Imagine."

But what if there *is* genuine truth and light to share? If so, then shutting your eyes tight, plugging your ears, and singing "Imagine" all the more loudly does not make absolute truth disappear. For all its haunting beauty, the song's idealism does not seem to have solved the problems of the world.[12] Simply imagining a better world does not seem to be working. What if there is more to this world than just people and place? What if there is something more than sky above us? What if the proliferation of religions indicates not just learned behavior but an innate need to worship? What if the difficult-to-eradicate longing for an Other to worship is a clue that such a One exists? What if our aching yearnings for peace and beauty harken back to a time when everything was good? What if our collective horror and moral outrage over innocent bloodshed reveals a deep brokenness in this world? What if our desire to fix it indicates the desperate need for a rescue mission? What if our seemingly unachievable longing for multicultural unity anticipates a day when things will be made right—where everything will be restored? And what if the nearly universal desire for life after death corresponds to a reality planted in hearts long ago? Maybe all of these unmet cravings for meaning and purpose point to a backstory that makes sense of all this after all. If such a narrative exists, it deserves a hearing, and those who know and live this story have an obligation to share its message of hope.

The narrative of the Bible is in fact just such a story. It teaches us that God is not only above us; he is also near each one of us. His purpose from the beginning has been to dwell—or tabernacle—in the midst of the people he has created. The Bible also proclaims that just such a rescue mission is already underway. Christopher Wright has, in fact, suggested that a missional hermeneutic is the key to unlocking the grand narrative of Scripture.[13] This study therefore traces the theme of God's tabernacling presence across the whole of Scripture, reading the story afresh through a missional lens in order to gain insights for mission and gospel witness.

12. Goheen, *Light to the Nations*, 3, observes that although the youthful counter-culture of Lennon's day failed to achieve the ideal world described in "Imagine," the church is the one community that can and should "embody [God's] work of healing in the midst of human history."

13. Wright, *Mission of God*, 51.

THE TABERNACLING PRESENCE OF GOD

Before defining the "tabernacling presence of God" as this book employs the phrase, it may be helpful to survey the biblical teaching on the divine presence. The biblical teaching on this subject suggests that there are three different degrees of the presence of God: 1) the extensive or general presence of God; 2) the intensive or special presence of God; and 3) the unique, full, and particular presence of God found only in Jesus.[14] Although the Bible assumes the general presence of God, the emphasis of Scripture is on the realization of his special presence.[15]

Scripture clearly teaches that God is omnipresent, transcendent, and immanent. The psalmist, for example, declares that there was no place he could go where God was not (Ps 139:5, 7–8). Isaiah affirms both the Lord's transcendence and immanence in the same verse: "For thus says the One who is high and lifted up, who inhabits eternity, whose name is Holy: 'I dwell in the high and holy place, and also with him who is of a contrite and lowly spirit, to revive the spirit of the lowly, and to revive the heart of the contrite'" (Isa 57:15). Solomon likewise acknowledged the surpassing transcendence of God at the dedication of his magnificent temple. He prayed, "But will God indeed dwell on the earth? Behold, heaven and the highest heaven cannot contain you; how much less this house that I have built!" (1 Kgs 8:27; cf. Isa 66:1–2). The idea that Almighty God, Maker of heaven and earth, could be confined to a dwelling place on earth is therefore impossible. The Lord, however, graciously condescended to manifest his glorious presence among his people in "a variety of terrestrial shrines . . . regarded as sacred points of contact between the 'God of glory and His creation.'"[16] These sacred points of contact are the essence of God's *tabernacling presence*.

Although no man-made structure can house his majesty, God himself initiated the construction of the tabernacle in Exod 25:8–9: "And let them make me a *sanctuary*, that I may dwell in their midst. Exactly as I show you concerning the pattern of the *tabernacle*, and of all its furniture, so you shall make it" (italics added). This passage illustrates how the tabernacle, in some sense, "dovetails" the two ideas of God's transcendence and immanence.[17] The most common word for the tabernacle complex—*miqdāš*, translated

---

14. Garrett, *Systematic Theology*, 201–2. Alternative concepts of the presence of God that are not biblical include the "divine spark" within human beings and the philosophical conception of omnipresence that is a neutral, spatial distribution of God that leans toward pantheism and panentheism (ibid.).

15. Bromiley, "Presence," 952.

16. Lioy, *Axis of Glory*, 38.

17. Hamilton, "שָׁכַן (*shākan*)," 1:925.

as "sanctuary" or "holy place"—expresses the holiness and transcendence of God. In contrast, this first occurrence of "tabernacle"—*miškān*, from the verb *škn* "to dwell"—emphasizes the presence and immanence of the Lord.[18] In this "text [that] binds the transcendence of God together with his immanence," the Lord of heaven and earth announces his astounding plan to pitch his tent in the midst of his people.[19]

The portable tabernacle is a particularly apt metaphor for the presence of God because it encompasses both God's local presence as well as his accompanying presence.[20] Later, when David expressed concern that the ark of God remained in a tent, the Lord's reply revealed his own missional priorities. God did not need for David to build him a house that endures (i.e., a temple); instead, he himself would build an enduring house (through royal offspring) for David (2 Sam 7:1–16). Even after the construction of the temple, the metaphor of God's tabernacling presence continues to surface (e.g., Isa 4:5–6, Ezek 11:16). A cursory survey of the canon reveals that the tabernacling presence of God is a major Old Testament theme that functions as a "highway" leading to the person and work of Christ.[21] This same theme of God's tabernacling presence continues to reverberate throughout the New Testament, as well (e.g., John 1:14; Heb 8–10; Rev 7:15; 21:3).

Although this study could trace the same material across the canon under the heading of a "temple motif," the "tabernacling presence of God" phrase seems to capture the intimacy of a holy God's expressed desire to dwell in the midst of his people. This study thus defines the tabernacling presence as the special, relational presence of God in the nexus of people and place.

As the following chapter will demonstrate, in some sense the divine mission stems from God's original purpose to create 1) a people in his image who reflect his glory, and 2) a world that functions as a sanctuary where he might dwell in communion with them. With the tragic advent of sin and its devastating consequences, this same purpose takes on a redemptive focus. Now, the *missio Dei* is to redeem and restore both people and place. In other words, the mission of God lies in the nexus of his tabernacling presence, people, and place. As Ryan Lister has pointed out, the presence of God in the midst of his people is both the means and the end goal of mission.[22] Thus, as this study traces the chronological succession of the various

18. Averbeck, "Tabernacle," 1:809.

19. Ibid.

20. Adams, "The Present God," 288.

21. Greidanus, *Preaching Christ from the Old Testament*, 267.

22. Lister, "'The Lord Your God.'"

sanctuaries where God interacts with his people, it essentially follows the contours of the unfolding mission of God.

THE PLAN OF THIS BOOK

An examination of this longitudinal theme generates practical suggestions for sharing the good news of Christ in Canada. Although religious decline has not been as steep in the United States, Canada's neighbor to the south appears to be on a similar trajectory. While 46 percent of Americans say they attend religious services at least once a month (as opposed to 27% of Canadians), the percentage who claim no religious affiliation has increased five percentage points in the last five years to 20 percent (24% in Canada).[23] Many of the thoughts shared in this book will therefore be relevant for believers south of the forty-ninth parallel as well. Perhaps missional strategies being developed and implemented in Canada may have an even bigger impact in the United States where the culture has not yet become as entrenched in its rejection of Christ. Undoubtedly, the missional dimensions of the tabernacling presence of God have significant implications for mission and gospel witness beyond the borders of Canada.

The framework of this book is essentially a triangulation of 1) the missional dimensions of the tabernacling presence of God across the canon, 2) a description of the current Canadian cultural context, and 3) a practical reflection that suggests insights for effectively communicating the truths of the gospel in a way that is biblically faithful. The purpose of this integrated, cross-disciplinary study is to develop a practice of evangelism that is both theologically grounded and contextually relevant. My hope is that this book will help Christians awaken wide-eyed to the wonder of God's tabernacling presence; that we will live in such a way that others exclaim, "God really is among you!"; and that we will boldly and joyfully share Jesus and his glorious gospel under the direction and power of his indwelling Spirit.

After an introduction to the topic in chapter 1, the first section of the book follows the theme of God's tabernacling presence from Genesis to Revelation. This motif is so central to the overarching biblical narrative that a host of sanctuary passages present themselves as possibilities for examination. The scope of this book, however, limits the number to select Old Testament and New Testament texts that are pivotal to the unfolding mission of God.

Chapters 2 and 3 trace the tabernacling presence of God through the first two divisions of the Hebrew Bible: the Law and the Prophets. Although

23. "Canada's Changing Religious Landscape," n.p.

the third division, the Writings—particularly the Psalms—are a rich source for imagery and insight into the nature of God's tabernacling presence, space limitations do not allow for their inclusion except in passing. Instead, the focus will be on the chronological succession of the various sanctuaries where God meets with his people. Chapter 4 examines the tabernacling presence of God in the New Testament. In some sense the theme of God's tabernacling presence permeates the entire New Testament because God is uniquely present in Jesus, and the Spirit indwells the church. This chapter, however, will focus primarily on those passages that use tabernacle/temple/dwelling language and imagery.

In the middle section of the book, chapter 5 examines the current Canadian cultural context. The first part of the chapter describes the characteristics of Canada in broad brush strokes, highlighting basic themes that characterize the nation as a whole. The second part narrows in focus to ethnographic interviews with a cross-generational sampling of individuals and concludes with a sample cultural exegesis of a specific Canadian cultural text—a music video by Avril Lavigne.

In the final section, chapter 6 is a practical reflection that synthesizes the missional dimensions drawn from Scripture with the Canadian cultural context for the purpose of uncovering insights for mission and gospel witness in this particular setting. Chapter 7 concludes the study with a summary of implications.

As Robert Martin-Achard has observed, there is an intricate relationship between mission, gospel witness, and the presence of God:

> [M]ission . . . is entirely dependent on the hidden activity of God within His Church, and is the fruit of a life really rooted in God. The evangelisation of the world is not primarily a matter of words or deeds: it is a matter of presence—*the presence of the People of God in the midst of mankind and the presence of God in the midst of His People.*[24]

After all, God is the source and author of mission. His presence indwells, compels, guides, and empowers the witness. His Spirit encounters, convicts, regenerates, and transforms sinners. In short, the tabernacling presence of God is both the means and the ultimate goal of God's redemptive mission. One day, both the redeemed people of God and his restored creation will be a sanctuary filled to the brim with the presence of God: "For the earth will be filled with the knowledge of the glory of the LORD as the waters cover the sea" (Hab 2:14).

---

24. Martin-Achard, *Light to the Nations*, 79; italics original.

—— 2 ——

The Tabernacling Presence of God in the Books of the Law

A STUDY OF THE longitudinal theme of God's tabernacling presence reveals that the mission of God is to redeem 1) a people who will display his glory and 2) a place where he may dwell in their midst. Because this purpose has been God's intention from the dawn of creation, a study of God's mission must start there, at the beginning, in the first pages of the Bible. This chapter traces the tabernacling presence of God through the Pentateuch: from creation to the patriarchs, from the exodus to the nation of Israel standing on the banks of the Jordan River preparing to enter the land of promise. Along the way insights for the mission of God will naturally rise to the surface.

THE TABERNACLING PRESENCE OF GOD IN GENESIS

Creation and the Mission of God

The *missio Dei* lies in the nexus of God, people, and place, and the first time these three converge is in the opening chapters of Genesis. The Bible opens with a majestic pronouncement of the presence and activity of God: "In the beginning God created the heavens and the earth" (Gen 1:1). After all, this preexistent God is the primary actor in the biblical drama about to unfold; it is his story. Thus, the ensuing theocentric narrative reveals much about the character of this one true God whose omnipresence permeates everything that he has made. Genesis 1:2 continues by describing the Spirit of God as a tabernacling presence "hovering over the waters"—language that evokes the image of a protective mother eagle shielding her young. A parental presence, God was intimately involved, carefully overseeing every aspect of his creation.

God's first act of creation was to make a place. He spoke, and by royal decree, God created an ordered cosmos out of that which was formless and empty. The Creator separated and formed in the first three days; in the last three, he filled that which he had formed, pronouncing it "good" at every juncture. God thus created a place perfectly suited for human habitation, but it was also a world that was "designed to be filled, flooded, drenched in God . . . ."[1] Craig Bartholomew notes that the opening chapters of the Bible provide a theology of place: "Genesis 1 is universal in its scope, with a developing focus on the whole earth as humankind's home, whereas . . . Genesis 2–3 is place specific in its focus."[2] Yet it is God's gracious gift of himself—his own presence—as co-inhabitant of this garden that makes the idea of place such a rich theological concept. Bartholomew notes, "Place is never fully place without God as co-inhabitant."[3]

As the Creator-King, God has sovereign authority and ownership over all that he created—including humanity. After God had made a place suitable for humankind to dwell, he created its inhabitants. In an astounding act of condescension, ". . . the LORD God formed the [first] man from the dust of the ground and breathed into his nostrils the breath of life . . ." (Gen 2:7). God is also loving, gracious, and relational. Human beings are designed to live in relationship with God and to reflect his character. As Michael Goheen describes it, "the very core of human existence is religious. Human life is dependent on and oriented toward God."[4]

The creation account contains several missional dimensions. The Creator designed the heavens and earth and its inhabitants for his own purposes. Mission, therefore, flows from the identity of *this* God and *this* story in which he reveals himself. Yahweh is not a generic god; rather, "[t]his is the God worshiped as the Lord by the Israelites and as Father, Son and Holy Spirit by Christians."[5] The very existence of a creation narrative

1. Wright, *Surprised by Hope*, 102.

2. Bartholomew, *Where Mortals Dwell*, 23.

3. Ibid., 31.

4. Goheen and Bartholomew, *Living at the Crossroads*, 42.

5. Wright, *Mission of God*, 54. The Old Testament primarily uses two Hebrew words to refer to God. The first is *Elohim* or "God" in the generic sense, and it can refer to pagan gods as well. The second is *Yahweh*, the specific covenant name that God revealed

demonstrates God's intention to make himself known as the one true God. Even before sin entered the world, he is a God on mission, directing the trajectory of human history to his desired ends. From the beginning, the purpose of God has been to create a people and a sanctuary where he might dwell in communion with them. Significantly, the place God made was not simply a habitation for the people he created. His express purpose was to dwell there with them—in their midst. The first man and woman were designed to worship this Creator who graciously made a place for them and welcomed them into his tabernacling presence. Allen Ross observes that this is the goal of creation: "Communion with the living God is at the heart of all worship; and where God is present with his people is a sanctuary."[6] Actually, there is strong evidence that the garden of Eden was, in fact, the first sanctuary of God.

The Garden of Eden as Sanctuary

Naturally, many scholars begin their discussion of the theme of God's tabernacling presence with the construction of the tabernacle in Sinai recorded in Exodus. After all, this was the first time that God prescribed the building of a shrine for his presence to dwell in. Others, however, argue convincingly that the first sanctuary is found in these opening chapters of Genesis.[7] Although there is "no architectural structure" in the garden of Eden, it is the "place of God's presence,"[8] and "it has the character of a royal temple of God."[9]

    The literature of the ancient Near East reveals that Mesopotamian religions often depict a close connection between the cosmos and temple building. People of the ancient Near East considered temples to be primordial and often defined cosmic origins in terms of a temple element. In other

---

to Moses in Exodus 3. Most English versions translate *Yahweh* as "Lord," using capital letters in order to distinguish it from *Adonai* (another Hebrew name translated as "Lord," with small letters). Unfortunately, the similarity makes it easy for English readers to overlook the import of the name. *Yahweh* has considerable significance for this particular study because its meaning ("I AM") points to the presence of God. It also conveys a missional polemic in that it indicates the personal identity of the one true God as opposed to any false gods. In the OT section of this book, I therefore refer to the Deity as "God" and "Yahweh" (rather than "Lord") in order to underscore these nuances—except when quoting Scripture or other authors.

6. Ross, *Hope of Glory*, 82.

7. Beale, "Eden," 7.

8. Ibid.

9. Kline, *Images*, 20.

words, they understood the cosmos as a temple and therefore constructed temples as microcosms symbolic of the cosmos. Once a newly constructed temple was inaugurated, they believed a deity would take up residence or "rest" in the temple. Thus, in the vocabulary of an ancient Near Eastern worldview, the Genesis account tells of a God who creates the cosmos as his temple dwelling; on the seventh day he "rests and rules from his residence."[10]

The Genesis story, however, also countered the pagan conception that an enthroned deity would rule over humans who labor to meet his needs. The numerous gods of the ancient Near East had many requirements: the image of the god "had to be awakened in the morning, washed, clothed, fed two sumptuous meals each day (while music was played in its presence), and put to bed at night."[11] This daily care constituted worship, and it ensured the continued presence of the deity in the image. The worship of these false gods stands in stark contrast to the one sovereign, living God who has no needs and who created man in *his* image instead of the reverse. While devotees might seek to appease their gods in order to acquire protection, there was no hint of relationship or exaltation.[12] In contrast, the biblical account describes how God provided everything that humans might need; he commissioned them as his stewards and invited them into fellowship with him. Although the Genesis account may have prompted a comparison with the cosmic temple motif found in other religions, the sharp dissimilarity would have opposed the wrong conceptions held by Israel's neighbors. John Stek argues that a careful reading of Genesis 1 "against the background of the several myths of the ancient Near East discloses a view of God, humanity, and world that, whatever its more or less incidental affinities with conceptions abroad in Israel's environment, stands in striking opposition to almost all that those religions had in common."[13] In fact, the entire creation account in some sense serves as a missional polemic. It lays bare the conflicting ideas—not by contentious dispute, but in a deliberate narration of creation by the One who rules over everything.

The case for the concept of Eden as a primordial temple finds additional support in the furnishings of the subsequent shrines of Israel that reflected this garden imagery.[14] For example, the tabernacle's gold lampstand bore flowerlike cups, buds, and blossoms extending from branches (Exod 25:31) and was likely a replica of the tree of life. The cedar paneling and doors

10. Walton, *Lost World*, 74.

11. Walton, *Ancient Near Eastern Thought*, 136.

12. Ibid., 161.

13. Stek, "What Says Scripture?," 231–32.

14. Beale, *The Temple*, 29–80.

of Solomon's temple boasted carvings of gourds, open flowers, and palm trees, while pomegranates and lilies adorned the pillars to the entrance of the holy place (1 Kgs 6:18, 29, 35; 7:18–20). Ezekiel's eschatological temple reverberates with garden imagery as well, as the life-giving river courses out from the sanctuary to flow past banks of trees that bear fruit for food and leaves for healing (Ezek 47:12). Finally, John's description of the New Jerusalem city-temple closely mirrors this imagery: "on either side of the river [flowing from the throne], the tree of life with its twelve kinds of fruit, yielding its fruit each month. The leaves of the tree were for the healing of the nations" (Rev 22:2). Thus the first sanctuary, the garden of Eden, serves as an archetypal pattern for all the succeeding worship centers of Israel. In the beginning God created a place where he might dwell with the people whom he made in his image.

People in the Image of God

Scholars have long debated the precise nature of the *imago Dei*. Richard Middleton observes that over the last century, exegesis of the broader context of Gen 1:1—2:3 has led to a virtual consensus of a functional interpretation of the *imago Dei* as mediation of power.[15] This interpretation is strengthened by comparative studies of ancient Near Eastern texts "in which kings (or sometimes priests) were designated the image or likeness of a particular god . . . [thus] representing the deity in question."[16] Middleton calls Genesis 1–11 "intentionally subversive literature" that stands in sharp contrast: the *imago Dei* is not reserved only for the king or priest, but rather this royal office characterizes and gives dignity to all of humanity. Astoundingly, all human beings—both male and female—are "granted authorized power to share in God's rule or administration of the earth's resources and creatures."[17] Middleton notes that this polemical interpretation of the image of God is not only functional, but also missional.

Richard De Ridder explains that the Genesis teaching on creation and the *imago Dei* is foundational to missions, noting that it forms the basis of Paul's apologetic message to the Athenians in Acts 17:24–28:

> The God who made the world and everything in it, being Lord
> of heaven and earth, does not live in temples made by man, nor
> is he served by human hands, as though he needed anything,

15. Middleton, *Liberating Image*, 25.
16. Ibid., 27.
17. Ibid.

since he himself gives to all mankind life and breath and everything. And he made from one man every nation of mankind
to live on all the face of the earth, having determined allotted
periods and the boundaries of their dwelling place, that they
should seek God, and perhaps feel their way toward him and
find him. Yet he is actually not far from each one of us, for "In
him we live and move and have our being" as even some of your
own poets have said.[18]

Other examples of gospel witness among Gentiles in Acts also follow this
pattern of beginning with an appeal to the unity of the human race (e.g.,
Acts 10:34–35) and/or creation (Acts 14:15). The fact that God made humanity in his image and that every nation traces its lineage back to one man
has huge implications for mission. All people everywhere are created for the
purpose of being people who display God's glory by knowing and worshiping the One whose glorious presence permeates his creation.

The identification of the garden of Eden as a sanctuary is thus a significant clue for understanding the original intention God had for the people
he created. Other hints arise from the commands God gave Adam and Eve.
He blessed them and commissioned them: "Be fruitful and multiply and
fill the earth and subdue it . . ." (Gen 1:28). By procreation Adam and Eve
were to participate in God's mission to fill the earth with more worshipers
made in his image. The fact that God made both male and female in his
own image underscores the idea that people were made for fellowship, for
community.[19] The image of God rightly configured included an outward,
missional focus: relationship to the Holy Other and relationship to others.
The command to multiply indicates that God intended to create a people
who would corporately worship him as Creator. The previously discussed
command to rule supports the idea that the image makes man "God's vice-
regent on earth" with the commission "to rule nature as a benevolent king,
acting as God's representative over them and therefore treating them in the
same way as God who created them."[20] Of course, God himself would enable
this stewardship of all aspects of creation. He gave humans the capacity for
creating culture as well as the command to do so. This cultural mandate extends to "every dimension of human culture and across the fabric of human

18. De Ridder, *Discipling the Nations*, 22. De Ridder quotes only Acts 17:26, but
the surrounding verses quoted here are particularly enlightening for the theme of the
tabernacling presence. God does not need a temple in which to dwell, but humans, on
the other hand, "live and move and have our being"—in him.

19. Goheen and Bartholomew, *Living at the Crossroads*, 43.

20. Wenham, *Genesis 1–15*, 32–33.

existence."[21] Lucien Legrand believes that this grand, creative adventure—which includes "the arts, technology, science, justice, and peace"—should be considered mission in a broad sense.[22]

In addition to the above commands, Yahweh further reveals his purposes in Gen 2:15: "The LORD God took the man and *put* him in the garden of Eden to *work* it and *keep* it" (italics added). The word translated "put" (*wayyannihēhû*) is elsewhere reserved for either God's "rest" or the "dedication" of an object in God's presence. For example, Yahweh later commanded that the following be set aside in his presence in the tent of meeting or before the altar: a jar of manna (Exod 16:33–34); Aaron's linen garments (Lev 16:23); the tribal staffs (Num 17:4); and the basket of first fruits (Deut 26:4, 10). Similarly, God "put" the first man in the garden before his presence for the express purpose of fellowship with God (cf. Gen 3:8).[23] Although the words describing Adam's role as "to work . . . and keep" (respectively, *'ābad* and *šāmar*) have common secular meanings, elsewhere in the Old Testament they are translated as "to serve and guard" and refer most often to the priestly duties of serving God in the temple. Ross explains that in the context of religious settings, *'ābad* (meaning "to serve, do") may describe "spiritual service in general but also specific duties in the sanctuary." He also notes that in similar religious settings *šāmar* ("to keep, observe") refers to keeping the commandments or religious practices.[24] Suggesting "to worship and to obey" as a more appropriate translation, John Sailhamer concludes that God created man to serve as a priest in his presence.[25] God's purpose for the people he created in his image thus included a priestly role and a life characterized by worship and fellowship.

Because God's purposes for Eden extended beyond the borders of the garden, he commanded Adam and Eve not only to worship in this first sanctuary, but also to be fruitful and multiply, filling the world with worshipers who extend God's praise—and his sanctuary—to the ends of the earth. G. K. Beale observes, "God's ultimate goal in creation was to magnify his glory throughout the earth by means of his faithful image-bearers inhabiting the world in obedience to the divine mandate."[26] In fact, Beale christens Gen 1:28 as the "first 'Great Commission' that was repeatedly applied to

---

21. Ashford, *Theology and Practice*, 2.

22. Legrand, *Unity and Plurality*, 4.

23. Sailhamer, "Genesis," 44–45.

24. Ross, *Hope of Glory*, 55. Beale, *The Temple*, 68, points out that a command—not to eat of the tree of knowledge of good and evil—follows in the next verse.

25. Sailhamer, "Genesis," 45.

26. Beale, *The Temple*, 82.

humanity."[27] In a similar vein, Yahweh articulates this mission through his prophets: "For the earth will be filled with the knowledge of the glory of the LORD as the waters cover the sea" (Hab 2:14). This well-chosen simile of waters covering the sea—they not only fill the sea, they *are* the sea—vividly captures the magnificent scope of the ultimate fulfillment of this mission: "It looks as though God intends to flood the universe with himself, as though the universe, the entire cosmos, was designed as a receptacle for his love."[28] As humans praise Yahweh and proclaim his excellence in every place, they fulfill the purpose God intended for them. Mission, therefore, begins with worship.

Finally, one last bit of evidence for Eden as tabernacle surfaces in the wording of Gen 3:8, a verse which also hints at the intimate relationship the first couple might have enjoyed in the unmediated presence of God. The verse implies that God would "walk" in the garden in fellowship with Adam and Eve. Beale notes that later, "[t]he same Hebrew verbal form (hithpael), *hithallek* used for Yahweh's 'walking back and forth' in the Garden (Gen 3:8), also describes God's presence in the tabernacle."[29] The concept of a pedestrian God who makes himself accessible to his creatures suggests astounding possibilities for relationship. Walking in close fellowship with a holy God was an incredible blessing, but with it came a correspondingly awesome responsibility of reverent obedience. Tragically, the possibilities had already been dashed in the preceding verses. The first couple failed to fulfill God's intended purpose for their lives when they allowed sin to enter their world.

Expelled from the Unmediated Presence of God

Sadly, the first mention of God's walking in the garden is juxtaposed with the first humans' ineffectual attempt to hide from an omniscient God. Yahweh had given the couple only one restriction; he could deny them no less and still offer them freedom. Adam and Eve willfully chose to yield to the serpent's temptation and disobeyed God's command not to eat from the tree of knowledge of good and evil. The essence of the temptation was a desire to be like God—to determine for themselves what is right or wrong. And so, the couple grasped for equality with God, taking the place that only God deserved. Unfortunately, after the fall they knew *good* because they

27. Ibid., 117.

28. Wright, *Surprised by Hope*, 102.

29. Beale, "Eden," 7. Cf. Lev 26:12; Deut 23:14; 2 Sam 7:6–7.

had rejected it; they knew *evil* because they had experienced it.[30] Sin immediately resulted in alienation—from God and from each other. In this context the mere sound of Yahweh walking in the garden struck fear in their hearts, and they tried to hide from his presence. Nothing had changed in the character or nature of God, but humanity had changed. The fall had devastating consequences for both the people and place God had created. Yahweh pronounced judgment on the serpent and the human couple, and the ground was cursed because of them.

Adam and Eve failed to fulfill their commission and forfeited their priestly calling. Unclean, they could no longer remain in the sanctuary of the full presence of God.[31] "[T]herefore the Lord God sent him out from the garden of Eden to work the ground from which he was taken. He drove out the man, and at the east of the garden of Eden he placed the cherubim and a flaming sword that turned every way to guard the way to the tree of life" (Gen 3:23–24). Interestingly, the task of guarding/keeping (*šāmar*) the garden, which had formerly belonged to Adam (Gen 2:15), is stripped from him and given to the cherubim, leaving the man with the sole task of working/tilling (*'ābad*) the now recalcitrant ground.[32] Yahweh also placed the cherubim ("literally, 'caused to dwell,' from the verb root *škn*; cf. *miškān*, 'tabernacle'")[33] at the entrance of the garden where he had intended for Adam and Eve to dwell in his presence. Instead, the couple and their future progeny were barred from the tree of life. As a tragic consequence of sin, God drove them out of the garden, expelling them from his unmediated presence.

Bartholomew, in his rich theology of place, observes that "[h]uman identity is deeply bound up with place, and in Genesis 3 *displacement* is at the heart of God's judgment."[34] This judgment radically transforms humankind's relationship to the ground, and thus his experience of place. Undoubtedly, the displacement includes this alienation between man and the ground from which he would wrest a living, but even more damning is the alienation between humanity and God. Surely this is the ultimate displacement. This profound sense of "not-being-at-home"[35] reverberates through every generation since the fall. Gordon Wenham observes that the narrator views this expulsion from the presence of God as death, "the real fulfill-

---

30. Kidner, *Genesis*, 63.

31. Greidanus, *Preaching Christ from Genesis*, 83.

32. Middleton, *Liberating Image*, 59.

33. Averbeck, "Tabernacle," 817.

34. Bartholomew, *Where Mortals Dwell*, 29; italics original.

35. Ibid., 30.

ment of the divine sentence" mandated in Gen 2:17.[36] This tragic chapter in history bears solemn witness: from the beginning, access to the immediate presence of God is restricted to those who are without sin.

Although sin resulted in judgment and death just as God had said it would, there were still hints of hope and grace even in the immediate context of judgment. The first sign of grace was that God did not immediately snuff out the lives of the man and woman. Adam named his wife Eve, meaning "living" or "lifegiver," which the narrator interprets as "the mother of all living."[37] Second, Yahweh also provided adequate clothing to cover the sinners' shame, replacing the withering fig leaves with the more acceptable and lasting solution of animal skins. Obviously, an animal was killed in order to procure the skins. Marcus Dods observes, "From the first sin to the last, the track of the sinner is marked with blood."[38] This first recorded death in the Bible would certainly have brought home the severity of sin which results in death.

A final hint of grace is the promise found in Gen 3:15. As early as the third century BC, the Septuagint and Jewish Targums understood this verse to refer to the coming Messianic victory over Satan.[39] In the same vein, the early church fathers called the verse the *protoevangelium*, or "first gospel." Although the meaning of the verse remains a matter of debate, at the very least, Gen 3:15 raised the hope that although the serpent will remain a pernicious enemy, one day a descendant of Eve would gain the upper hand and deal the serpent a mortal blow.

With the advent of sin and the fall, God begins to reveal his rescue mission. From this point on, the Bible records the history of God's redemptive activity. Lister observes that the fall resulted in a change in both the functionality and the experience of the presence of God. Whereas before the fall humans had access to the unmediated relational presence of God, after the fall God's presence is redemptive and mediated. The goal of this redemptive activity is that in the eschatological new creation redeemed humanity will once again have access to the unmediated relational presence of God. That the story continues at all bears witness to the incredible grace of God. Lister explains, "God's purpose in drawing near to humanity after the Fall is to reconcile sinners to himself, and for those who reject the Gospel, God

36. Wenham, "Sanctuary Symbolism," 404.

37. Ross, *Creation and Blessing*, 148.

38. Dods, *Book of Genesis*, 25. Ross, *Creation and Blessing*, 150, explains that later, any priest of Israel reading this passage would have associated this exchange of the animals' lives for their skins with the sacrifices offered in exchange for human atonement.

39. Greidanus, *Preaching Christ from the Old Testament*, 248.

is also present to judge."[40] These two responses to the redemptive activity of God yield starkly contrasting results.

Two Responses, Two Results

Cain and Abel

In a warped distortion of God's mandate to fill the earth with worshipers, the ravages of sin spread like cancer as the number of humans multiplied. The initial glimpse of life outside the garden introduces the first couple's two sons, Cain and Abel, in the context of worship. The two brothers provide "archetypical representations of two kinds of people."[41] While Yahweh received the fat portions from the firstborn of Abel's flock, he rejected Cain's fruit of the ground either because of the quality of his gift or because of an underlying wrong attitude (Gen 4:4–5). Gerhard von Rad, however, argues that the real basis of God's preference was that "the sacrifice of blood was more pleasing to Yahweh."[42] It is intriguing that the first recorded act of worship that pleased God after the fall was the sacrifice of the firstborn from Abel's flock. Even though God did not look on Cain's offering with favor, he still held out the possibility for acceptance in Gen 4:7. But disregarding Yahweh's warning, Cain yielded to the wickedness crouching at his door and murdered his younger brother. Shockingly, the first recorded sin after the fall was fratricide. As judgment God cursed Cain, who "went away from the presence of the LORD" to live in the land of Nod or "wandering" (Gen 4:16). Bartholomew describes Cain's punishment as "permanent displacement."[43]

This account underscores the truth that the One who is worshiped sets the parameters for acceptable worship. Access to even the mediated presence of God was restricted to those who were properly related to God. Ross explains this same enduring principle in the context of a later period: "As unforgiven sinners they could not participate freely in sanctuary worship . . . but as confessing believers they would be restored to a proper relationship with God and able to enter his courts once again."[44] Although God still desired to fill the world with worshipers, it did not mean that any form of worship would suffice. In order for worshipers to be restored to a proper relationship with God, their sin must be covered in his prescribed way.

40. Lister, "Lord Your God," 38.
41. Ross, *Creation and Blessing*, 153.
42. Rad, *Genesis*, 101.
43. Bartholomew, *Where Mortals Dwell*, 33.
44. Ross, *Creation and Blessing*, 114.

The contrast between these two types continues with the juxtaposition of the godless line of Cain and the line of Seth, whose descendants "began to call upon the name of the Lord" (Gen 4:26). Ross translates this as they "began to make proclamation of the Lord by name."[45] He contends that their faithful worship was accompanied with a verbal witness to the character of God. But even most of Seth's lineage must have drifted away so that by Noah's day, the number of righteous had dwindled down to just one man and his family.

Noah and His Generation

The universal scope of sin resulted in universal judgment in the days of the flood. Still, even then, God faithfully preserved a remnant through his servant Noah. Genesis 6–9 recounts the wholesale judgment of Noah's day because "every intention of the thoughts of [the human] heart was only evil continually" (Gen 6:5). This wickedness was so pervasive that it filled Yahweh's heart with pain and called for drastic measures. Ross points out that the verb *māḥâ* literally means "to blot out," resulting in "a complete removal of one thing from another."[46] God's judgment on such endemic evil was to wipe from the face of the earth every living creature—except for those who had experienced his grace. In contrast to the perversity of his day, "Noah was a righteous man, blameless in his generation. Noah walked with God" (Gen 6:9). Although he was not without sin, Noah was rightly related to God, and his life stood out in contrast to the rest of humanity. Furthermore, not only was Noah righteous in character, but he also was a "herald of righteousness" (2 Pet 2:5).

Alas, Noah's proclamation had little effect on his wicked generation. While every living creature outside the ark perished in the flood, God spared Noah and his family as a remnant. The earth was covered with water, reverting to "its primeval state at the dawn of Creation."[47] When the waters receded, the doors of the ark opened to an essentially new creation. Like Adam, Noah received a commission to be fruitful and to refill the earth. Significantly, Noah's first act after disembarking from the ark was worship. He built an altar and offered burnt animal sacrifices which Yahweh accepted as a "pleasing aroma" (Gen 8:21).

Many other cultures also preserved the memory of a great flood. While scholars have noted various similarities—in particular with the stories from

45. Ibid., 169.
46. Ibid., 184.
47. Ibid., 183.

Mesopotamia—the differences "shed light on the theological interests of Genesis."[48] The extrabiblical accounts reveal a pluralistic pantheon whose petty gods sought to destroy humans for their irritating noisiness. These capricious deities displayed fear, greed, and weakness; and they lacked both omniscience and the power to control the flood. In other words, some ancient pagan theologian(s) recast the memory of an ancient flood, filling it with anthropomorphic gods and elevating the status of the story's human protagonist to a heroic king who then morphed into a god. The sharply contrasting details of the monotheistic Noah story stand as a polemic against such pagan accounts. Although Genesis uses anthropomorphic language to describe Yahweh's thoughts and actions (e.g., God was grieved by human depravity, and he accepted Noah's sacrifice as a sweet aroma), this personal God is the omniscient, omnipotent Creator who judges unrepentant sinners and yet shows grace toward those who walk in faith. Those who heard the Noah story would recognize its challenge to their own worldviews.

Unfortunately, in spite of the flood, sin continued to plague the lives of Noah and his descendants. The Table of Nations in Genesis 10 records the lineage of each of Noah's three sons. Rad reflects, "The broad range of vision [of the table] is amazing for an inland people like Israel; It extends northward to the Black Sea, eastward to the Iranian plateau, southward to Nubia and westward to the Mediterranean coast of Spain."[49] He also draws attention to the table's striking omission of the nation of Israel, who is hidden in the neutral name of Arpachshad (Gen 10:24). Rad explains that "Israel looked at herself in the midst of the international world without illusion."[50] This perspective demonstrates God's universal sovereignty over all peoples everywhere. Bartholomew, however, observes that Israel's presence is still implicit in the Table of Nations, in that the entire table reflects the inner map of the author whose ordering of the names places the central focus on the nation of Israel. He offers the commentary: "The vision is not an ethnocentric one, but as is typical of the biblical story, one in which particularity (Israel) is always connected with universality (the nations) in God's purposes of redemption."[51] The account that follows provides a vivid depiction of the universal need for such a redemptive plan, because sin tainted every member of the fallen race—no matter their racial or ethnic background.

---

48. Wenham, *Genesis 1–15*, 164.
49. Rad, *Genesis*, 139.
50. Ibid., 141.
51. Bartholomew, *Where Mortals Dwell*, 45.

The Babel Builders and . . .

Genesis 11 describes the human effort to build a temple-like structure that would reach to the heavens. The builders' motivation was to make a name for themselves and so avoid being scattered over the face of the whole earth. Although God's general presence is everywhere, he is conspicuously absent from all the planning and activity. Yahweh did not instigate the building of this temple whose purpose was not to magnify his name but rather to bring fame to its builders. The folly of this massive building project was exposed when God had to "go down" to observe the people's feeble attempts to control the Almighty. Naturally, this presumptuous display of human arrogance to reach for the heavens attracted the judgment of the one true God who confused their language and scattered the nations listed in chapter 10 over the face of the earth. Ironically, their plan to avoid being scattered actually precipitated their dispersion.

This section that narrates the fall and thus the need for mission also highlights several other missional dimensions. God's intention for creating a people and a place shifted into a mission with a redemptive focus: to redeem a people who would display his glory and to restore the sanctuary where he would dwell in their midst. The results of the fall led to a shift in the mission of God's people as well. After the fall there are two kinds of responses to God's grace: those who obey God and those who rebel against God. Just as before the fall, those rightly related to Yahweh would still be a display people for his glory; but now, in the midst of a world twisted by sin, they would also be a contrast community.[52] The life of a person who walked with God stood out markedly from those who did not (e.g., Enoch in Gen 5:24; and Noah in 6:9). At times it appeared that their numbers dwindled to the verge of extinction. God, however, remained committed to fulfill his redemptive mission on behalf of all mankind. The mission would not succeed or fail based on human faithfulness. The mission moved forward based on the faithfulness of the One who had determined to redeem a people who would display his glory and walk in communion with him in the place he would restore. Genesis 1–11 ends with humankind's pathetic attempt to construct their own idolatrous religious system, rather than walk with the one true God.[53] At first glance it appears that a godly counterpart to the tower builders is missing. Genesis 12, however, opens with the absolutely pivotal words to a descendant of Shem: "Now the Lord said to Abram . . ."

---

52. I am indebted to Durham, *Exodus*, 263, for the concept of "display people" and to Goheen, *Light to the Nations*, 195, for "contrast community."

53. Ross, *Hope of Glory*, 133.

Abraham: Elect for the Sake of the Nations

Genesis 12 is crucial in the unfolding of the mission of God because it acts as a hinge between the prologue (Genesis 1–11) and the entire rest of the Bible. In fact, "Genesis 12:1–3 is God's gracious response which reverses the sin and downward spiral of chapters 3–11."[54] In this pivotal text God elects a particular man through whom he will bless *all* the peoples of the earth—a promise ultimately fulfilled in Abraham's descendant, Jesus Christ. Genesis 12 opens with Yahweh's command to Abraham to leave his country, his people, and his father's household—and presumably, his father's religion.[55] In turn, God promised him a great name, a great nation of descendants, and a new land. He also promised to bless Abraham and to bless "all the families of the earth" through him (Gen 12:2–3). It is noteworthy that the covenant promises feature both a people and a place. Obedience to this command required faith, however, because Abraham's wife was barren and Canaanites filled the land of promise.

Having obeyed God's command by faith, Abraham arrived in Canaan at Shechem. There Yahweh appeared to him and promised this land to his offspring. Abraham responded by building an altar and presumably offering a sacrifice (Gen 12:7). Here, in the patriarch's worshipful response to God's reiteration of the promises, we see the nexus of people, place, and the tabernacling presence of God. Abraham then moved on to Bethel, pitched his tent, built an altar to Yahweh, and worshiped (Gen 12:8). As he traveled throughout the land, he followed this same pattern, worshiping at Hebron and Beersheba, as well (Gen 13:18; 21:33). Although God continually blessed Abraham so that he became "very rich in livestock, in silver, and in gold," the richest blessing he gave him was his own presence: "I am your shield" (Gen 13:2; 15:1). Finally, after twenty-five years, God blessed Abraham with the birth of the child of the covenant. It is through this lineage that all the nations of the world will be blessed.

The fulfillment of this long-awaited promise made God's abrupt command to Abraham all the more shocking: "Take your son, your only son Isaac, whom you love, and go to the land of Moriah, and offer him there as a burnt offering on one of the mountains of which I shall tell you" (Gen 22:2).[56] Although the preceding verse alerts the reader that what follows

54. Köstenberger and O'Brien, *Salvation*, 28.

55. According to Josh 24:2, Abraham's father, Terah, was an idolater. The residents of Ur and Haran worshiped the moon god.

56. Bartholomew, *Where Mortals Dwell*, 51, notes that the use of the divine name "Elohim"—in contrast to the use of "Yahweh" in the six previous visitations of God to Abraham—indicates "the cosmic implications of this test."

was a test, Abraham did not have the luxury of this knowledge. Nevertheless, he promptly moved to obey. The tension he must have felt builds as the writer draws out the narrative with "excessive and deliberate details" of both the preparation and the journey.[57] Finally, carrying the wood for the sacrifice, the promised heir broke the silence with the incredibly ironic question: "Where is the lamb for a burnt offering?" Abraham's answer forms the structural center of the passage and anticipates the resolution to the situation: "God will provide for himself the lamb for a burnt offering, my son."[58] Ross describes what followed: "At the moment of truth Abraham did not look around for an animal or wait hesitatingly for God to intervene; he raised his hand to slay his son. . . . The divine intervention came when the sacrifice was made—in the mind of Abraham, if not in fact."[59] Pleased with Abraham's devotion and obedience, Yahweh stayed his hand and provided a substitute—a ram caught in the thicket.

Abraham marked the significance of the event by naming the place, "The LORD will provide," which the narrator relates to an enduring proverb in his day: "On the mount of the LORD it shall be provided." The proverb would therefore preserve not only the abiding significance of what took place on this mountain, but also its location. Later, the chronicler actually identifies the site of Solomon's temple-mount construction as Mount Moriah in 2 Chr 3:1.[60] God's provision of a substitute sacrifice on Mount Moriah typifies the ultimate sacrifice of Jesus Christ, "the Lamb of God, who takes away the sin of the world" (John 1:29). In response to Abraham's obedience, Yahweh reiterates his promises of land and descendants—through whom all the nations on earth will be blessed (Gen 22:18).

Abraham: Witnessing Worshiper

The content of Abraham's worship in the places where he acknowledged the presence of Yahweh would have stood in marked contrast to that of his neighbors. Even though his God had required a willingness not to withhold his firstborn son, it became clear that Yahweh was not pleased with the child sacrifice of the Canaanites. Instead, he had provided a substitute.

---

57. Sailhamer, "Genesis," 168.

58. Brueggemann, *Genesis*, 186.

59. Ross, *Creation and Blessing*, 399.

60. Although some may attempt to dismiss the mention of Mount Moriah in Gen 22:2 as a later insertion (to equate the location of the patriarch's sacrifice with Jerusalem), the word "Moriah" is integral to the narrative because the name itself contains the first hint that "the LORD will provide" (*rā'āh*, "provide").

Even the preservation of the place name, "The LORD Will Provide," would have been a continual reminder of the identity and activity of Abraham's God. In addition, Abraham's worship likely included some sort of proclamation about the character and nature of the God in whom he placed his faith. Ross draws attention to the clause in Gen 12:8—"and he called on the name of the LORD" or "he worshiped"—and explains that the Hebrew verb *qārā'* carries a number of meanings including, "call, call out, cry out, proclaim, read aloud, name, or summon." He argues that the expression means proclamation rather than invocation based on the translation of the same word in Exod 34:5–8 where Yahweh is the subject of the same verb. Ross, therefore, concludes that "Abraham was a witnessing worshipper."[61] Even speaking the actual names by which God had revealed his identity would have communicated great truths. For example, when God changed Abram's name to Abraham, he also revealed a new name of his own: *El-Shaddai*, which is translated as "God Almighty" (Gen 17:1). Whatever Abraham may have said as part of worship, it surely differentiated his worship of the living God from the surrounding pagan religions. The content of Abraham's worship proclaimed the identity and character of his God before his neighbors.

Undoubtedly, Abraham's witness to the presence of God in his life was also borne out in his deeds as God had commanded, "I am God Almighty; walk before me, and be blameless."[62] Abraham's faith had an immediate impact on those within his household as he obeyed God's very next command to circumcise all the male members of his household along with his son and himself as a sign of the covenant. This action would have included at least the 318 trained men born in Abraham's household (cf. Gen 14:14). Scripture records that Abraham's faith in Yahweh also inspired similar faith in the lives of his nephew Lot, the Egyptian Hagar, and Eliezer of Damascus. In Abraham's contacts with his neighbors, he surely acknowledged the God whom he worshiped. For example, when Melchizedek—priest of the "God Most High, Possessor of heaven and earth"—blessed Abraham, the patriarch later clarified in an oath to the king of Sodom that he himself served the "LORD [*Yahweh*], God Most High, Possessor of heaven and earth" (Gen 14:19, 22, emphasis added). Others, like Abimelech, witnessed the power of Abraham's God first hand. Waltke suggests that in the midst of a pluralistic world, ". . . Abraham walks with divine sensitivity, tailoring his relationships

61. Ross, *Hope of Glory*, 145. A similar understanding led the rabbis to consider Abraham to be "the first proselyte and that he made converts and brought them under the wings of the Shekinah" from Makilta, Mishpatim 18, cited in De Ridder, *Discipling the Nations*, 27. Likewise, Luther translates the verb in Gen 12:8 as *predigte* ("preached") in his 1545 German translation.

62. Gen 17:1. HCSB translation of 17:1b: "Live in my presence and be devout."

to people's level of relationship with God."[63] Repeatedly, the blessings God poured out on Abraham spilled over onto those around him.

Not surprisingly, Paul labels the oft-repeated promise—"in you all the families of the earth shall be blessed" (Gen 12:3; repeated in 18:18; 22:18; 26:4)—as "the gospel in advance" (Gal 3:6–9). Along those same lines, Christopher Wright suggests that it would also be appropriate to label God's command to Abraham to "Go . . . and be a blessing" (Gen 12:1–3) the "Great Commission" in advance.[64] Wright observes that in this promise God is "totally, covenantally and eternally committed to the mission of blessing the nations through the agency of the people in Abraham."[65] This promise of universal blessing does not automatically extend to every individual but to every major people group in the world. In short, God's covenant with Abraham has profound missional dimensions.

This section also highlights the "twin poles of Israel's mission": universality and election.[66] The goal of God's mission is universal, and his purpose is to redeem all the peoples of the world through the descendants of one particular man. God chose Abraham—"'a wandering Aramean' (Deut 26:5) out of an idolatrous family (Jos. 24:2) . . . [as] a true representative of the fallen race."[67] Therefore, because every person from every people group descends from the one man, Adam, no one people group can consider itself superior to another. God's election of Abraham is the means to bring redemption to all nations. Thus, the history of God's activity among Abraham's descendants is also the story of God's plan of redemption for the world.

Bethel: The House of God

Following Abraham's example, Isaac and Jacob also built altars and worshiped God as they traveled through the land of promise. Although the patriarchs did not construct any buildings, Beale considers these impermanent "sanctuaries" to be echoes of the original non-architectural sanctuary of Eden and observes that they were frequently connected to an appearance of God and a restatement of the Adamic commission to multiply.[68] Samuel Terrien also notes that these patriarchal accounts of "epiphanic visitation

63. Waltke and Fredericks, *Genesis*, 289.

64. Wright, *Mission of God*, 214.

65. Wright, "Mission as a Matrix," 134.

66. Legrand, *Unity and Plurality*, 15.

67. De Ridder, *Discipling the Nations*, 32.

68. Beale, *The Temple*, 97.

reveal the unique character of the Hebraic theology of presence."[69] The patriarchs' priestly activities and sacred spaces are also important because they anticipate Israel's later tabernacle and temple. Tremper Longman suggests that these altars, which marked the patriarchs' encounters with the special presence of God, were in essence staking a flag to claim the land in the name of Yahweh.[70]

One of the more significant patriarchal worship sites was Bethel. Abraham himself had built an altar near Bethel and returned to worship there a second time (Gen 12:8; 13:3–4). But the naming of this sacred space actually occurred later, in the Jacob narrative. Esau was furious that Jacob had stolen his blessing, and Jacob, in fear, fled for his life. His solitary journey led him to "a certain place" where he stopped to sleep for the night. While sleeping, his spiritual eyes were opened to the reality of the tabernacling presence of God in this place: "his hard place is transformed into an awe-inspiring sanctuary, the axis between heaven and earth."[71] Jacob dreamed of "a ladder [NIV: "stairway"] set up on the earth, and the top of it reached to heaven. And behold, the angels of God were ascending and descending on it!" (Gen 28:12). Yahweh, who stood at the top, extended the Abrahamic covenant to Jacob and promised him, "I am with you . . . wherever you go." Upon awaking, Jacob set a stone upright and poured oil over it, naming the place *Bethel*, because it was "the house of God . . . the gate of heaven" (Gen 28:17).

The description of Jacob's dream contains obvious parallels to the above discussion of ziggurats in regards to the Tower of Babel. The contrast between the two accounts underscores the differences between false and true worship. Whereas the proud human effort of the tower-builders ended in failure, God graciously appeared to Jacob who was not even aware that "the Lord is in this place." Jacob marked the event and the place with a simple upright stone—quite the contrast to the massive tower structure of Genesis 11. Standing the stone on end would naturally attract attention; likewise, naming the place Bethel, the "House of God," would invite worship of Yahweh in this place for generations to come. Thus, the self-initiated appearance of God at Bethel stood in contrast to false religions and welcomed worship of the one true God.

In Jacob's vision, Yahweh extended his covenant promise to bless all the peoples on earth through Jacob and his descendants. Furthermore, God's promise to be with Jacob wherever he traveled demonstrated the universal scope of God's rule and authority. Jacob responded to the presence of

---

69. Terrien, *Elusive Presence*, 93.

70. Longman, *Immanuel*, 20.

71. Waltke and Fredericks, *Genesis*, 395.

God with fear and worship, as well as with a vow to worship and serve this God who had promised, "I will be with you." This promise given at Bethel is an excellent example of what David Adams calls the bipolar Hebraic notion of the presence. Adams argues that the biblical concept of presence contains two elements: 1) a local presence and 2) an accompanying presence. In the former, a sacred space associated with a visual appearance of God takes on cultic significance; in the latter, God gives a spoken word promising to be with a specific person wherever they go.[72] This episode illustrates both of these concepts: God fulfilled his promise to accompany Jacob in his travels beyond the borders of Canaan, and Bethel became a sacred space with enduring cultic significance. Because of his encounter with the tabernacling presence of God, Jacob became a living display of the promises and provision of *this* God, wherever he went.

When Jacob returned twenty years later, he was not alone; his large household and flocks testified to God's faithful presence during his travels. Jacob charged "his household and all who were with him" to get rid of their foreign gods, purify themselves, and travel to Bethel where they might worship the God who had revealed himself to Jacob. The impact of Jacob's proclamation extended well beyond his household as "a terror from God fell upon the cities that were around them" (Gen 35:5). When the patriarch finally returned to Bethel, he once again built an altar and worshiped *El Bethel*, the God of Bethel whom he now knew by experience.

One final missional dimension that surfaces in these stories of the patriarchs is the constant reminder that this mission belongs to God; *he* will accomplish his purposes to redeem a people and to provide a place to dwell in their midst. The promises of God, however, seemed to be threatened time and time again. The land promised to Abraham by all appearances remained in the hands of others. The promise of a great nation of descendants seemed laughable in view of the recurring barrenness in every generation. And unfortunately, all too often the people of God failed to be a display people or a contrast community. Frequent family discord threatened to tear the clan apart long before they could become a nation: bargained birthrights, stolen blessings, wife-swapping, brother-selling—the list goes on and on. In spite of their failures, the forward movement and trajectory of God's mission did not falter. After all, Exod 6:3 records that the God of the covenant had revealed himself to the patriarchs as *El Shaddai*, a name that stressed God's power in contrast to human helplessness, as "God Almighty, who was well able to perform what he had promised, even against all odds . . . ."[73] The

---

72. Adams, "The Present God," 288–89.

73. Baldwin, *Genesis 12–50*, 63.

mission belongs to this God, and he would accomplish his purposes for the descendants of Abraham—even after four hundred years of slavery in a foreign land.

THE TABERNACLING PRESENCE OF GOD IN EXODUS

After the detailed accounts of God's activity among the patriarchs in Genesis, the uninitiated reader may be surprised to find that centuries have elapsed between the close of this book and the opening pages of Exodus. The biblical narrative fast-forwards over the four-hundred-year enslavement in Egypt that Yahweh had predicted to Abraham (Gen 15:13). Compared to the previous patriarchal accounts, there is a noticeable absence of the mention of God in the opening chapters of Exodus.[74] In fact, until the end of chapter 2, the only reference to God is in relation to the midwives who feared him. What was God doing while the Israelites were being oppressed?

Further reflection reveals that while Yahweh waited for the sin of the Amorites to reach full measure (Gen 15:16), he was fulfilling the historical promises that echo back to Adam and Abraham: "But the people of Israel were fruitful and increased greatly; they multiplied and grew exceedingly strong, so that the land was filled with them" (Exod 1:7). This piled-up series of verbs emphasizes the exponential increase. The seventy members of Jacob's family who entered Egypt had indeed become "a people" whom God considered his own (Exod 3:7). Terence Fretheim notes that whereas "the sons of Israel [Israelites]" occurs only twice in Genesis, it occurs 125 times in Exodus.[75] Although the plaintive cries of the Israelites are not mentioned until the end of chapter 2, God had set in motion his plans to deliver his people some eighty years earlier.

The seeming lack of divine presence at the outset only serves to heighten the effect of the final verses of Exodus where the presence of God filled the tabernacle with the fullness of his glory. Longman believes that the presence of God is "the most explicit and pervasive theme of the book."[76] John Durham also notes that it serves as both theological anchor and compass for the entire book.[77] Thus, Yahweh is very present; he is actively fulfilling his promises, unveiling his mission to redeem a people and to provide a place where they may worship him as he takes up residence in their midst.

74. Fretheim, *Exodus*, 39.
75. Ibid., 24.
76. Longman, *Exodus*, 39.
77. Durham, *Exodus*, xx.

Presence of God in the Burning Bush

In Exodus 3 Yahweh revealed himself to Moses in a theophany—as flames of fire that inexplicably engulfed a bush but did not consume it. In doing so, he revealed that he was in control of the forces of nature and therefore not confined to "specific sacred spaces." Any place he intervened was "a veritable sanctuary."[78] God cautioned Moses to remove his sandals as a sign of reverence; the ground was holy because of the presence of a holy God. Instead of directly answering Moses' question "Who am I?" God's response answered the self-doubt behind Moses' query with the promise of his accompanying presence: "I will be with you." In response to Moses' second question "What is [your] name?" God revealed his covenant name: "I AM WHO I AM" (Exod 3:14). Peter Toon explains that it is a matter of scholarly debate whether this clause should be read "as present tense, 'I am who I am,' or future tense, 'I shall be who I shall be,' or even as the causative-factitive, 'I cause to be whatever I cause to be' (or even as all three tenses) . . . ."[79]

The meaning of the related but shortened tetragrammaton, YHWH (Yahweh; "I AM"), is also a matter of great debate. After summarizing recent scholarly research, Toon suggests the following meanings for the name: 1) the positive assurance of YHWH's communing presence with his people (e.g., Exod 3:14); and 2) the declaration that ". . . YHWH is the only God who actually exists and there is no other" (e.g., Deut 4:39).[80] Fretheim notes that God is not given a name but that he reveals his own name. In doing so, Yahweh makes himself accessible to his people; he invites encounter and communication.[81] This is significant because in the ancient Near East, the name of a deity was more than a moniker; it communicated the god's identity and function.[82] Durham contends that the presence of God is closely tied to the name: in spite of his seeming absence, "Yahweh Is, and his Is-ness means Presence." This Yahweh is the same God that their forefathers worshiped (Gen 6:2), and it is by the name Yahweh that he will "make his Presence a reality to the generations to come."[83] Terrien offers the following qualification: "the name indeed carries the connotation of divine presence, but it also confers upon this presence a quality of elusiveness." He calls this

78. Robinson, "Burning Bush," 121.

79. Toon, *Triune God*, 87.

80. Ibid., 97.

81. Fretheim, *Exodus*, 65.

82. Walton, *Ancient Near Eastern Thought*, 92.

83. Durham, *Exodus*, 39–40.

ambivalence "the mark of the Hebraic theology of presence."[84] Although God graciously reveals the name of his presence to his people, he remains beyond their understanding.

Upon reflection, the name of Yahweh has several missional dimensions. Yahweh reveals his name and his identity to humanity; no one, therefore, has the right to define God for themselves. The very mention of the name Yahweh is polemical: He is unique, the one and only God who exists; any other god is false. Although he reveals himself, he is still elusive and inscrutable, beyond human understanding. Still, this ineffable God desires to be with his people that they might worship him. Furthermore, the context of the revelation of the name Yahweh is quite significant. It is an integral part of God's sending Moses on a mission that includes the worldwide impact of proclaiming his name in all the earth (Exod 9:16). Yahweh commissioned Moses, promising to accompany him and to empower him for the task: "I will be with you" (Exod 3:12).[85]

This phrase which capsulizes the presence of God with his people— "I will be with you"—occurs in some form almost one hundred times in the Old Testament.[86] Terrien observes that this offer marks "a shift from one mode of presence to another." Moses' experiential encounter with God transitions to "a psychological mode of presence." This promise of "divine companionship and help" would long outlast "the temporal limits of the 'appearance' at the Burning Bush."[87] Interestingly, Moses' experience closely parallels the experience of Jacob at Bethel. Their encounters with God in a specific place included God's promise to accompany them in their travels and to bring them back to the same location. This sign served as "proof of [God's] promised Presence with Moses": all the Israelites would gather with Moses on this very same spot to worship the God who had delivered them.[88] Yahweh would meanwhile accompany and empower him. Moses had received a divine commission, but the mission belonged to God. God had taken the initiative; the mission moved forward under his authority, at his timing, and according to his plan.

Exodus 6:4–8 is a concise, forceful outline of that plan—a passage that Fretheim calls "*the gospel of the exodus*."[89] The repeated assertion of "I am

---

84. Terrien, *Elusive Presence*, 119.

85. The comparison to a similar promise by Jesus in the Great Commission is striking. Cf. Matt 28:19–20.

86. Durham, *Exodus*, 33.

87. Terrien, *Elusive Presence*, 113.

88. Durham, *Exodus*, 33. Durham calls the ten plagues the "Proof-of-Presence Sequence" (ibid., 89).

89. Fretheim, *Exodus*, 92; italics original.

the LORD" in these verses underscores the identity of the Israelites' God as well as his activity among them. The stipulation that Yahweh is the name by which God is to be remembered "throughout all generations" carries a missional dimension, as well (Exod 3:15). Not only are the Israelites charged with the faithful transmission of the name, but also they are to rehearse continually the identity, character, and mighty acts of Yahweh so that future generations may know that he alone is God.

The "Proof of Presence" Plague Cycle

Fretheim points out that the entire plague cycle exhibits a fundamental mission orientation. When Moses first appeared before Pharaoh, a standoff quickly developed. Moses declared,

> Thus says the Lord, the God of Israel, "Let my people go, that they may hold a feast to me in the wilderness." But Pharaoh said, "Who is the Lord, that I should obey his voice and let Israel go? I do not know the Lord, and moreover, I will not let Israel go" (Exod 5:1b–2).

Yahweh responded to this arrogance with an incredible demonstration of his "outstretched arm and . . . great acts of judgment" (Exod 6:6). He also revealed the purpose of this very public display of his power: "so that my name may be proclaimed in all the earth" (Exod 9:16). God ordered the plagues so that everyone would know that *he* is the one true God. Negatively, the Egyptians would experience his judgment for their cruelty to the Israelites. Positively, the Israelites would know that it was Yahweh who delivered them out of bondage.[90]

The showdown took on a cosmic character as well, as the divine activity testified "that this God is the God of all *creation*."[91] Yahweh intended to use the plagues to execute judgment on all the gods of Egypt (Exod 12:12). While these mighty acts were proofs of his presence, they also exposed the false religion of the Egyptians. Many have pointed out that certain plagues seem to have been directed at various gods in the Egyptian pantheon: for example, the frog-headed goddess Heqt who assisted in childbirth; the goddess Isis who was associated with the inundation of the Nile River; and the sun-god Re. Of course, the Pharaoh himself—and later, presumably, his firstborn son—was considered to be a divine incarnation of Horus, the falcon. "As a god, Pharaoh [was] responsible for maintaining what the

90. Ibid., 94–95.
91. Ibid.; italics original.

Egyptians called *ma'at*, or order in the cosmos or creation."[92] His rule was supreme; "no other form of rule was an option—the choices were king or chaos."[93] In the presence of the true Creator and sustainer of the universe, however, Pharaoh's claim to divinity quickly evaporated, and the Egyptian pantheon was demythologized.[94] The contrast between the one true God and a host of false deities was pronounced. In the end the plagues were not only the means by which God accomplished his mission; they were also the megaphone through which God proclaimed his message: Yahweh alone is God.

The plagues not only pointed out the contrast between Almighty God and the impotent gods of the Egyptians, but they also highlighted the contrast between the people of God and those who were not. While Yahweh wreaked absolute devastation upon the Egyptians—their land, their king, and their gods—he dealt differently with the land of Goshen, shielding the sons of Israel from the effects of the last six plagues. In the tenth and final plague, the distinction between the two peoples was actually marked with a visible sign. God instructed the people to place the blood of a perfect lamb on the doorframes of their houses. The people's response to the command was immediate: they bowed down and worshiped, then obeyed. That night, when the presence of Yahweh passed through Egypt to strike down every firstborn, he saw the blood that distinguished his people and "passed over" those homes, sparing their residents. A great cry of anguish arose from all the households that were not covered by the blood.[95]

These chapters in Exodus highlight the twin poles of mission—universality and particularity. Legrand observes that "[t]o assert the power of Yahweh over Pharaoh of Egypt was itself a universalism of sorts."[96] As Creator, God is sovereign over the whole earth and all its peoples, but the Egyptians had failed to recognize him and instead exchanged the truth for a lie, worshiping the inanimate creation instead of the Creator. Yahweh was the source of the Nile, which overflowed year after year to water their crops. During the famine of Joseph's days, God had visibly demonstrated that he alone was sovereign over all creation, and he had graciously provided grain for all of Egypt as well as his own people. Confronted by God's power in the signs and plagues, Pharaoh's sorcerers came to recognize that these events

92. Bartholomew and Goheen, *Drama of Scripture*, 63.

93. Walton, *Ancient Near Eastern Thought*, 283.

94. Legrand, *Unity and Plurality*, 14.

95. Fretheim, *Exodus*, 141, reminds sensitive readers that Pharaoh had ordered the deaths of all the Hebrew male infants in Exodus 1. The judgment of the tenth plague fits the crime. In some sense Yahweh showed mercy by sparing all but the firstborn.

96. Legrand, *Unity and Plurality*, 11.

were the work of the "finger of God" (Exod 8:19). The Egyptians could have submitted to Yahweh and worshiped him, but they refused. Recognition does not equal submission. As the universal God of all earth, Yahweh through his activity would either harden or convict; his presence evoked faith or defiance. An encounter with the Almighty resulted in worship or judgment. The contrast between those who responded in faith and those who did not was quite distinct.

These chapters also focus on God's redemptive activity on behalf of his people. Through the plagues Yahweh displayed his power over creation in front of both the Egyptians and the Israelites so that all would know that he is alone is God. Although his people did nothing but "stand firm" and "be still," they served as a foil to the Egyptians. Yahweh himself shielded them, all the while dismantling the false religion of the Egyptians. The Israelites thus served as both a display people and a contrast community.

The night of the first Passover was an unforgettable reminder of the awesome power of God's presence—both to slay and to shield. Yahweh instructed his people to recount this astounding deliverance in an annual memorial feast that would undoubtedly prompt questions about its meaning. As generation after generation narrated these events, they repeatedly remembered that their redemption from slavery required a sacrifice. This annual recitation had a missional dimension. The Passover celebration preserved not only the memory of the mighty acts of God on behalf of his people, but also the significance of the redemptive message behind the events. This memorial meal pointed forward to a day when, through the lineage of Abraham's descendants, God would bring the promised deliverer who would ultimately bless all the nations of the world.

The Accompanying Presence

When Pharaoh finally relented, the Israelites departed quickly. The divine presence accompanied them in the visible symbol of the pillar of cloud and fire. The defined shape and maneuverability of the pillar point to the supernatural character of the phenomena.[97] It came as a surprise, therefore, when it seemed that God intentionally led his people into a trap. After Pharaoh changed his mind and the entire Egyptian army gave chase, the Israelites found themselves hemmed in by the sea. But then God revealed that the

---

97. Caudill, "Presence of God, 216, suggests that the pillar was not a manifestation of God's presence (as compared to *kābôd*; "glory"), but rather it was a tangible, impersonal sign of the presence of God, who used them as his agent to lead and protect his people.

trap was for their captors: "I will get glory over Pharaoh and all his host, and the Egyptians shall know that I am the LORD" (Exod 14:4).[98] The pillar moved to stand between the two camps all night long while a strong wind blew, making an escape route of dry land in the midst of the sea. Not only did the pillar serve as a divine guide for the Israelites, but it also served as a fearful battle-post for the divine presence. The text narrates how from the pillar Yahweh "glared" down on the Egyptian army, throwing them into confusion (Exod 14:24).[99] The Israelites crossed safely, but the Egyptians perished in the sea. In response to this overwhelming display of God's presence and power, the Israelites feared Yahweh and put their trust in him (Exod 14:31). Naturally, their worship burst forth in praise of the God who delivered them.

The Song of Moses and Miriam, which commemorated the event, memorialized God's mighty acts of salvation for future generations. The tenfold repetition of the name "Yahweh" emphasized that all the credit and glory go to God alone. Although God may have seemed absent in the opening pages of Exodus, this song reverberated with his presence. The Israelites attributed the marvelous victory to the divine Warrior and assumed that the surrounding nations—Philistia, Edom, Moab, and Canaan—would hear it and tremble in anticipation of their own demise. In fact, "[t]he reputation of Israel's God goes out ahead of Israel like a veritable pillar of smoke and fire."[100] The song also proclaims the character of Yahweh: he is "majestic in holiness, awesome in glorious deeds, doing wonders" (Exod 15:11). His love is unfailing toward the people he has redeemed, yet his burning anger consumes those who oppose him (Exod 15:7, 13). Clearly, his presence convinced the Israelites that there is no God like Yahweh. They declared their allegiance to him and anticipated that he would establish a sanctuary in order to dwell in their midst (Exod 15:2, 13, 17).

Significantly, God chose to save his people in the sight of the nations. His activity benefited the Israelites primarily, but it also addressed non-Israelites secondarily.[101] The massive crowd that fled the oppression of Egypt was a "mixed multitude" (Exod 12:38). Included in their numbers were many other people—non-Israelites who also benefited from God's liberation of his people. Fretheim notes that "God's redemption is not for the chosen few; it is for the sake of the whole world."[102] Because the bond

---

98. Durham, *Exodus*, 198.

99. Mann, "Pillar of Cloud," 26.

100. Fretheim, *Exodus*, 165.

101. Legrand, *Unity and Plurality*, 20.

102. Fretheim, *Exodus*, 143. There were distinctions, however, for those foreigners

that held Israel together was the covenant more than race, "it was always possible for individuals of other nations to be admitted as members of the particularistic covenant with Israel and join with Israel in the service required by her election."[103] From the beginning, God's intention was to incorporate others into the community of faith.

Another missional dimension of this portion of Exodus is the focus on proclamation. In some sense, the entire plague cycle proclaimed the identity of the one, true God before the Egyptians and the Israelites. The Passover meal became an annual commemoration through which the Israelites would continually proclaim how God had delivered them out of slavery. Likewise, the Song of Moses and Miriam proclaimed the presence and activity of Yahweh through praise. This public praise that honored God accomplished his divine objective for the entire exodus event: "But for this purpose . . . to show you my power, so that my name may be proclaimed in all the earth" (Exod 9:16). As Fretheim notes, *"Praise enhances the attractiveness of God."*[104] Magnifying Yahweh's name in worship increases his fame among those who do not know him.

Unfortunately, the people's memory of the mighty acts of God dimmed with surprising rapidity in the harsh realities of desert life. Even though the pillar of cloud accompanied them and Yahweh miraculously provided manna, quail, and water, the Israelites repeated their basic refrain: "Is the LORD among us or not?" (Exod 17:7).

Still, in spite of their whining, others outside the Israelite community could see the presence of God in their midst. For example, when Moses' father-in-law arrived, Moses testified about all Yahweh had done for them in Egypt and how he had saved them as they encountered hardships in their journey. Jethro was delighted and praised the God of Israel: "Now I know that the LORD is greater than all gods . . ." (Exod 18:11). Jethro then offered sacrifices to God and ate bread with all the elders of Israel in the presence of God. The proclamation of the extraordinary deeds of Yahweh could have a significant impact on those outside the covenant community.

---

who were not circumcised. For example, only those who had demonstrated their commitment to become full covenant members through circumcision were allowed to celebrate the Passover (Exod 12:48).

103. Legrand, *Unity and Plurality*, 47.

104. Fretheim *Exodus*, 164; italics original.

God's Presence Manifested

Three months after the Israelites left Egypt, they arrived at the mountain in Sinai—in fulfillment of God's promise to lead Moses back to the site of the burning bush. The importance of this time is reflected in the fifty-eight chapters of Scripture that record this one-year period (Exodus 19–40; Leviticus 1–27; Numbers 1–10).[105] The entire section begins on the mountain where God instructed Moses to tell the people:

> You yourselves have seen what I did to the Egyptians, and how I bore you on eagles' wings and brought you to myself. Now therefore, if you will indeed obey my voice and keep my covenant, you shall be my treasured possession among all peoples, for all the earth is mine; and you shall be to me a kingdom of priests and a holy nation (Exod 19:4–6a).

Acting as a prologue to the covenant, this "eagles' wings speech" echoes the imagery hinted at in Gen 1:2 and developed more fully later in Deut 32:11. Walter C. Kaiser Jr. explains the metaphor: "As the young eagles were carried on the adult wings and brought out of their nests and taught to fly, so Yahweh had lovingly carried and safely delivered Israel."[106] Based on this relationship forged with his people through his redemptive activity, God expected them to obey fully the covenant that was to follow. In short, the narrative of grace preceded the covenant.

The Israelites' affirmation of the covenant would then result in a unique relationship with God described in "three separate but interrelated images."[107] 1) They would be *segullah*: the king's "personal treasure set aside for his own use"; "the 'crown jewel' of a large collection . . . the one-of-a-kind piece." Against the backdrop of the whole earth—which belongs to Yahweh —"Israel [would] be the means by which God accomplishes [his] goal: the renewal of creation and all nations."[108] 2) They would be his priestly agents. Terrien explains the functions of priests in the ancient Near East: "Their function is to administer the sacred acts in sacred places at sacred times. They are therefore sacred persons."[109] But as a "kingdom of priests," the entire nation of Israel was to serve as priests—with no clergy/laity distinction. "All were to be agents of God's blessing to all on earth."[110] 3)

---

105. Kaiser, "Exodus," 414.

106. Ibid., 415.

107. Durham, *Exodus*, 262.

108. Goheen, *Light to the Nations*, 37–38.

109. Terrien, *Elusive Presence*, 124.

110. Kaiser, *Mission*, 16. Of course, God also commissioned the priesthood for the

And precisely because they were to "mediate the presence of Yahweh to the world," the people of God were called to be "a holy nation."[111] They were to be a contrast community, "different from all other people by what they are and are becoming—a display people, a showcase to the world of how being in covenant with Yahweh changes a people."[112] The contrast seen in the lives of God's display people should attract the attention of a watching world.

Following the "eagles' wings speech," God gave Moses extensive instructions to prepare the Israelites to meet with him. For two days they were to consecrate themselves, wash their clothing, and abstain from sexual relations. Even from a distance the presence of Yahweh demanded holiness.[113] Because his holiness would render the entire mountain holy, they were told to erect barriers so that no one would touch the mountain. If a person or animal crossed the barriers, the punishment was immediate death by stoning or arrows. On the morning of the third day, Yahweh descended on Mount Sinai in a theophany that was both awe-inspiring and dreadful. Thunder, lightning, thick cloud, and trumpet blast attended his presence, and billowing smoke covered the mountain. As the tabernacling presence of God converged on people and place, both are reduced to trembling (Exod 20:18).

From the midst of the theophany, Yahweh spoke the Ten Words and the Book of the Covenant. He began with a historical prologue: "I am the LORD your God, who brought you out of the land of Egypt, out of the house of slavery" (Exod 20:2). Bartholomew observes that "Old Testament law is always embedded in narrative . . . ."[114] In fact, the Torah derives its validity from that communal story. The first of the Ten Commandments reads: "You shall have no other gods before me" (Exod 20:3). The phrase "before me" is literally 'al-pānāya, "before my face," meaning, "in my presence." Because Yahweh was the one who rescued them out of Egypt while exposing the emptiness of the pagan pantheon, he demanded their exclusive devotion. Although he would be truly present in their midst, the second command—no idolatry—guards against any idea that they could control or confine him.[115] The third command deals with the central concern of God with the declaration of his name "in all the earth" (Exod 9:16). Negatively, God's people must not dishonor the name by their misuse of it; "[p]ositively,

---

cultic ministry in the tabernacle. But the entire nation was to function in a mediatorial role to the nations.

111. Terrien, *Elusive Presence*, 125.

112. Durham, *Exodus*, 263.

113. Caudill, "Presence of God," 220.

114. Bartholomew, *Where Mortals Dwell*, 61.

115. Ibid., 62.

God's name is to be used in prayer and praise, one important dimension of which is witness."[116] The fourth word sets aside the Sabbath day as holy to Yahweh, "a sanctuary of time," that echoes back to creation.[117] The remaining six words deal with interpersonal relations, yet these commands still have a "fundamentally Godward orientation," in that sin against a fellow human being involves God.[118] The Ten Commandments and the Book of the Covenant are crucial because they create "the moral space for Israel to inhabit in order to become a royal priesthood."[119]

Terrien explains that God's unique presence among his people is the source of the Torah. The focus of the Decalogue is not on a legal system but on "the prophetic attunement to a living power which surrounds and penetrates the wholeness of human existence."[120] Obedience grows out of relationship and maintains that relationship. Living as a kingdom of priests and a holy nation in covenant with a holy God required hearing and keeping God's words. Exodus 19:4–6, therefore, paves the way for the Ten Words and the Book of the Covenant that follow, which is the climax of the Sinai theophany. When the lightning and thunder had ceased and the cloud had dissipated from view, these commands remained and instructed the people how to live as God's special treasure, a kingdom of priests, and a holy nation. The commands covered everyday aspects of life and thus enabled a holy God to dwell among his people on an everyday basis.

When Moses relayed God's instruction to the people, they all agreed to obey everything Yahweh had commanded. Moses built twelve pillars and an altar, sacrificed burnt offerings and fellowship offerings, and sprinkled both the altar and the people with the blood of the covenant (Exod 24:3–8). This blood on the altar makes the keeping of the words (the Decalogue) and laws (the Book of the Covenant) possible. Kaiser notes, "The blood by which the covenant was ratified and sealed was the basis for the union between Yahweh and the people."[121] The covenant thus ratified, God invited the elders to join Moses and Aaron in a covenant meal in his presence. He invited Moses to ascend the mountain with his aide Joshua, and the glory of Yahweh "settled" (*šākan*; "tabernacled")[122] on the mountain with the appearance of a consuming fire. Moses remained on the mountain for forty days, during

---

116. Fretheim, *Exodus*, 228.
117. Patrick, *Old Testament Law*, 50.
118. Fretheim, *Exodus*, 239.
119. Bartholomew, *Where Mortals Dwell*, 62.
120. Terrien, *Elusive Presence*, 129–30.
121. Kaiser, "Exodus," 449.
122. Ibid., 450.

which time he received careful instructions for the construction of the place where Yahweh might tabernacle continually in the midst of his people.

The amount of space in Exodus devoted to the tabernacle and its furnishings underscores its significance. God explained the purpose and pattern for the structure in Exod 25:8–9: "And let them make me a sanctuary (*miqdāš*), that I may dwell in their midst. Exactly as I show you concerning the pattern of the tabernacle (*miškān*), and of all its furniture, so you shall make it."[123] Exodus 25–31 records God's instructions for the construction of the sanctuary; chapters 35–40 detail the Israelites' faithful completion of them. The only interruption in this section is the completely unexpected and inexplicable debacle of the golden calf, an event which jeopardized the very concept of Yahweh's tabernacling presence in the midst of his people.

God's Presence Forfeited?

The Israelites at the foot of the mountain grew restless in Moses' forty-day absence. Incredibly, they convinced Aaron to make an idol of a golden calf, before which they bowed down and worshiped as the gods "who brought [them] up out of the land of Egypt"—a pathetic parody of the words God spoke in Exod 20:2 and a flagrant transgression of the first two commandments (Exod 32:4). When God expressed his desire to destroy the Israelites for this horrific blasphemy, Moses mediated on their behalf, appealing to Yahweh's reputation among the Egyptians and his promises to the patriarchs. The depth of Moses' anguish is reflected in his offer to substitute himself as atonement: he pled for God to blot out his own name "from the book" in exchange for forgiveness of the people's sin.[124] Yahweh refused Moses' offer explaining that ". . . [w]hoever has sinned against me I will blot out of my book" (Exod 32:33).

Alas, the Israelites who had been spared the plagues of Egypt now had to endure a plague of their own because of their idolatry. God commanded Moses to lead the people to the land of promise, but he announced that he would not accompany the stiff-necked Israelites on their journey. He warned, "[I]f for a single moment I should go up among you, I would consume you" (Exod 33:5). Moses, however, refused to settle for this, remonstrating,

123. According to Averbeck, "Tabernacle," 807–10, there are three Hebrew terms associated with the desert shrine: 1) The most common term is *miqdāš*, ("sanctuary") from the root word *qdš*, meaning "holy" and connoting transcendence; 2) *miškān* ("dwelling place" or "tabernacle"), which focuses on the immanence of the Lord dwelling in their midst; and 3) *'ōhel mô'ēd* ("tent of meeting"), which emphasizes the place where God meets with his people.

124. Kaiser, "Exodus," 481.

> If your presence will not go with me, do not bring us up from here. For how shall it be known that I have found favor in your sight, I and your people? Is it not in your going with us, so that we are distinct, I and your people, from every other people on the face of the earth? (Exod 33:15–16).

In response, Yahweh mercifully yielded to Moses' appeal to the mission of God—to create a distinct community who will display his glory before the nations. Moses followed this bold request with one even more audacious: "Please show me your glory." Evidently, the risk of losing the tabernacling presence of God evoked an impassioned cry from Moses' lips to know him more fully.[125] Explaining that no one may see the unmediated glory of his face and live, God agreed to allow Moses to see his goodness and to hear his name pronounced: "Yahweh." When God proclaimed this covenant name, he also communicated his character:

> The Lord, the Lord, a God merciful and gracious, slow to anger, and abounding in steadfast love and faithfulness, keeping steadfast love for thousands, forgiving iniquity and transgression and sin, but who will by no means clear the guilty, visiting the iniquity of the fathers on the children and the children's children, to the third and the fourth generation (Exod 34:6–7).

This episode highlights the deep tension between the understanding that God's presence is essential to his people's well-being, yet on the other hand "that very presence is likely to consume them."[126] Gordon McConville proposes that these "theophanic terms [i.e., 'name' and 'glory'] are marshaled in such a way as to provide a solution to the problem raised by Israel's need to approach and be intimate with one who by his nature was holy and unapproachable."[127] While "glory" is a manifestation of God that is so dangerous it must be enshrouded in a cloud, the "name" expresses God's goodness and mercy, and worshipers are invited to be familiar with it.[128] The preceding narrative had revealed the holiness of God; in these verses Yahweh revealed more of his character in a list of piled-up adjectives: He is compassionate, gracious, slow to anger, forgiving, and abounding in love

125. Terrien, *Elusive Presence*, 140.

126. McConville, "God's 'Name,'" 154.

127. Ibid.

128. Ibid., 157. This distinction also provides an explanation for the frequency of "glory" in Exodus, which is full of "dramatic, exceptional divine manifestations," as compared to the preference for "name" in Deuteronomy, which deals with "the routine of worship in the new land" (161). "Name" and "glory" are thus complementary aspects of the presence of God.

and faithfulness.[129] It is on the basis of this divine revelation of his character that a holy God is able to take up residence among his people.

In response to this gracious disclosure Moses fell to his knees in the presence Yahweh and worshiped, pleading for forgiveness on behalf of the Israelites and for God's continued tabernacling presence. Yahweh answered that he would do "marvels, such as have not been created in all the earth or in any nation . . ." so that the surrounding peoples would watch and be amazed at the glory of God displayed among his own people (Exod 34:10). Moses descended from the mountain, unaware that his own face was radiant. Time spent in God's presence resulted in Moses' becoming a literal display of his glory.

God's Presence Dwelling in Their Midst

Then, as if the golden calf catastrophe had never taken place, the remainder of the book of Exodus details the people's careful adherence to God's plan for the construction of the tabernacle—a testimony to his astounding grace. The text suggests "that the Israelites understood the tabernacle, and accordingly the temple, to be patterned on a heavenly model."[130]

The plan for the tabernacle design revealed a series of "gradations of holiness" and therefore gradations of access, as well.[131] A hanging veil divided the tent structure (ten by ten by thirty cubits) into two chambers: the holy place and the holy of holies (a perfect ten-cubit cube). The veil (*paroketh*, meaning "to separate") "acted as a barrier between God and man, shutting God in and man out."[132] Yahweh's command that cherubim be embroidered on the veil (Exod 26:31) recalled those guarding the entrance to the garden of Eden, as if saying, "Thus far, but no further!"[133] A courtyard surrounded the structure and contained the bronze altar for sacrifices and the bronze laver for priestly purification. This courtyard formed a "buffer zone" without which the Israelites could not have lived safely beside the presence of their holy God.[134]

The tabernacle furnishings and daily ministrations—e.g., lighting the lampstand, burning the incense, and maintaining the bread of

129. The significance of this revelation of God's identity is seen in its frequent repetition throughout the OT.

130. Spatafora, *Temple of God*, 25. This is the clear teaching of Heb 8:5 as well.

131. Caudill, "Presence of God," 221.

132. Levy, *Tabernacle*, 61.

133. Ibid., 62.

134. Alexander, *Paradise*, 197.

presence—give the impression that "someone is home": Yahweh has truly taken up residence in his tabernacle tent.[135] The chief furnishing of this "tabernacle of testimony" was the ark of the covenant, sometimes translated as the "ark of testimony." The covering of the ark supported two cherubim who mirrored the pair guarding the way to the tree of life. The ark also contained the two tablets of the law which stood as "evidential, legal 'testimony' of God's saving and preserving presence as it had been manifested in various ways to Israel." Beale notes that the Hebrew word 'ēdût can mean "testimony" and that the Greek translation of the Hebrew Bible most often translated it as *martyrion* related to *martys* or "witness."[136] The "testimony" tablets were housed in the ark of the testimony in the tabernacle of testimony—all bearing witness to Yahweh. Thus, by their very existence, the tabernacle and the ark bear witness to the worldwide scope of the mission of God. Their "testimony" proclaimed to future generations of Israelites and to the surrounding nations that the God of creation was present in the midst of his people.

At the completion of the construction, the glory of God descended on the tabernacle, so filling it with his manifest presence that for a time Moses was unable to enter. As R. E. Averbeck explains, the tabernacle was, in effect, a "moveable Sinai": "The tabernacle became the medium through which the Lord in his true presence traveled from the mountain of God (Sinai) to accompany and guide Israel from there to the Promised Land."[137] The pillar of cloud settled over the tabernacle and remained, functioning as a guide for the Israelites in their desert wanderings. The Shekinah, which to this point had only appeared in "extraordinary, temporary manifestations, [made] its presence felt permanently."[138]

Exodus 19–40 contains significant missional dimensions concerning God's presence in the midst of his people. When God had accompanied the Israelites on their three-month journey to Sinai, they had repeatedly asked: "Is Yahweh among us or not?" (e.g., Exod 17:7). Now, the abiding presence of God in the tabernacle removed all doubt. Yahweh's desire to dwell among his people has both a functional and a teleological aspect: "God's presence among the Israelites brought about their deliverance and redemption . . . and simultaneously, his presence in their midst was the goal

---

135. Averbeck, "Tabernacle," 815.

136. Beale, *The Temple*, 118–19.

137. Averbeck, "Tabernacle," 824.

138. Donaghy, "Holy Scripture," 279. The term "Shekinah" (from *šākan* "to dwell") refers to "a special presence, a localization, so to speak, of His power in a given time and a given place." Donaghy also notes, "The Shekinah is for its people a directive, a provident, presence" (277–78).

of that salvation."[139] The goal of God's mission is to redeem a people with whom he dwells in communion—to the praise of his glory. In fact, "My people" is a major emphasis in Exodus, and as Terrien observes, "Presence is what creates a people."[140] The shared experience of God's presence in the Passover, on the shore of the Sea, and at the foot of Sinai transformed this unorganized mass of slaves into a community centered—literally—around the God who delivered them, named them as his own, and chose to make his abode in their midst.

God's purpose for this unique relationship with Israel surfaces in the words, "all the earth is mine" (Exod 19:5). This phrase makes Yahweh's universal authority and concern explicit and sheds light on Israel's missionary function.[141] Exodus 34:10 clearly articulates God's purpose for the covenant: "Before all your people I will do marvels, such as have not been created in all the earth or in any nation. And all the people among whom you are shall see the work of the LORD, for it is an awesome thing that I will do with you." The passage continues with the command that the Israelites separate themselves completely from any aspect of the false religions of their neighbors. The harsh language that followed is understandable on the heels of the golden calf episode. Because the Israelites served "Yahweh, whose name is Jealous," they were to deconstruct—literally—the false gods of the peoples living within the land of promise (Exod 34:13–14). An overwhelming experience of God's presence in their midst at Sinai called for exclusive worship of Yahweh and the "revolutionary requirement of aniconism."[142] His presence was also the foundation of the moral and ethical requirements for the people of God. The Torah served to preserve the Israelites' relationship to a holy God and their witness to the watching nations.

---

139. Lister, "Lord Your God," 186.

140. Terrien, *Elusive Presence*, 124. Fretheim, *Suffering of God*, 208, notes that with the single exception of Lev 26:12, this book contains all the occurrences of this phrase in the Pentateuch: Exod 3:7, 10; 5:1; 7:4, 16; 8:1, 20–22; 9:1, 13, 17; 10:3–4; cf. 5:23; 15:16.

141. Block, *I Love Your Torah*, 159.

142. Terrien, *Elusive Presence*, 130.

THE TABERNACLING PRESENCE OF GOD IN THE REST OF THE PENTATEUCH

Restricted Access to the Presence of God

Yahweh promised the Israelites that if they would observe his commands, he would bless them with the ongoing manifestation of his presence: "I will make my dwelling among you, and my soul shall not abhor you. And I will walk among you and will be your God, and you shall be my people" (Lev 26:11–12). But how is a holy God to dwell in the midst of a sinful people? The book of Leviticus outlines an extensive cultus that manages the relationship of Yahweh and his people.[143] It shows that if something has become unclean, a blood sacrifice can reverse that process, making it clean again; similarly, sacrificial blood can consecrate the clean, making it holy.[144] While assembling this religious framework for the Israelites, Leviticus also lays a foundation for the New Testament understanding of the atonement. The sacrifices offered through the mediation of a consecrated priesthood brought expiation for sin, expressed gratitude, and celebrated communion—all of which find their ultimate fulfillment in the once-for-all sacrifice of Jesus Christ.[145] Holiness is a central characteristic of the tabernacle and serves as the theme of the entire book of Leviticus, as summarized in the command of Lev 19:2: "You shall be holy, for I the LORD your God am holy." God had called Israel to be a kingdom of priests. Leviticus begins, therefore, with a focus on the responsibilities of the priests (Lev 1–16) and concludes with a call to congregational holiness (Lev 17–26).[146]

Clearly, access to the presence of a holy God had severe restrictions. The vast majority of the people "were not permitted near the sanctuary or anything sacred . . . under pain of death."[147] All the people of Israel had to observe the cleanliness laws that distinguished between clean and unclean. "Unlike cleanness, though, uncleanness is contagious and incompatible with holiness."[148] Out of all the people of Israel, only the priests could enter the holy place. The priests were required to be consecrated and ceremonially clean, exemplary in their marriages, restricted in their mourning practices, and free of physical impediments.[149] Out of all the priests, only the high

---

143. Bartholomew, *Where Mortals Dwell*, 70.

144. Wright, *Mission of God*, 337.

145. Ross, *Holiness*, 15, 30.

146. Averbeck, "Tabernacle," 820.

147. Spatafora, *Temple of God*, 20.

148. Wenham, *Leviticus*, 20.

149. Ibid., 290–92.

priest could enter past the veil into the holy of holies once a year on the Day of Atonement when he would sprinkle the blood of sacrifices for his own sin and for the sin of the Israelites. Even then, a cloud of incense obscured the seat of atonement lest the high priest see it and die (Lev 16:13).

God also laid out careful prescriptions for the various sacrifices through which he graciously provided a means of reinstating and sustaining communion with his people. Wenham observes, "These verses clearly express the notion that sin defiles men and particularly God's sanctuary, and that the proper means of purification is animal blood. If there is no purification, death will follow."[150] For the Israelites, having Yahweh dwell in their midst was a great privilege attended by great danger. Wenham notes, "Fierce judgments and sudden death stud [the] pages [of the whole Pentateuch]. Sacrifice is the appointed means whereby peaceful coexistence between a holy God and sinful man becomes a possibility."[151] God's presence in the midst of his people demanded a corresponding holiness in every facet of their lives.

A vivid example of these truths appears at the juncture of Leviticus, chapters 9 and 10. After Moses and Aaron carefully followed Yahweh's instructions for the inauguration of worship in the tabernacle, the results were breathtaking: "the glory of the LORD appeared to all the people. And fire came out from before the LORD and consumed the burnt offering and the pieces of fat on the altar, and when all the people saw it, they shouted and fell on their faces" (Lev 9:23–24). Although understated, the verses which immediately follow could not offer a sharper contrast: "Now Nadab and Abihu, the sons of Aaron . . . offered unauthorized fire before the LORD, which he had not commanded them. And fire came out from before the LORD and consumed them, and they died before the LORD" (Lev 10:1–2). In the first instance, God's presence graciously consumed the sacrifice that met his requirements; in the second, his presence consumed those who presumptuously attempted to skirt his requirements. Thus, the commencement of worship in the tabernacle underscored the need for holiness.

There are some obvious missional dimensions in Leviticus. Although no sinner could ever approach the unmediated presence of a holy God, Yahweh graciously provided a way for his people to worship him through the mediation of sacrifice. However, because *he* is the object of worship, *he* sets the parameters for worship. Entering the restricted presence of God can be deadly if the worshiper attempts to come on his own terms. The tragic story of Nadab and Abihu highlights the fact that there are two kinds of responses

---

150. Ibid., 94–95.
151. Ibid., 56.

to the holiness of God that result in two outcomes: those who follow God's prescriptions for worship are welcomed by grace into his presence; those who attempt unauthorized access will face destruction. God's people should be a display people—those who approach a holy God on his terms and live life in his presence.

The twin poles of mission—particularity and universality—are also present in Leviticus. These religious and ethical distinctions in Leviticus had universal implications. They set Israel apart from her neighbors, giving "clear evidence of Yahweh's rule over her"; she was to be "a model of his lordship over the whole world."[152] The people of God, however, were not a closed group.[153] Non-Israelites living among God's people were required to obey these same laws and abstain from "detestable things" (Lev 18:26, NIV). Yet Yahweh also commanded, "You shall treat the stranger who sojourns with you as the native among you, and you shall love him as yourself, for you were strangers in the land of Egypt: I am the LORD your God" (Lev 19:34). Although God's provision for a perfect sacrifice was embedded in the lineage of Israel, his concern extended to all peoples.

The multitude of regulations found in Leviticus related to every dimension of daily life, shattering any dualistic concept of sacred versus secular. The holistic holiness required of the Israelites to dwell alongside God extended to the food they ate, the clothes they wore, the loans they made, and even to their sexual practices. The Sabbath year demonstrated Yahweh's deep concern for both people and place: every seven years the Israelites were to cancel debts, free slaves, and give their fields a rest. Similarly, in addition to the theological dimensions of the Jubilee, this fifty-year celebration was designed to be a socioeconomic institution that ensured equitable distribution of the land based on kinship units.[154] The Israelites' observance of the religious calendar with its Sabbaths and Passover and other annual feasts gave a rhythm to life that undoubtedly stood in contrast to others. Their worship and praise magnified the mighty works of God and reflected the glory of God to a watching world. All of these would have attracted the notice of their neighbors, causing them to marvel at the privileges the Israelites enjoyed by virtue of God's presence tabernacling among them.

---

152. Köstenberger and O'Brien, *Salvation*, 34.

153. Ibid., 35. The authors note that "Israel related to the nations in two ways: first, *historically* through incorporation, and then *eschatologically* through ingathering" (135; italics original).

154. Wright, *Mission of God*, 290.

Divine Warrior Dwelling in Their Midst

The book of Numbers takes its name from the two census lists that function as military rosters of the Israelite men (chapters 1 and 26). The book also describes the organization of the Israelite camp where the twelve tribes were grouped in units of three around each of the four sides of the tabernacle. The Levites camped in the area between the tribes and the tabernacle, acting as a buffer, "so that there [might] be no wrath on the congregation of the people of Israel" (Num 1:53). This arrangement reflects the centrality of the tabernacle in this theocracy. Wenham observes, "The fiery cloud covering the tabernacle showed that it was no empty royal palace, but that 'the LORD their God is with them, and the shout of a king is among them' (23:21)."[155] Amazingly, the sovereign God who had utterly defeated the Pharaoh and his army now deigned to take up residence in a tent in the middle of his people.

Michael Homan observes that the outlay of the tabernacle resembles that of an Egyptian war camp in the days of Ramesses II. He contends that the tabernacle, which was built along similar dimensions and configuration, may have portrayed Yahweh in a Divine Warrior role just as Ramesses led his troops into battle from a mobile military war tent.[156] If the Israelites were indeed familiar with this model for military encampment, the parallel design of the tabernacle would have underscored the fact that Yahweh was their King living in their midst. The Song of Moses and Miriam celebrated this realization: Yahweh is a warrior who will fight for his people (Exod 15:3). Just as he had already defeated Pharaoh and his army, God would lead them and fight future battles on their behalf. But the King of Israel was not only their commander-in-chief; more importantly, he had demonstrated—through the plagues, the parting of the sea, and the manna from heaven—that he ruled supremely over all of his creation. The same God who settled on Mount Sinai in the midst of a storm was now settling in the midst of their camp.

The Divine Warrior would continue to lead this people in formation by the movements of the cloud which continued to cover the tabernacle (Num 9:15–23). Wenham explains, "Both at rest and on the move the camp was organized to express symbolically the presence and kingship of the LORD."[157] The mobility of the tent-tabernacle illustrated that God was not confined to a particular place. The ark of the covenant actually led the way, heralded by

155. Wenham, *Numbers*, 40.

156. Homan, "Divine Warrior," 22–27. Kitchen, "Desert Tabernacle," 14–21, notes that Ramesses' war tent stood inside its own fenced-off precinct in the midst of the rectangular military encampment.

157. Wenham, *Numbers*, 56.

Moses' triumphant pronouncement: "Arise, O LORD, and let your enemies be scattered, and let those who hate you flee before you" (Num 10:35). With the Divine Warrior in their midst, it appeared that no enemy could stand against them. According to Num 14:14, news of Yahweh preceded the Israelites' progress: ". . . the inhabitants of this land . . . have heard that you, O LORD, are in the midst of this people. For you, O LORD, are seen face to face, and your cloud stands over them and you go before them, in a pillar of cloud by day and in a pillar of fire by night." This was exactly what Yahweh had intended: the missional proclamation of his glorious presence on display in the midst of his people.

Tragically, however, the Israelites fell prey to the one enemy who could defeat them—their own sin nature. They failed to live as a contrast community, and the rest of Numbers records numerous outbreaks of sin and judgment within the ranks of the Israelites. Ironically, the entire roster of soldiers destined for triumph in battle becomes a tragic memorial of combatants who out of fear refused to obey the orders of their commander-in-chief. Because of their failure, the Israelites were consigned to displacement for forty years. Amazingly, however, God preserved a second generation through the wilderness wanderings, names that fill a second roster whom he would lead into the land of promise. The two lists represent two kinds of responses to the divine King: those who obey God and those who rebel against his authority.

Wenham points out that "[r]unning through all the legislation in Numbers are warnings about the danger of unholy men approaching God."[158] Yet the book of Numbers is also replete with examples of those who rebel, like Korah and his followers who tried to wrest control of the priestly functions. Moses declared that Yahweh would "show who is his, and who is holy" (Num 16:5). Indeed he does. The ground swallowed Korah and his family, "[a]nd fire came out from the Lord and consumed the 250 men offering the incense" (Num 16:35). When the Israelites blamed Moses for this turn of events, the glory of God suddenly appeared over the tabernacle, and a plague swept through the people, killing 14,700 before Aaron could make atonement for them. Although the Israelites were the people God had elected to work through to bring redemption to the nations, they were not exempt from his wrath for their sin. God would judge the rebellious among the Israelites, just as he judged those among the nations. Even if his wrath threatened to consume his own, still Yahweh was faithful to accomplish his goal of blessing all the nations through the descendants of this chosen people. Just as there were rebellious Israelites who would be excluded from

158. Ibid., 47.

the covenant community, there were also non-Israelites who would be incorporated into the community of faith. The mission belonged to the King whose presence in their midst brought both peril and privilege.

Blessed to Be a Blessing

According to Ronald Allen, God's blessing of Israel is the heart of both the book of Numbers and the Torah.[159] The familiar Aaronic benediction captures the essence of the privilege of the tabernacling presence of God. Beale observes that it is no coincidence that the familiar blessing was first pronounced on the day of the dedication of the tabernacle:[160]

> "The LORD bless you and keep you;
> the LORD make his face to shine upon you and be gracious to you;
> the LORD lift up his countenance upon you and give you peace."

> So shall they put my name upon the people of Israel, and I will bless them (Num 6:24–26).

Beale concludes that the blessing at that time was the glorious presence of Yahweh in the midst of his people.[161] Leviticus 9:22–24 clearly links the blessing and the presence. After Aaron offered the sacrifices and pronounced the blessing, the glory of God appeared to all the people; fire from the presence of Yahweh consumed the offerings, and the people fell down in worship. The atoning sacrifice had preceded the blessing of God's presence, and it is on the basis of the atoning sacrifice that God grants grace and peace. The words of the blessing are from God; they are, therefore, efficacious.[162]

This priestly blessing also demonstrated how these people belonged to Yahweh. By pronouncing this blessing on the Israelites, the priests would "put" Yahweh's name on them, essentially branding them as the people belonging to God. Daniel Block notes that, "wearing the name of YHWH as a badge or brand of ownership" is the central concept of "name theology," a prominent theme in Scripture. Because the Israelites bore his name, they would be the objects of his blessing.[163] God's mission includes assembling a people who bear his name.

---

159. Allen, "Numbers," 677.

160. Beale, *The Temple*, 402, bases his conclusion on Num 7:1.

161. Ibid.

162. Ross, *Hope of Glory*, 288.

163. Block, *I Love Your Torah*, 63–64.

Yet the blessing in this text, which harkens back to the promised Abrahamic blessing of Gen 12:3, has a much broader scope than just the Israelites and thus a missional dimension, as well. This Aaronic benediction captivated a later psalmist who "turn[ed] the blessing inside out" and made it his prayer for the nations:[164]

> May God be gracious to us and bless us
> and make his face to shine upon us—
> *that* your way may be known on earth,
> your saving power among all nations.
> Let the peoples praise you, O God;
> let *all* the peoples praise you! (Ps 67:1–3; italics added).

The purpose of God's blessing the descendants of Abraham is *so that* the whole world will know God's way and salvation, and the ends of the earth will fear him. Just as the priests had the role of blessing the Israelites, Israel as a whole had the priestly role of blessing the nations by sharing their knowledge of God and his ways.[165]

This blessing motif surfaces again in Numbers in the account of Balaam, a pagan sorcerer hired by the Moabite king to curse the Israelites. Although Balaam considered the God of the Israelites as just another deity he might manipulate, he soon discovered otherwise. Not only was Balaam unable to curse the Israelites, but instead, the Spirit of God came upon the prophet, causing him to pronounce a series of oracles that rose to a crescendo of blessing on these descendants of Abraham.[166] God used Balaam to acknowledge the presence of Yahweh in their midst: "The LORD their God is with them, and the shout of a king is among them" (Num 23:21b). He also caused Balaam to prophesy about a future deliverer: "a star shall come out of Jacob, and a scepter shall rise out of Israel" (Num 24:17b). Although this prophecy may have found an initial fulfillment in David, ultimately it reaches beyond him to the coming messianic Ruler, who in days to come will reign as King over all his enemies.[167] In spite of the faithlessness of his people, God remains faithful to his promises. His blessing on the Israelites will ultimately result in the blessing of all nations.

---

164. Wright, *Mission of God*, 232.
165. Ibid., 331.
166. Allen, "Numbers," 895.
167. Ibid., 909–10.

Proclaiming His Presence before the Nations

The last book of the Pentateuch, Deuteronomy derives the name "second law" from the repetition of the law for the second generation following the exodus event—a community consisting primarily of the offspring of Abraham.[168] Moses reminded the Israelites that their unique status as the chosen people of God was based on the grounds of God's love and his oath to their forefathers (Deut 7:7–8). Therefore, they could claim neither "exceptional physical nor spiritual qualifications." Neither could they claim that God gave them the land because of their moral superiority: "Not because of your righteousness or the uprightness of your heart are you going in to possess their land, but because of the wickedness of these nations the LORD your God is driving them out from before you . . . for you are a stiff-necked people" (Deut 9:5–6). "On the contrary, their election was an act of *sheer grace*."[169]

Wright notes that although Deuteronomy does not feature the other nations very often, when they are mentioned, "it is of considerable missiological interest."[170] Deuteronomy 4:6–8 clearly ties the Israelites' obedience to the law to their mediatorial role to the nations. Keeping these commands would impact the surrounding nations:

> Keep them and do them, for that will be your wisdom and your understanding in the sight of the peoples, who, when they hear all these statutes, will say, "Surely this great nation is a wise and understanding people." For what great nation is there that has a god so near to it as the LORD our God is to us, whenever we call upon him? And what great nation is there, that has statutes and rules so righteous as all this law that I set before you today?

The Torah was not a burden for the Israelites to bear, but rather it was a revelation of the character of a holy God and the means for abiding in communion with this God who had revealed himself—in contrast to the mute idols of the nations. Moses reminded this generation of the theophany at Sinai which provided the dramatic backdrop for the Ten Commandments. Moses' first address builds to a final climax:

> For ask now of the days that are past, which were before you, since the day that God created man on the earth, and ask from one end of heaven to the other, whether such a great thing as this has ever happened or was ever heard of. Did any people ever hear the voice of a god speaking out of the midst of the fire,

168. Block, *Gospel*, 15.
169. Ibid.
170. Wright, *Mission of God*, 226.

as you have heard, and still live? Or has any god ever attempted
. . . all [that] the Lord your God did for you in Egypt before your
eyes? To you it was shown, that you might know that the LORD
is God; *there is no other besides him* . . . [K]now therefore today,
and lay it to your heart, that the LORD is God in heaven above
and on the earth beneath; *there is no other* (Deut 4:32–35, 39;
italics added).

Peter Craigie calls this a "loaded" rhetorical question.[171] Never at any
time and never in any place has any other nation experienced all that Yahweh has done on behalf of the Israelites. Block concludes that from beginning to end Deuteronomy proclaims grace; the gospel, therefore, confronts
the reader on every page.[172] The only correct response to such grace is to
love Yahweh with the entirety of one's being and to forsake all others (Deut
6:5). After all, *there is no other god*—in heaven above or on the earth below—besides the God of the Israelites. If the God who has so graciously
revealed himself to Israel is indeed the *only* true God, then knowledge of
this truth carries huge implications for the people of God. Those who know
the one true God have a tremendous obligation to make him known to others. Israel's monotheism thus contained an embedded missional impulse.

This exclusive relationship with God also called for the sons of Israel
to expunge the names of every false deity from the land of promise (Deut
12:3)[173] and to seek the place Yahweh chooses "to put his name and make his
habitation there" (Deut 12:5). As Block notes, this is the first of twenty-one
occurrences of the "place formula" found in Moses' speeches in Deuteronomy.[174] Just as God elected a *people* for himself, he would also choose a *place*
for his name, or *presence*, to dwell in their midst. These three elements are
the essence of the mission of God from creation.[175] Just as Yahweh had put
his name on the Israelites with the Aaronic Blessing, once they entered the
Promised Land, Yahweh would stamp his name on the place he chose to
dwell in their midst. This place would function not only as a symbol of the

171. Craigie, *Deuteronomy*, 142.

172. Block, *Gospel*, xii.

173. Ibid., 252–53.

174. Block, *I Love Your Torah*, 105.

175. Block, *Gospel*, 259, diagrams these same three elements in a triangle, which he
labels "The Triadic Covenantal Relationship Involving Deity, People, and Territory." See
also Block, "Stones," 17–41. Wright, *Mission of God*, 394–95, uses a similar diagram to
describe the conceptual framework of Paul's sermon in Athens. Wright places a smaller
triangle (labeled God, Israel, and the Land) within a larger triangle (labeled God, Humanity, and the Earth). This framework has obvious parallels to the mission of God as
expressed in this study.

Lord's claim on the land, but "it would also signify YHWH's delight in his people and his desire to fellowship with them."[176] The people of God would have the incredible privilege of sharing a communion meal in that place— *rejoicing* in his very presence (Deut 12:7, 12, 18).

Because they were a display people who belonged to God, Yahweh had placed his name on them, in essence, branding them as his own. Block suggests that a better translation of the idiom found in Deut 28:9–10 would read as follows: "YHWH will establish you as his holy people, as he has sworn to you, if you keep the command of YHWH your God and walk in his ways. Then all the peoples of the earth shall see that you bear the name of YHWH, and they shall be in awe of you."[177] Like the high priest whose turban-medallion read, "Holy. Belonging to YHWH," Israel, too, was consecrated as a holy priesthood and bore the stamp of the Lord's name. In other words, the people of God had a missional role to play before the surrounding nations. The moral and ethical character of the people of God would "advertise the name of the God whose name they bore."[178] In contrast to the religious pluralism of the surrounding nations, however, the Israelites were prohibited from bearing the brand of any other god.

The book of Deuteronomy reflects several missional dimensions, including the main components of the mission of God: a people and a place that both bear his name. The twin poles of mission are clearly in view. While Deuteronomy outlines the covenant for the elect people of God, it is in light of their mediatorial role before the nations. The nations will see that the people of Israel bear the name of Yahweh and that God is present in the place he chooses for his name to dwell. God therefore called Israel to be a display people and a contrast community who "by their ethical and cultic performance might bring praise to his name."[179] Living a life consecrated to Yahweh would bring God's blessings and pique the curiosity of those who do not know him.

Proclaiming His Presence to the Next Generation

A cursory reading of the blessings and curses (Deut 27–30), however, reveals the anticipation that the Israelites would fail to keep their covenant commitment. But even after their failure resulted in their being banished— "dis-placed"—to "the uttermost parts," when they repented, God would

---

176. Block, *Gospel*, 255.

177. Ibid., 246.

178. Ibid., 247.

179. Ibid., 246.

have compassion and restore them to the land of promise (Deut 30:1–5). Yahweh, through Moses, set a clear choice before his people:

> If you obey the commandments of the Lord your God that I command you today, by loving the Lord your God, by walking in his ways, and by keeping his commandments and his statutes and his rules, then you shall live and multiply, and the Lord your God will bless you in the land that you are entering to take possession of it. But if your heart turns away, and you will not hear, but are drawn away to worship other gods and serve them, I declare to you today, that you shall surely perish . . . I call heaven and earth to witness against you today, that I have set before you life and death, blessing and curse. Therefore choose life . . . (Deut 30:16–19).

God's gracious offer of a relationship with him called for a response. Being a physical descendant of Abraham did not guarantee devotion to God. Block draws attention to the frequent shift between the "you" singular and "you" plural forms of direct address in the book of Deuteronomy.[180] While Yahweh was at work in and through the community of his chosen people, each individual was responsible for his or her own response to God's gracious offer of relationship.

Not surprisingly then, Deuteronomy contains a strong emphasis on the need to recall the mighty acts of God and to remember his instruction. Moses warns the people, "Only take care, and keep your soul diligently, lest you forget the things that your eyes have seen, and lest they depart from your heart all the days of your life. Make them known to your children and your children's children" (Deut 4:9). Thus, a primary missional task is to pass on the faith to the next generation. The following verses describe the heart of the Torah and how to imprint it on succeeding generations:

> Hear, O Israel: The Lord our God, the Lord is one. You shall love the Lord your God with all your heart and with all your soul and with all your might. And these words that I command you today shall be on your heart. You shall teach them diligently to your children, and shall talk of them when you sit in your house, and when you walk by the way, and when you lie down, and when you rise. You shall bind them as a sign on your hand, and they shall be as frontlets between your eyes (Deut 6:4–8).

This message of the *Shema* was absolutely critical for a generation of Israelites poised to enter a land steeped in religious pluralism. The fundamental

180. Ibid., 17.

reason for the tabernacling presence of God in their midst was for relationship.[181] And, because Yahweh alone is God, theirs was to be an exclusive relationship. The faithful transference of this understanding to the next generation was what would make or break their future success in the land. The success of God's mission, however, depended not on the spiritual fidelity of the people but rather on the faithfulness of the God who conceived it.

CONCLUSION

As this chapter demonstrates, the mission of God flows from the purposes of God at the beginning of time: to create a people who would display his glory and a place where he might dwell in their midst. God commissioned the first man and woman to fill the earth with the knowledge and praise of God's glory. After they disobeyed, he drove them from the garden, and they no longer had access to his unmediated presence. Although sin resulted in judgment, the outlines of God's mission to redeem both people and place began to unfold. Yahweh graciously allowed access to his mediated presence for forgiven sinners who were rightly related to him.

God's redemptive plan began to take shape in the calling of one particular man, Abraham, through whose offspring all the nations of the world would be blessed. In the period that followed, from time to time God manifested his presence to the patriarchs, reiterating his promises of people, place, and blessing for the nations. His faithfulness to the promises crystallized in the exodus when he miraculously delivered the fledgling nation from slavery and accompanied them on their way to the Promised Land. He appeared to the Israelites in a glorious theophany, tabernacling on the mountain at Sinai. Establishing a covenant whereby this treasured people would become a kingdom of priests and a holy nation, Yahweh graciously condescended to take up residence in a tent in their midst. The tabernacle represented a fundamental shift in the way God was present with his people. The occasional appearances gave way to his ongoing presence. He was no longer on a distant mountain but rather in the middle of the camp. The portability of this dwelling place also assured them that his own presence would accompany them as they made their way to the place he had reserved. Such an incredible privilege was matched only by its attendant responsibility: The tabernacling presence of this holy God called for his people to live as a contrast community on display for the sake of the watching world. With the bilateral relationship between God and his people established in the Torah, the focus of the biblical text then turns toward the completion of the

181. Fretheim, *Suffering of God*, 230.

covenantal triangle—the establishment of the land where God will place his name and dwell in their midst.[182]

---

182. Block, "Stones," 34, uses a pair of triangles to illustrate 1) the bilateral covenant relationship between Yahweh and Israel and 2) the tripartite covenant between Yahweh, Israel, and the Land of Canaan.

— 3 —

The Tabernacling Presence of God in the Prophets

This chapter takes up the theme of God's tabernacling presence at a significant point in the unfolding *missio Dei* as the people of God entered the land he had chosen as a dwelling place for his name (e.g., Deut 12:11). Why this particular place? Clearly God did not just spin the globe and pick a random spot to plant his treasured people. Even a brief geographical survey reveals that the homeland of the Israelites lay at the crossroads of three continents: Europe, Asia, and Africa. This tiny nation straddled the Levant land-bridge that was all the more narrow because of the natural barriers formed by mountains, desert, and sea. Because the international highways of the ancient Near East threaded through this thin strip of land, camel caravans long traversed these routes in search of trade, and marching armies surged through in quest of power.

Christopher Wright observes that "Israel lived on a very public stage. . . . [T]his visibility of Israel was part of its theological identity and role as the priesthood of YHWH among the nations."[1] In fact, God articulated his purpose for planting his people here: "This is Jerusalem. I have set her in the center of the nations, with countries all around her" (Ezek 5:5). God thus perfectly positioned his people to display his presence in their midst before a watching world. Unfortunately, rather than being a light to the nations, the Israelites more often succumbed to the influence of the sur-

---

1. Wright, *Mission of God*, 378–79.

rounding nations. Still, even by their negative example, God was faithful to carry out his mission.

THE TABERNACLING PRESENCE OF GOD IN THE CONQUEST

The first book of the Former Prophets opens with the people of God poised to enter this long-promised place. Significantly, Yahweh promised to accompany Joshua with his very own presence: "Just as I was with Moses, so I will be with you. I will not leave you or forsake you" (Josh 1:5b). The success of Joshua's leadership, therefore, did not hinge on his "administrative or military genius—although he appears to have had abilities in both areas—but on his devotion to God" and his continual meditation in the Law of Moses (Josh 1:8).[2] In one sense God had already given both the land and the peoples of the land into the hands of the Israelites.[3] Yet, even though the land already belonged to Israel, they would have to enter and take possession of their inheritance. Still, God himself would go with them and guarantee the process.

The Conversion of a Canaanite

The news of Yahweh's deeds had already reached the inhabitants of Canaan and paved the way before the Israelites even stepped foot in the land. When Joshua sent the two spies into the land, they took refuge in the house of Rahab, who hid them from the king of Jericho. She revealed her motivation—and the emotional state of her fellow citizens:

> I know that the Lord has given you the land, and that the fear of you has fallen upon us, and that all the inhabitants of the land melt away before you. For *we have heard* how the Lord dried up the water of the Red Sea before you when you came out of Egypt, and what you did to the two kings of the Amorites who were beyond the Jordan, to Sihon and Og, whom you devoted to destruction. And as soon as *we heard it*, our hearts melted, and there was no spirit left in any man because of you, for the Lord your God, he is God in the heavens above and on the earth beneath . . . (Josh 2:9b–11; italics added).[4]

2. Howard, *Joshua*, 62–63.

3. Ibid., 81. The land belonged to God, and it was his to give. Cf. Deut 7:1.

4. Hess, *Joshua*, 88, observes that this statement by Rahab, the Canaanite, is "one of

Rahab's confession began with a statement of the basic theological premise of the entire book: "I know that the Lord has given you the land." She then described the great fear that had fallen upon the Canaanites, causing their hearts to melt. The reason for this rampant fear was that they had heard the accounts of God's great works in drying up the Red Sea in Egypt and in devoting to destruction the kings of the Transjordan. Richard Hess notes that the verses in Josh 2:9–11 form a chiasm that pivots on the repetition of the clause, "We have heard."[5] The telling of the mighty acts of God had a powerful effect on the people of the land, causing their courage to fail before the advent of the Israelites.

This same proclamation, however, "opened a line of witness,"[6] which had an even greater effect on Rahab as her "cosmological confession"[7] in Josh 2:11 reveals: "for the Lord your God, he is God in the heavens above and on the earth beneath." As David Howard notes, this declaration is "a most remarkable statement in the mouth of a foreigner," for in it she affirms that Yahweh has dominion over the realms that her own religious tradition had ascribed to Baal, Asherah, and others.[8] This statement is Rahab's declaration of personal faith. Like her compatriots, she trembled upon hearing of the stories of Israel's powerful God; in contrast to them, Rahab cast her lot with Yahweh.

Rahab's words of faith echoed in her deeds as she showed "kindness" (*ḥesed*, "steadfast love") to the spies.[9] Later, her faithfulness resulted in her family's deliverance and incorporation into the Israelite community (Josh 6:25).[10] Hess observes that in "one of the most nationalistic books in the Hebrew Bible," the focus of the narrative shifts from Joshua, the Israelite male leader who finds his success through faith in Yahweh, to Rahab, his

---

the longest uninterrupted statements by a woman in a biblical narrative."

5. Ibid., 91.

6. Kaiser, *Mission*, 20.

7. Hess, *Joshua*, 90.

8. Howard, *Joshua*, 103.

9. Auld, *Joshua, Judges, and Ruth* points out that this word is one of the terms God used to reveal his character to Moses in Exod 34:6; therefore, it is "a vital element in the character of God, and of any true servant of his" (20–21). Rahab, a fledgling convert, had already begun to reflect the character of the God she professed.

10. While Rahab's actions earned her a commendation in the New Testament "Hall of Faith" (Heb 11:31), Auld, *Joshua*, 21, notes that ". . . Joshua himself is passed over in silence." Similarly, when James searched the Old Testament for examples of faith demonstrated by works, he proffered only two: Abraham and—surprisingly enough— "Rahab the prostitute" (Jas 2:25). Even more amazing, Matthew mentions Rahab's name in his genealogy as the ancestor of King David as well as the long-awaited Messiah. Matthew's inclusion of Rahab points to the inclusiveness of the mission of God.

female Canaanite counterpart who likewise finds success through faith in the same God.[11] Howard concludes that Rahab is "a prime example of a foreigner who responded in faith to Israel's God." In shifting her allegiance to the God of Israel, "[Rahab] was, in effect, no longer a Canaanite"; she was therefore spared the destruction that awaited the inhabitants of Canaan.[12] The news of God's presence and power resulted in the promise of salvation for at least one woman and her family before the Israelites even crossed over the Jordan. Presumably, the other citizens of Jericho could have likewise embraced Israel's God. Instead, they shut the gates tight.

The Ark Leads the Way

When the time finally came for the Israelites to enter the Promised Land, Yahweh led the procession—literally—through his presence symbolized in the ark carried by the priests. Graeme Auld comments, "The Ark of the Covenant of the Lord does not make many appearances in the pages of the Scriptures; but it is an extraordinarily potent presence when it is there. . . . [I]t seems to embody the very power and presence of God himself."[13] God gave careful instructions to the people that balanced the immanence of his presence with his transcendence: the people were to consecrate themselves and to keep a distance of at least one thousand yards from the ark itself (Josh 3:4–5). By properly revering the holiness of God in their midst, the people were prepared to witness his wondrous work in their midst.

Auld remarks that crossing the Jordan River did not necessarily require a miracle. After all, the Jordan was a barrier in only a limited sense because "it is readily fordable at several points . . . ."[14] However, although a miracle was not required, it was important. Yahweh explained the purpose of the Jordan-crossing, which so closely mirrors that of the parting of the Red Sea: "Here is how you shall know that the living God is among you and that he will without fail drive out from before you the Canaanites, the Hittites, the Hivites, the Perizzites, the Girgashites, the Amorites, and the Jebusites" (Josh 3:10). Crossing the Jordan on dry ground demonstrated to the Israelites that God was truly in their midst. The polemical reference to the "living

11. Hess, *Joshua*, 96–97.

12. Howard, *Joshua*, 104.

13. Auld, *Joshua*, 24. Howard, *Joshua*, 120, observes that the ark is a prominent feature of Joshua 3 and 4: the ark is mentioned ten times in Joshua 3 and seven times in Joshua 4. Adams, "The Present God," 291, notes that during the period of the settlement and the judges, the emphasis is on the accompanying presence rather than the localized presence.

14. Auld, *Joshua*, 23.

God" also highlighted the contrast between Israel's powerful God and the false gods of the peoples listed in the verse. The inhabitants of Canaan were not a unified foe, but "a number of different small city-states, each with its own tradition, people, culture, and god"—none of which was "any match for the living God of Israel."[15] The miraculous crossing gave notice to every one of these peoples that Yahweh alone is God. Indeed, the living God of all the earth was personally and powerfully leading his people into the land he had promised to hand over to them.

Once all the Israelites had crossed over the Jordan, Joshua ordered representatives from each of the twelve tribes to pick up twelve stones from the place where the priests stood holding the ark. When the ark finally came up out of the riverbed, "the waters of the Jordan returned to their place and overflowed all its banks, as before" (Josh 4:18). At Gilgal, Joshua erected a memorial from the stones as a perpetual testimony to both the miracle and God's presence with them.[16] Joshua reiterated that when their children would ask "What do these stones mean?" the Israelites were to recount Yahweh's miracle on their behalf (Josh 4:6, 22). The first time, Joshua explained that "these stones shall be *to the people of Israel* a memorial forever" (Josh 4:7, italics added). The second time, he acknowledged a wider audience as well: "*so that all the peoples of the earth may know* that the hand of the LORD is mighty, that you may fear the LORD your God forever" (Josh 4:24; italics added). The very next verse shows that God's amazing work displayed among his own people had the desired effect on the watching world:

> As soon as all the kings of the Amorites who were beyond the Jordan to the west, and all the kings of the Canaanites who were by the sea, heard that the LORD had dried up the waters of the Jordan for the people of Israel until they had crossed over, their hearts melted and there was no longer any spirit in them because of the people of Israel (Josh 5:1).

Like a forward guard, news of the mighty acts of God preceded the Israelites, debilitating their foes.

This paralyzing fear allowed the Israelites time for important spiritual preparations before launching the conquest. These rituals were not unnecessary interruptions in the "action" but were essential elements precisely because a proper relationship with God would be the key to the Israelites' success.[17] Then Joshua encountered a divine messenger, the commander of the army of Yahweh. When Joshua asked, "Are you for us, or for our adver-

15. Butler, *Joshua*, 47.

16. Howard, *Joshua*, 135.

17. Ibid., 61.

saries?" the reply corrected his perspective. God was on mission, assembling his heavenly hosts to accomplish his purpose in the conquest of Canaan.[18] The more appropriate question was whether or not the Israelites were rightly related to the God of all the earth. Significantly, the messenger commanded Joshua to remove his sandals, "for the place where you are standing is holy" (Josh 5:15). Yahweh was present; the place was holy; the people of God must likewise be holy.

God's Presence Brings Judgment

This clear echo of Moses' commission was a fitting prelude to Yahweh's careful instructions to Joshua concerning the capture of Jericho. Rather than crafting carefully orchestrated strategies, taking the land required sanctification and reliance on the presence and power of God. The unorthodox plan—consisting of spiritual ceremony rather than military tactics—underscored that God himself would deliver the city into the hands of the Israelites. Symbolized in the ark, the presence of Yahweh led the daily procession of Israelite soldiers around Jericho, preceded by seven priests blowing seven trumpets. On the seventh day the same procession encircled the city seven times; the Israelites shouted, and the wall "fell down flat" (Josh 6:20). Thus, the entire city was exposed and slated for absolute destruction—the sole exception being Rahab and her family. Appropriately, the account capsulizes the military matters in one terse statement that emphasizes the effortlessness with which God accomplishes his purposes.[19]

At this point one may wonder why God commanded the wholesale destruction of the Canaanites. Deuteronomy 20:16–18 makes it clear that the practice of ḥērem ("devotion to complete destruction") was very limited: it was enjoined only against the inhabitants of Canaan for the express purpose "that they may not teach you to do according to all their abominable practices that they have done for their gods . . . ."[20] Sadly, the Israelites had already demonstrated their proclivity to adopt these "abominable practices" at Baal-peor (Num 25). Also, God had already pronounced judgment against the inhabitants of Canaan in the days of Abraham but had patiently

18. Ibid., 157.

19. Ibid. Cf. Josh 6:20b.

20. Howard, *Joshua*, 185, explains that the sins of the Canaanites were particularly wicked, as reflected in his summary of the abominations catalogued in Leviticus 18: "incest, adultery, child sacrifice, homosexual activity, and bestiality." While the mitigations in this section are true, in the final analysis, this command echoes the sweeping judgment of the great flood and anticipates the sobering NT descriptions of hell. Although God is slow to anger, the time does come for judgment.

delayed fulfillment for 400 years, until the iniquity of the Amorites was complete (Gen 15:16).

Finally, it is also important to remember that God does not show favoritism. Craig Bartholomew observes that while "[t]he conquest is perilous for the Canaanites ... it is also dangerous for the Israelites, since they are dealing with Yahweh."[21] In fact, the sin of just one Israelite who violated the ḥērem placed the entire nation in grave danger. As in the golden calf incident, God threatened to remove his protective presence from their midst (Josh 7:12). Because of his rebellion, Achan had essentially become a Canaanite; thus, he suffered the same fate pronounced on the Canaanites (Josh 7).[22]

Although at first glance the destruction of the Canaanites may appear to be at odds with a universal mission, God was in fact advancing his plan to redeem a people and a place where he might live among them. Marten Woudstra observes that God's promise to bless all the peoples of the earth through Abraham "must be understood in its proper context": Canaan's "frantic preparations for war against Israel" demonstrated that they were among those who cursed Abraham and his offspring, and so they fell under God's curse (Gen 12:3).[23] Therefore, calling the nations that Yahweh intended to dispossess *enemies* "is not out of accord with the mission of Israel to be a blessing to the nations. . . . While Israel was meant to be a channel of salvation for the nations, it was also called to represent provisionally the kingdom of God on earth."[24] Those nations who opposed them were actually opposing God himself. Howard explains, "The special emphasis at the time of Joshua was that Israel was to keep itself holy, undefiled, and the land itself was to be undefiled. In the particular circumstances of the Israelites entering the long-promised land as a newly constituted nation, it was vitally important that they do so uncontaminated by pagan worship."[25] Hess also notes that the Hebrew account of the destruction of Jericho consists of 102 words, while the concluding account of Rahab's rescue is 86. He therefore concludes, "The salvation of Rahab was as important as the destruction of Jericho."[26] Those who repented and turned to God would be spared.

---

21. Bartholomew, *Where Mortals Dwell*, 77.

22. Conversely, as a Canaanite who became an Israelite, Rahab provides the perfect foil to Achan.

23. Woudstra, *Joshua*, 38. Both Testaments teach the truth that "God is 'a consuming fire.'"

24. Ibid., 133.

25. Howard, *Joshua*, 183.

26. Hess, *Joshua*, 134. The NT acknowledgments of Rahab also lend weight to this missional observation.

Likewise, when the Gibeonites heard the name of Yahweh and a report of his powerful deeds, they concocted an elaborate ruse posing as distant foreigners in order to avoid sure destruction. In exchange for their lives, they gladly accepted perpetual servitude as "cutters of wood and drawers of water for the congregation and for the altar of the Lord" (Josh 9:27).[27] The stories of Rahab and the Gibeonites clearly reveal that any Canaanites who transferred allegiance to Yahweh would be incorporated into the faith community of the Israelites. Rahab's salvation gained her a place in the genealogy of the Savior; the Gibeonites' deliverance gained them a significant—albeit menial—role of service directly related to the worship of the one true God. The call for the eradication of the Canaanites was therefore contingent upon their response to God.[28] Clearly, there was a universal scope to the mission of God as it unfolded in the land.

God's Presence Requires Covenant Renewal

Meditation on the Book of the Law was crucial to maintaining a right relationship with God. After the initial cities of the conquest fell to the Israelites, Josh 8:30–35 recounts the careful enactment of the covenant renewal ceremony prescribed in Deut 27:1–8. As per Moses' instructions, Joshua wrote out a copy of the law on a memorial stone covered in plaster. Daniel Block argues that this performative act formally incorporates the land into the tripartite covenant between Yahweh, Israel, and the land.[29] Before the entire congregation, Joshua read "all the words of the law, the blessing and the curse . . . . There was not a word of all that Moses commanded that Joshua did not read . . ." (Josh 8:34–35). Significantly, the passage emphasizes that *all* Israel participated, twice stipulating that the assembly included both "sojourners" and "native born" (Josh 8:33, 35). Howard explains that the presence of "true 'converts'" at the covenant affirmation ceremony demonstrates that the Israelite faith was not a closed system: "In the case of its aliens, Israel was to treat those within its own borders in such a way that they would be desirous of entering fully into a relationship with Israel's

27. Placing the Gibeonites in service at the sanctuary may have had a missional role in bringing them into the faith. Later references to the Gibeonites suggest that it was successful (e.g., Neh 3:7; 7:25).

28. Bartholomew, *Where Mortals Dwell*, 77.

29. Block, "Stones," 34. Block points out that this ceremony not only formalizes the Israelites' claim to the land, but it also portrays the land as an "animate . . . vital and responsive partner in the covenant relationship" (36). Just as Yahweh sealed the bilateral covenant relationship between himself and Israel in Exodus 24, here he binds the land to himself, thus completing the "deity-nation-land covenantal triangle" (37).

God."[30] Living as covenant people in relationship with the living God had missional implications.

The book of Joshua celebrates the faithfulness of Yahweh who fulfills his promise to give the Israelites the land. Chapters 18 and 19 emphasize that it is God himself who determines the distribution of the land to the various tribes. The backdrop of this land distribution was the tabernacle— newly assembled in Shiloh where it would remain until Samuel's day. It is noteworthy that at the same time God gave each of the tribes a home, he also chose a place for his own "home." This is an important development in God's mission to establish a place where he might dwell in the midst of a people who rightly worship him.

The book of Joshua closes with a second covenant renewal ceremony at Shechem. Nearing the end of his life, Joshua reminded the Israelites that God had fulfilled his part of the covenant: ". . . not one word has failed of all the good things that the LORD your God promised concerning you" (Josh 23:14). After recounting the mighty acts of God on their behalf, Joshua called the people to fulfill their part of the covenant: ". . . choose this day whom you will serve, whether the gods your fathers served in the region beyond the River, or the gods of the Amorites in whose land you dwell" (Josh 24:15). Auld observes that because Yahweh tolerates no other gods before him, the choice is quite exclusive and carries attendant dangers.[31]

The only way that the people of God would be able to resist the strong pull of the Canaanite religions would be if they followed Yahweh's injunction to Joshua at his commissioning in Josh 1:8. The speeches at the end of Joshua's life revealed that he had indeed meditated on the Book of the Law: his words were steeped in both the indicatives and imperatives found in Deuteronomy (Joshua 23–24). Clinging to Yahweh and loving him would only be possible if they, too, continually rehearsed his mighty acts and commands (Josh 23:6–11). Surrounded by people who espoused a pagan worldview diametrically opposed to their own, the Israelites must immerse themselves—and their children—in a biblical worldview if they desired to remain faithful to the God who tabernacled among them. God had abundantly proven his promise-keeping faithfulness; the Israelites' faithfulness, however, remained in question.

30. Howard, *Joshua*, 217.

31. Auld, *Joshua*, 126.

THE TABERNACLING PRESENCE OF GOD IN THE PERIOD OF THE JUDGES

The Canaanization of the Israelites

Unfortunately, the opening of the book of Judges reveals that the Israelites abysmally failed to keep their end of the covenant. How could they have gone so wrong? The text contains the telling clue: "And there arose another generation after [Joshua's generation] who did not know the LORD or the work that he had done for Israel" (Judg 2:10). In other words, the Israelites had failed to make an impact on the innermost concentric circle of missional living—the members of their immediate families. The people of God had failed to remember and pass on to the next generation the stories of God's powerful deeds on their behalf. Cut loose from their indicative moorings, the imperatives were no longer convincing, and the Israelites failed to fear, love, and obey the God who had so graciously condescended to live in their midst.

Block articulates the theme of the book of Judges as "the *Canaanization of Israelite society during the period of settlement*."[32] When the Israelites found it difficult to drive the Canaanites from the land, they compromised by allowing them to live alongside them as forced laborers (Judg 1:35). When toleration for the surrounding pagan practices turned into attraction, the Israelites abandoned Yahweh who had done so much for them, and "whored after other gods," serving and bowing down to the Baals and the Ashtaroth (Judg 2:17).[33] Block observes that "this nation had exchanged Yahweh its patron God for worthless idols—gods that were not god at all."[34] In essence, the Israelites had become Canaanites. In response, "the anger of the LORD kindled against Israel, and he gave them over to plunderers . . . [a]nd he sold them into the hand of their surrounding enemies . . ." (Judg 2:14). The Israelites must have been shocked to discover that "their real enemy was God."[35] Eventually, "moved to pity by their groaning," Yahweh would raise up a judge to deliver his people (Judg 2:18). Then, when the

---

32. Block, *Judges*, 58; italics original.

33. According to Auld, *Judges*, 143, the Baals and Ashtaroth are simply a "shorthand reference" to a disturbingly long list of divinities such as the one found in Judg 10:6: "The people of Israel again did what was evil in the sight of the LORD and served the Baals and the Ashtaroth, the gods of Syria, the gods of Sidon, the gods of Moab, the gods of the Ammonites, and the gods of the Philistines."

34. Block, *Judges*, 126.

35. Ibid., 127.

Israelites inevitably slid back into apostasy, the cycle would begin again (Judg 2:19).

Tragically, the book of Judges records six episodes that follow this basic pattern of sin, oppression, repentance, and deliverance. These cycles are not simply repeated, but rather, "Israel is depicted as increasingly Canaanized, spiraling downward into worse and worse apostasy."[36] Becoming more and more like the surrounding pagan peoples, the nation of Israel was in danger of either total assimilation or self-destruction. Block comments, "Only by the repeated gracious intervention of God do they emerge from the dark pre-monarchic period as a separate people and nation . . . [God] intervenes repeatedly presumably because his long-range goal of using Israel as a light to the nations depends upon the nation's survival of this dark period of her history."[37] Thus, the sole hero in the book of Judges is Yahweh, and he is determined to fulfill his mission.

The Deliverance of God

This concept of God as the true hero is particularly evident, for example, in the expanded Gideon cycle. In every instance God took the initiative. When the Israelites did evil, Yahweh himself gave them over to the ruthless Midianites. Later, when God sent an angel, Gideon voiced his doubt: "[I]f the LORD is with us, why then has all this happened to us?" (Judg 6:13). Like the rest of the Israelites, Gideon did not recognize that their plight was the direct result of their failure to worship exclusively the God who tabernacled among them. Still Yahweh reassured this hesitant warrior with the exact same promise he had given Moses at his commissioning—"I will be with you" (Judg 6:16; Exod 3:12). Indeed, "the Spirit of the LORD clothed Gideon" (Judg 6:34), and a miraculous victory ensued.

When the band of three hundred prevailed over an army numbered at 135,000, the glory belonged to the only true hero who was present. Still, neither Gideon nor the Israelites gave God the glory that he alone deserved. Although Yahweh had done so much for Gideon, the once-hesitant leader brazenly led the Israelites into further idolatry, "steepen[ing] the slope of their spiritual declension."[38] Fittingly, the narrator penned a summary evaluation of this period of the Judges: "In those days there was no king in Israel. Everyone did what was right in his own eyes" (Judg 17:6; 21:25).

36. Ibid., 132.
37. Ibid., 58.
38. Ibid., 301.

The chapters framed by this evaluative inclusio include stories that feature Levites fully participating in the nation's deep spiritual depravity. Even the supposed spiritual leaders of the Israelites fell prey to an insidious, internal enemy. As Block observes, the time period covered in the book of Judges serves as "[an] eternal testimony to the grim reality that God's people are often their own worst enemy. It is not the enemies outside who threaten the soul but the Canaanite within."[39] Tragically, this evaluation held true of the priests serving at the tabernacle during this period as well.

A Faithless Priesthood and a Promised Priest

The opening chapters of 1 Samuel—which immediately follows Judges in the Hebrew Scripture—reveal that even the members of the priesthood had abysmally failed to be a contrast people who displayed the presence of God in their lives. In actuality, the sons of the high priest were "worthless men [who] did not know the LORD" (1 Sam 2:12).[40] God therefore announced an irrevocable judgment against the family of Eli. In their place Yahweh promised, "I will raise up for myself a faithful priest, who shall do according to what is in my heart and in my mind. And I will build him a sure house, and he shall go in and out before my anointed forever" (1 Sam 2:35). Finally there was hope that the religious, moral, and social chaos of the period of the Judges would come to an end. The mission of God was about to advance.

The story of this promised priest had, in fact, already been introduced in the first chapter of 1 Samuel where the actions of a simple godly couple stood out in bright relief against the dark backdrop of the period. Before the tabernacle, the barren Hannah poured out her heart to Yahweh promising that if he would give her a son, she would give him back to God. When he granted her request, she named the child Samuel and brought the weaned boy back to the house of Yahweh "so that he may appear in the presence of the LORD and dwell there forever" (1 Sam 1:22). Samuel grew up in the tabernacling presence of God—literally—as he slept "in the temple of the LORD, where the ark of God was" (1 Sam 2:21; 3:3). In time Yahweh spoke to the young boy, revealing himself and his word, and promised to be with Samuel (1 Sam 3:19-21). The presence and power of God were on obvious display in the life of Samuel—in stark contrast to the wicked priests who did not even know God.

39. Ibid., 585.

40. They slept with the women who served at the entrance to the tabernacle, and they treated the offering of Yahweh with contempt by demanding the fat portions that rightfully belonged to God and should have been burned on the altar (1 Sam 2:15-17).

The Glory Departs Israel

Walter Brueggemann explains that 1 Samuel 4–7 is often called "'the ark narrative' because, apart from the powerful, invisible working of Yahweh, the ark is the only 'character' who acts in the story."[41] When the Israelites suffered the loss of four thousand troops to the Philistines, the elders of Israel determined to manipulate the outcome of the next battle by sending for the ark of the covenant. Undoubtedly, they recalled the ark's role in the fall of Jericho and hoped to harness the power of God's presence in a repeat performance. They failed to realize, however, that "the ark was neither an infallible talisman nor a military palladium that would insure victory."[42] In fact, Yahweh had a different agenda for the battle: the demise of Eli's house. Nevertheless, when "the ark of the covenant of the LORD of hosts, who is enthroned on the cherubim," arrived on the battlefield, the Israelites rallied with a great shout (1 Sam 4:4). Hearing the news that "a god has come into the camp," the Philistines quaked at the muddled memory of Israelite gods who had struck the Egyptians with plagues. Brueggemann observes that this knowledge did not cause the Philistines "to collapse, surrender, submit, or pray," but rather it emboldened them to fight all the more fiercely.[43]

The outcome of the battle seems to have surprised both sides: Israel suffered a staggering defeat in which thirty thousand soldiers were slaughtered, including the sons of Eli. Even more stunning was the unbearable news that the ark had fallen into the hands of the Philistines. This was the piece of news that toppled the aged and heavy (kābôd) Eli from his chair and broke his neck. Likewise, the shocking report sent Eli's daughter-in-law into labor. With her last breath she named her newborn son Ichabod ('i-kābôd, lit., "Where [is] glory?" or "Nothing of glory"),[44] saying, "The glory has departed from Israel, for the ark of God has been captured" (1 Sam 4:21).

The Ark Bears Witness among the Philistines

The victorious Philistines paraded the ark back to Ashdod, setting it up in the temple of Dagon, next to the pagan idol. Inconceivably, it appears as though "YHWH is a prisoner of war put on exhibit," an attendant to the supposedly superior Philistine god.[45] The Philistines, however, understood nei-

41. Brueggemann, Samuel, 28.
42. Youngblood, "Samuel," 595.
43. Brueggemann, Samuel, 31.
44. Bergen, Samuel, 94.
45. Brueggemann, Ichabod, 26.

ther the power of God nor the first two of his commandments.[46] The light of dawn revealed the statue of Dagon in "an act of obeisance," facedown before Yahweh who would never be any pagan god's acolyte.[47] Quickly the priests set Dagon back in place, but the next morning the idol was once more prostrate before the Judge of the ends of the earth—only this time the impotent idol had lost both head and hands. Yahweh displayed his formidable power by slaying the Philistine god in a "ritual execution."[48] Indeed, God himself literally deconstructed the false religion of the Philistines. Dagon, however, did not suffer alone, as the ark's presence wreaked havoc on the general populace in the form of a deadly plague. Finally, the desperate Philistines admitted defeat and resolved to return the ark to the Israelites in a way that would "give glory [*kābôd*] to the God of Israel" (1 Sam 6:5).

Significantly, the glorious "God of Israel" returned to Israel under his own power and direction. After all, he is "a self-emancipating, initiative-taking, glory-getting God."[49] The apparent capture of the ark turned out to be "a divine ruse" to display his unparalleled majesty among the nations.[50] Ironically, when the Israelites failed to live as display people, God himself bore witness among the Philistines through the ark of testimony. Presumably, the Philistines could have recognized Yahweh's exclusive authority and yielded their allegiance to him alone. Instead, they sent the ark on its way while clinging to their worldview and worship of Dagon with one alteration—the added taboo of not treading on the threshold where his lifeless head and hands had lain.

When the ark returned to the Israelite city of Beth-shemesh, the inhabitants took the ark, chopped up the cart, and sacrificed the calves on its wood. Their celebration was cut short, however, when Yahweh struck down seventy irreverent Israelites who dared to look inside the ark (1 Sam 6:19). They quickly learned that God's presence judged and blessed Israelites and Gentiles without partiality. The great stone beside which they placed the ark stood as a witness to future generations of all that had transpired. Because of the Israelites' sin, the glory had truly departed the tabernacle. That the ark remained at Kiriath-jearim[51] rather than returning to Shiloh points to the

---

46. Brueggemann, *Samuel*, 34.

47. Brueggemann, *Ichabod*, 47.

48. Bergen, *Samuel*, 96.

49. Brueggemann, *Ichabod*, 43.

50. Bergen, 1, 2 *Samuel*, 97.

51. Cf. 1 Sam 7:1–2. It is noteworthy that the city of Kiriath-jearim belonged to the Gibeonites who had made a treaty with the Israelites (cf. Josh 9:17). Similarly, the tabernacle and altar were located in the city of Gibeon during this same time period (cf. 1 Chr 16:39–40).

likelihood that the religious center at Shiloh had been destroyed soon after the infamous capture of the ark.

With the demise of the Elide dynasty, Samuel challenged all Israel to return to the exclusive covenant relationship with Yahweh. The people complied and Samuel gathered all Israel together at Mizpah for a solemn assembly in which they fasted, prayed, and confessed their sin. Alarmed at the massive gathering, the Philistines drew near to attack Israel. This time, however, the outcome of the battle was completely different. Yahweh himself thundered, throwing the Philistines into confusion that contributed to their sound defeat. Although the ark did not make an appearance in the battle, this time the repentant Israelites had something far more powerful: they were rightly related to the God who was present in their midst. Samuel acknowledged God's role in the battle with a memorial stone called "Ebenezer" ("The Stone of [the] Help"; 1 Sam 7:12).[52] Thus, Samuel and the Israelites rightly ascribed the victory to Yahweh who alone deserved the glory.

Under Samuel's leadership, Israel continued to walk in a covenant relationship with Yahweh. When he grew old, however, the nation rejected this theocratic arrangement designed to display the glory of their divine King. Rather than being a contrast people, the Israelites begged for a human king: "so that we also may be like all the nations, and that our king may judge us and go out before us and fight our battles" (1 Sam 8:20). God acquiesced to their demands by giving them Saul: "a clear example of leadership at odds with the Lord." Robert Bergen points out the contrast in the similar names: Samuel ("Requested from God") and Saul ("Requested"). The theophoric element that is present in Samuel's name and absent from Saul's reflects "the essential difference between the two leaders: Samuel's life and career were marked by the presence of God; Saul's were not."[53] Not surprisingly, then, Yahweh stripped the monarchy from a disobedient Saul and bestowed it on David, a man after God's own heart (1 Sam 13:14).

THE TABERNACLING PRESENCE OF GOD AND THE MONARCHY

David Prepares for the Temple

The aging Samuel anointed the eighth son of Jesse with oil—which "symbolized the divine presence entering into the one being anointed"[54]—and

52. Bergen, *Samuel*, 108.

53. Ibid., 119.

54. Ibid., 180.

"the Spirit of the LORD rushed upon David from that day forward" (1 Sam 16:13b). David's mounting political and military successes were directly attributable to the presence of God displayed in his life: "And David became greater and greater, for the LORD, the God of hosts, was with him" (2 Sam 5:10). Once all of Israel recognized David's rule, he captured the Jebusite stronghold and named this "City of David" as his political capital. More importantly, Jerusalem was the place where Yahweh had chosen for his name to dwell.

The Ark Arrives in Jerusalem

Desiring to make Jerusalem the religious center of the nation, David assembled thirty thousand men to help bring the ark up to the city. This jubilant procession came to a sudden halt when oxen pulling the new cart stumbled, and God struck Uzzah dead for reaching out to steady the ark.[55] While the presence of a holy God in their midst was an incredible privilege, it also introduced the inherent danger of presumptuous familiarity. Brueggemann rightly observes, "When people are no longer awed, respectful, or fearful of God's holiness, the community is put at risk." Any possible "hint of political calculation and manipulation"[56] on David's part immediately evaporated into a proper fear of God: "How can the ark of the LORD come to me?" (2 Sam 6:9). The sobering event was a clear reminder that this holy God would enter Jerusalem only on his own terms. Consequently, David left the ark at the house of a man named Obed-edom the Gittite, whom Yahweh blessed along with his entire household (2 Sam 6:11). Although the presence of God could be deadly among those who failed to revere him, it could also bring great blessing to those who were rightly related to him.

Three months later, David exercised proper reverence in transporting the ark into Jerusalem. The Levites carried the ark in the prescribed manner, and the king offered sacrifices when they "rested" after taking six steps. Dressed in a linen ephod, "David danced before the LORD with all his might" (2 Sam 6:14), having "shamelessly abandoned himself to the glory, exposing and ceding himself over to the presence."[57] The ark arrived in the midst of jubilant shouting and singing accompanied by trumpets, horns, cymbals, harps and lyres; and David placed the ark inside the tent he had

55. Gordon, *Samuel*, 232, suggests that although Uzzah's action may have been an unintentional reflex, the failure to transport the ark in the prescribed manner (Exod 25:12–15) made his error a possibility.

56. Brueggemann, *Samuel*, 249.

57. Brueggemann, *Ichabod*, 60.

prepared for it.[58] After sacrificing burnt offerings and peace offerings, the king blessed the people and distributed meat and cakes of bread and raisins to "the whole multitude of Israel" (2 Sam 6:19). With this extravagant worship and communal meal, the Israelites welcomed the ark of God's presence into Jerusalem. David's song of thanksgiving for this occasion calls for the Israelites to recall Yahweh's wondrous works and to remember his "everlasting covenant to Israel" (1 Chr 16:8–22).[59] The hymn balances this particularity, however, with a marvelous universality:

> Sing to the Lord, *all the earth*!
> Tell of his salvation from day to day.
> Declare his glory *among the nations*,
> his marvelous works among *all the peoples*!
> For great is the LORD, and greatly to be praised,
> and he is to be feared above all gods.
> For all the gods of the peoples are worthless idols,
> but the LORD made the heavens (1 Chr 16:23–26; italics added).

This global proclamation of Yahweh's exclusive reign and glorious salvation requires an equally expansive missional summons to worship:

> Ascribe to the Lord, *O families of the peoples*,
> ascribe to the LORD glory and strength! . . .
> Let the heavens be glad, and let the earth rejoice,
> and let them say *among the nations*, "The LORD reigns!"
> Let the sea roar, and all that fills it;
> let the field exult, and everything in it!
> Then shall the trees of the forest sing for joy
> before the LORD, for he comes to judge the earth.
> O give thanks to the LORD for he is good;
> for his steadfast love endures forever! (1 Chr 16:28–34; italics added).

Remarkably, David's song of thanksgiving does not stop with the worship of all peoples everywhere. It rightly commands all creation to join in worship: the heavens and earth, the sea and field and all that fill them, even the very trees of the forest! Every people *and every place* are to worship and tremble before the glory of this one true God. This song of David illustrates how worship is inherently missional. A heart full of praise recognizes that "no

---

58. This was a different tent than the tabernacle, which remained at Gibeon. There the Zadokite priesthood continued to oversee daily sacrifices, thanksgiving, and "sacred song" (cf. 1 Chr 16:39–40).

59. Although citations from Chronicles are part of the *Writings* and not the *Prophets*, the chronicler's material helps fill in gaps in the Samuel narrative.

corner of creation [should] be exempt from exposure to the glory of God."[60] This is precisely the goal of God's mission: to extend the praise of God's glory to every people group in every place. The glory that had departed when Yahweh surrendered the ark into the hands of the Philistines had indeed returned to Israel. Thus the true King of Israel entered the city where he had chosen to place his name.

A Tent versus a House

After a time the blatant contrast began to weigh on David: while he dwelt in a sumptuous palace, the ark of God dwelt in a simple tent (2 Sam 7:2). David therefore proposed to rectify this imbalance by building a similar house of cedar for God. After all, kings in the ancient world frequently crowned their achievements by erecting a temple to their god. However, even though Nathan initially had approved of the king's plan, Yahweh himself revoked permission in an oracle through the prophet (2 Sam 7:5–16). This monologue of 197 words—the longest recorded statement by Yahweh since the time of Moses—is extremely significant.[61] Brueggemann describes it as "the dramatic and theological center of the entire Samuel corpus," and "one of the most crucial texts in the Old Testament for evangelical faith."[62] Although these descriptors may seem effusive, the content of the passage holds up to the superlatives.

In the oracle Yahweh pointed out that he did not need a house in which to dwell. Instead, his presence had accompanied the Israelites as they left Egypt—even before there was a tabernacle. Therefore, the portable tent had been particularly suited to symbolize his presence in all their wanderings. Furthermore, God had not commanded David or any past leader to build him a house. If Yahweh did desire a temple, he himself would initiate the plan, name the place, and tap the person to build it. As the object of worship, God rightfully dictates the parameters of worship.

In the next section of the oracle, God recounted all he had done for his servant David; then he outlined what he would do—in language that clearly echoed his covenant with Abraham.[63] Instead of accepting David's offer to build a house for him, Yahweh promised to build a "house" for David—a

60. Liederbach and Reid, *Convergent Church*, 131.

61. Bergen, *Samuel*, 336.

62. Brueggemann, *Samuel*, 253; Gordon, *Samuel*, 235, calls the monologue the "ideological summit" of the entire Old Testament; Kaiser, *Mission*, 22, maintains, "It will stand forever as one of the grand high points in God's revelation to humankind."

63. Youngblood, "Samuel," 888.

dynasty, a throne, and a kingdom that would endure forever. He declared, "I will raise up your offspring after you, who shall come from your body . . . . I will establish the throne of his kingdom forever" (2 Sam 7:12–13). Although God did concede that David's son would eventually build a house for his name (2 Sam 7:13), the emphasis is on the dynastic house, rather than the temple. This passage focuses on "Yahweh himself, and his covenant promises that remain when all else fails, and the houses of cedar have turned to dust."[64] Even when David's successors would fail so miserably that they would eventually be removed from power, the "Davidic hope" of an everlasting kingdom anticipated that one day a deliverer would arise from his offspring—"a shoot from the stump of Jesse" (Isa 11:1). Robert Gordon therefore christens the Nathan oracle as "the matrix of biblical messianism."[65]

Yahweh's covenant with the house of David is a major development in the unfolding mission of God. The hope for all the families of the world would not be fulfilled in a *temple* filled with the presence of God, but in a *person* filled with the presence of God. Bergen suggests that David did not need to construct a lifeless temple for God's dwelling place because Yahweh had already constructed just such an edifice in the life of David: "Though the ark resided in a lifeless tent of skin, in a very real sense the Lord resided in the living tent of David."[66] Indeed, the covenant promises of God find their ultimate fulfillment in one of the offspring from David's own body—the Messiah, the Word of God who would take on a tent of flesh (cf. John 1:14).

Both the oracle and David's response emphasize the particularity of God's mission. Overwhelmed with God's extravagant promises, David evidently entered the sacred tent and sat in the presence of God. His worshipful adoration is inherently polemical in its exclusive monotheism: "For there is none like you, and there is no God besides you . . . And who is like your people Israel whom God went to redeem to be his people . . . driving out before your people a nation and its gods?" (2 Sam 7:22b–24a). Because God's revelation concerned the house of David, the king's response naturally mirrored its particularity.

There is evidence, however, that David's prayer may also point to the universality of the mission of God. Marveling at the magnitude of Yahweh's kindness, David remarks, "And yet this was a small thing in your eyes, O Lord GOD. You have spoken also of your servant's house for a great while

---

64. Amerding, "House of Cedar," 47.

65. Gordon, *Samuel*, 236.

66. Bergen, *Samuel*, 339. Bergen, ibid., notes that later prophets refer to the Davidic dynasty as the "tent of David" (cf. Isa 16:5; Amos 9:11; Acts 15:16).

to come, and *this is instruction for mankind*" (2 Sam 7:19; italics added).[67] The antecedent for "this" is the content of the oracle just pronounced about the offspring of David. Just as God had promised Abraham, the offspring promised to David would be a blessing to all the nations of the earth. God's blessing on David's house was not limited to the Israelites.

The Purchase of the Temple Site

The concluding appendix in 2 Samuel 24 narrates the backstory of the temple location. After King David stubbornly insisted on conducting a census of the Israelites, he later recognized it as sin and repented of his actions (2 Sam 24:10). God allowed him to choose his own punishment—three years of famine, three months of war, or three days of plague. David chose the latter, preferring to cast himself on God's mercy. Indeed Yahweh showed mercy, staying the angel's hand before the pestilence—which had already killed seventy thousand—destroyed Jerusalem. The sincerity of David's repentance reflects in the shepherd-king's offer to lay down his own life: "Behold, I have sinned, and I have done wickedly. But these sheep, what have they done? Please let your hand be against me and against my father's house" (2 Sam 24:17).[68]

Instead, Yahweh commanded David: "Go up, raise an altar to the LORD on the threshing floor of Araunah the Jebusite" (2 Sam 24:18). Refusing to give God a sacrifice that cost him nothing, David purchased the land from Araunah along with the oxen for the burnt offering and the yokes and threshing sledge for wood. There on the hill overlooking Jerusalem, David built an altar and offered burnt offerings and peace offerings, and Yahweh averted the punishment for sin. The chronicler adds the following footnote to this narrative in his parallel account: "Then David said, "Here shall be the house of the LORD God and here the altar of burnt offering for Israel" (1 Chr 22:1). It is intriguing that *this* is the place LORD chose as a dwelling for his name (cf. Deut 12:11). Allen Ross observes, "This episode symbolized the drama of worship that would unfold here: sinful people who would appeal to God's grace on the basis of the sacrifices would find true peace with

---

67. Similarly, the HCSB translates the phrase (*torat ha'adam*) as "this is a revelation for mankind." Kaiser, *Mission*, 23, translates it as "this is the charter/instruction for all mankind." Regarding this suggestion of universality, Kaiser exclaims, "Surely that is mission at its highest watermark!" (ibid., 24).

68. Gordon, *Samuel*, 320.

God . . . ."[69] Certainly this incident highlighted the need for atonement if the presence of God was to continue dwelling in the midst of the Israelites.

This episode has other missional dimensions as well, as seen in the added details of Chronicles, where the chronicler identifies this same location as Mount Moriah, where God had commanded Abraham to offer Isaac (2 Chr 3:1; cf. Gen 22:2). This identification recalls God's provision of a substitute sacrifice as well as the place name "The LORD will provide" and the proverb: "On the mount of the LORD it shall be provided" (Gen 22:14). Because Abraham had not withheld his only son, Yahweh had reiterated his missional promise to the patriarch: "in your offspring all the nations of the earth shall be blessed" (Gen 22:18). The ancient promise contains the hope that God will provide for the atonement of Gentiles as well.

A Gentile with a Front-Row Seat

It is certainly intriguing that a Gentile played a supporting role at this critical juncture in the life of Israel. Araunah the Jebusite had been an inhabitant of Jebus, one of the last Canaanite holdouts against the Israelites, before David conquered this "fortress of Zion" and claimed it as his own "City of David" (2 Sam 5:6–12). Evidently the capture of the city did not involve a wholesale slaughter or displacement of the Jebusites—as evidenced by the cordial negotiations between David and Araunah. When David offered to buy the threshing floor to build an altar, Araunah bowed facedown before David and graciously supplied all that was needed: "See, I give the oxen for burnt offerings and the threshing sledges for the wood and the wheat for a grain offering; I give it all" (1 Chr 21:23b).[70]

Even though David insisted on paying, Araunah still had a vested interest in the events that immediately followed. When David offered the oxen as a sacrifice, "the LORD answered [David] with fire from heaven upon the altar of burnt offering . . . and [the angel] put his sword back into its sheath" (1 Chr 21:26–27). Araunah may very well have witnessed this visible fulfillment of his "prayerful wish"[71] voiced earlier: "May the LORD [Yahweh] your God accept you" (2 Sam 24:23b). For some reason Yahweh afforded this Gentile a front-row seat to this powerful scenario of both the wrath and mercy of God. On the mountain called "The LORD will provide," Arau-

69. Ross, *Hope of Glory*, 243.

70. Perhaps Araunah's largesse was prompted by the sight of the angel of Yahweh with "drawn sword stretched out over Jerusalem" (1 Chr 21:15–16, 20)—a scene that recalls the cherubim with a flaming sword restricting the access to Eden (Gen 3:24).

71. Bergen, *Samuel*, 479.

nah had experienced firsthand his providential provision of the essential elements for an atoning sacrifice—the same place that Yahweh had chosen to place his name forever. While David's purchase of the threshing floor extended the Israelites' rule over one of the last of the Canaanite holdouts in the land, the events that unfolded there raise at least the possibility that Yahweh may have also extended his rule over the heart of Araunah.

Solomon Builds the Temple

Andrea Spatafora notes that the Hebrew terms used to designate the temple are *bêt* (house) and *hekal* (palace or temple). He observes that the use of these terms reveals that, "the Jerusalem shrine was considered to be God's house, his palace, for he was understood to be the king of Israel."[72] Appropriately, then, the writer of 1 Kings crafts his account of Solomon's reign (chapters 3–11) as a chiasm that serves to focus the reader's attention on Solomon's most significant accomplishment (chapters 5–8)—the construction of a dwelling place for the true King of Israel.[73]

God is always the one who initiates his own worship. Not only had Yahweh revealed the site for the temple and selected David's son, Solomon, for the task of construction, but he had also given David the actual plans for the temple (see 1 Chr 28:11–12; 19). These and many other details recall God's similar activity in the construction of the tabernacle. The tabernacle served as the prototype for Solomon's temple, both structures having an outer courtyard, a Holy Place, and a Most Holy Place. Just as embroidered cherubim adorned the veil separating the innermost sanctuary of the tabernacle, a massive pair of carved cherubim guarded the ark in Most Holy Place of the temple (Exod 26:31–33; 1 Kgs 6:27). Both sets of cherubim recall those stationed as sentries at the entrance to Eden (Gen 3:24). Additionally, the garden symbolism depicted in the blossoms of the tabernacle lampstand was amplified in the beautifully carved flowers, palm trees, and pomegranates of the temple. These art motifs "graphically transferred" the meaning of the "original garden sanctuary" to the temple, reflecting in some measure the primordial sanctuary where the first humans had unrestricted access to the presence of God.[74]

Similarly, the glorious theophany of God's immanent presence at the temple dedication echoed the same event that occurred at the tabernacle dedication. Just as in Moses' day, the priests were unable to continue serving

---

72. Spatafora, *Temple of God*, 17.

73. Brueggemann, *Solomon*, 87.

74. Dumbrell, *End of the Beginning*, 52.

after they set the ark in place under the sheltering wings of the cherubim, and the Shekinah glory-cloud filled the temple (1 Kgs 8:11; cf. Exod 40:34). Solomon declared, "The LORD has said that he would dwell in thick darkness. I have indeed built you an exalted house, a place for you to dwell in forever" (1 Kgs 8:12–13). In the king's dedicatory prayer, however, he acknowledged that such a miniscule structure cannot hold the Creator of the heavens and earth: "But will God indeed dwell on the earth? Behold, heaven and the highest heaven cannot contain you; how much less this house that I have built!" (1 Kgs 8:27).

Solomon's Dedicatory Prayer

This awareness of the transcendence of God is also reflected in Solomon's petition that envisioned various scenarios when the people of Israel might call on Yahweh for help. The king repeatedly prayed, "Hear from heaven, your dwelling place, and when you hear, forgive" (1 Kgs 8:30, 32, 34, 36, 39, 43, 45, 49). Terence Fretheim explains the balance of immanence and transcendence in this passage: "[T]his text claims that God dwells in *both* temple and heaven, and these claims should be kept in constant interaction with each other so as not to lose the concern that each individually expresses."[75] This perspective would prove to be crucially important for the Israelites who found themselves in exile by the end of the book of Kings. Although Yahweh had deigned to tabernacle among his people in the temple (1 Kgs 6:13; 8:6–7, 10–13; 2 Kgs 19:15), Fretheim observes that the theology of presence presented in Solomon's prayer is replete with qualifications and "comes with no guarantees." This inscrutable God who "dwell[s] in a dark cloud" (1 Kgs 8:12) remains "a mystery and cannot be domesticated."[76]

Solomon's prayer of dedication also contains elements of restrictivity. The king of Israel was keenly aware of the nation's propensity to rebel and the judgment that sin would necessitate. Kneeling in prayer, Solomon beseeched Yahweh to hear the prayers of his people, to forgive their sins, and to amend the consequences of their sins. When he had finished praying, Solomon blessed the people: "The LORD our God be with us, as he was with our fathers. May he not leave us or forsake us, that he may incline our hearts to him, to walk in all his ways and to keep his commandments, his statutes, and his rules, which he commanded our fathers" (1 Kgs 8:57–58).

---

75. Fretheim, *Kings*, 54; italics original.

76. Ibid., 53. Fretheim also mentions that the odd notation of 1 Kgs 8:8—the ark's carrying poles were so long that they were visible from the Holy Place—seems to underscore the concept that Yahweh is free to move on whenever he so chooses.

The king also pled with the people to be completely devoted to Yahweh. As always, God's presence in their midst required cleansing from sin and total consecration. After the dedicatory prayer, Solomon had to consecrate the entire temple courtyard because the bronze altar could not hold all the burnt offerings, the grain offerings, and the fat of a staggering number of 142,000 fellowship offerings (1 Kgs 8:62–64). When God's people were thus rightly related to him, they enjoyed a massive communion meal with Yahweh, rejoicing in the very place that he had chosen "to put his name and make his habitation there"—just as Moses had instructed (Deut 12:5–12). This two-week festival was a wonderful foretaste of God's ultimate goal for mission.

In fact, the temple itself was designed for activities that pointed to the *missio Dei*. Michael Goheen summarizes the importance of the temple for mission:

> The temple provides the sacrificial system as a way to repair the people's failure and set them on the right path again; it provides worship to nurture faithfulness, celebrates an alternative world-view to that of paganism, stands as a witness to the true God and the real world, and exhorts Israel to exercise a universal vision. To miss the missional significance of the temple is to misunderstand profoundly the role of the temple in Israel's life.[77]

Clearly, the construction of the temple—the meeting point for God and humankind—was a momentous development in the unfolding theme of God's tabernacling presence.[78]

Solomon's Missional Petition

Naturally, Solomon's prayer at the dedication of the temple focused on the God of Israel dwelling in the midst of his own people. But what is remarkable is that embedded in this particularity is "possibly the most marvelously universalistic passage in the Old Testament."[79] One of the scenarios Solomon envisioned concerns those outside the nation of Israel:

> Likewise, when a foreigner, who is not of your people Israel, comes from a far country for your name's sake (for they shall hear of your great name and your mighty hand, and of your

77. Goheen, *Light to the Nations*, 58–59.

78. Adams, "Present God," 291, observes that these circumstances also resulted in a pendulum swing from the accompanying presence of God toward a localized presence.

79. DeVries, 1 *Kings*, 126.

outstretched arm), when he comes and prays toward this house, hear in heaven your dwelling place and do according to all for which the foreigner calls to you, in order that all the peoples of the earth may know your name and fear you, as do your people Israel, and that they may know that this house that I have built is called by your name (1 Kgs 8:41–43).

The underlying assumption is that the fame of Israel's God would spread even to peoples who live in distant lands. These foreigners would not only learn the name "Yahweh" but also his identity represented in the name. News of God's power and mighty acts would so intrigue them that they would be drawn to seek the God of the Israelites; they would even be willing to travel great distances for his name's sake.

Solomon beseeched Yahweh to answer the prayers of foreigners who pray to him, in order that "*all* the peoples of the earth" may know and fear him—just as the Israelites do. Fretheim notes, "[T]his petition on behalf of foreigners is also grounded in God's promises to Israel and God's presence in Israel's temple. The monotheistic faith of Israel is 'ecumenical' in that it understands its God not only to be active in the lives of such foreigners but also eager to attend to their prayers."[80] This prayer which began with a polemical praise statement of the incomparability of the God of Israel (1 Kgs 6:23), closes with a missional benediction that God would be with the Israelites so "that all the peoples of the earth may know that the LORD is God; there is no other" (1 Kgs 8:60). Solomon's prayers on behalf of those outside of the faith community reflect God's heart for the nations and his purpose to spread his glory to the ends of the earth.

The rest of the book of Kings offers evidence that God was actively answering Solomon's prayers regarding foreigners.[81] A prime example is the queen of Sheba, who "heard of the fame of Solomon concerning the name of the LORD" in the distant land of southwest Arabia (1 Kgs 10:1). She traveled from this far country all the way to Jerusalem in order to test Solomon with hard questions. When she saw the king's wisdom and prosperity with her own eyes and witnessed his burnt offerings at the temple, it literally took her breath away (1 Kgs 10:5). She therefore praised Solomon's God, declaring, "Blessed be the LORD your God who . . . set you on the throne of Israel . . . that you may execute justice and righteousness" (1 Kgs 10:9). In a second example, God directed Elijah to travel outside of the land of Israel to Sidon, where he had commanded a widow to feed the prophet—from the very last

80. Fretheim, *Kings*, 51.

81. Fretheim, ibid., 52, suggests that the testimonies of Naaman and the Queen of Sheba demonstrate the missional impact of Solomon's prayer.

handful of her provisions. This obedient Gentile witnessed not only God's gracious provision of an unending supply of flour and oil, but also the far greater miracle of her dead son being restored to life. In light of Yahweh's activity in Sidon—the epicenter of radical Baal worship—the widow reached the unerring conclusion: "Now I know that you are a man of God, and that the word of the LORD in your mouth is truth" (1 Kgs 17:24).

A final example is Naaman, the Syrian army commander who suffered with leprosy. This time, however, the proclamation of Yahweh's power came not through a king or a prophet, but through someone with the lowest social standing imaginable—a captured Israelite slave-girl who dared to offer what her master needed most. Desperate for healing, Naaman traveled to Samaria and eventually humbled himself by obeying Elisha's orders. Once healed, the Syrian made the astounding confession: "Behold, I know that there is no God in all the earth but in Israel . . . . [F]rom now on your servant will not offer burnt offering or sacrifice to any god but the LORD" (2 Kgs 5:15, 17). Fretheim comments, "Naaman's confession is remarkably sophisticated in its understanding of God in both particular and universal terms ('in Israel'; 'all the earth'). . . . The confession excludes all gods that other lands may have to offer (the universal dimension), but the confession is linked to a particular community, namely, Israel . . . ."[82] Significantly, Jesus held up each of these Gentiles as positive examples of faith in contrast to his own unbelieving generation (cf. Matt 12:42; Luke 4:24–27).

Solomon Slips into Syncretism

Unfortunately, not all of the Israelites' encounters with outsiders had a missional impact. Solomon evidently sealed many of his international treaties with marriage, resulting in a surprising list of nationalities. Contrary to the Deuteronomic prohibitions against pagan partners, "King Solomon loved many foreign women along with the daughter of Pharaoh: Moabite, Ammonite, Edomite, Sidonian, and Hittite women" (1 Kgs 11:1; cf. Deut 7:3–4; 17:17). Instead of leading these women to worship Yahweh, Solomon not only tolerated their idolatry, but he actually built high places "on the mountain east of Jerusalem"—in full view of the temple—to facilitate their worship of false gods: Ashtoreth, Milcom, Chemosh, and Molech (1 Kgs 11:5, 7). Tragically, Solomon's compromise led to syncretism in his own heart, and he began to worship these "abominations" as well. Paul House therefore

---

82. Fretheim, *Kings*, 155.

lays the blame for the nation's initial descent into pluralism at the feet of Solomon.[83]

In fact, Daniel Hays observes that "a very negative characterization of Solomon emerges" in the narrative of 1 Kings 1–11. He argues that the account of Solomon's temple construction, which is the climax of the narrative, exhibits "the same kind of ironic critique underlying the superficial surface praise."[84] Contrasting the descriptions of how the temple was built vis-à-vis the tabernacle, Hays concludes that whereas the account of tabernacle construction emphasizes the role of Yahweh, the Kings account of the temple construction "is dominated by Solomon and two Canaanites from Tyre."[85] Tellingly, the only time that the construction account in Kings records a word from God to Solomon, it is a jarring interruption in which "Yahweh is cautionary rather than congratulatory," reminding Solomon that his presence in the midst of his people is contingent on obedience rather than the construction of a temple.[86] Significantly, following the dedication of the structure, the temple receives very little mention in the book of Kings.[87]

Certainly, the progression of God's mission had revealed a growing emphasis on the house (descendants) of David rather than the house (temple) of God (cf. 1 Kgs 8:16). But in view of the difficulties that worship in the high places posed, the people of God needed one centralized location "where their communion with [Yahweh] would be most meaningful and beneficial."[88] Sadly, Solomon seemed to value erecting the stone structure more than maintaining his relationship with the living God tabernacling in their midst. In the end his love for his foreign wives outweighed his love for Yahweh, and his example set the entire nation on the road to apostasy.

The Northern Kingdom's Apostasy and Exile

The syncretism that Solomon slipped into gradually, Jeroboam plunged into headlong. When Solomon's heir, Rehoboam, refused to end his father's practices of heavy taxation and labor conscription, Jeroboam led the revolt against the house of David. Anxious to consolidate his leadership over his foundling northern kingdom, Jeroboam realized that if his subjects traveled south to worship at the temple, they could easily renew their allegiance to

83. House, *Kings*, 74.

84. Hays, "Just How Glorious," 2–3.

85. Ibid., 11.

86. Walsh, 1 *Kings*, 105.

87. Fyall, "Curious Silence," 50–58.

88. Ross, *Hope of Glory*, 248.

the Davidic king. As a preventative measure, Jeroboam made golden calves and set them up at Bethel and Dan, declaring: "Behold your gods, O Israel, who brought you up out of the land of Egypt" (1 Kgs 12:28; cf. Exod 32:8). Jeroboam installed non-Levitical priests in high places everywhere and instituted festivals in months of his own choosing (1 Kgs 12:31–33). Jeroboam's actions launched the kingdom into wholesale idolatry, and future northern kings were held up to Jeroboam's wicked benchmark (e.g., 1 Kgs 15:34). Replicating the external religious trappings of the temple failed to secure God's favor or the nation's future; rather, it provoked Yahweh's wrath and insured Israel's demise.

One of the most intriguing examples of God's missional activity occurs during the reign of King Ahab, who made Jeroboam's sins seem "light" by comparison (1 Kgs 16:31). Ahab had facilitated the radical Baalism of his Sidonian wife, Jezebel, by building her a temple of Baal. Jezebel, however, "insisted on attempting to promote Baal as a replacement for Yahweh" and systematically set out to extinguish all the prophets of Yahweh who opposed her. House observes, "Her successes moved Israel beyond tolerance of high places and syncretism to outright worship of another god."[89]

Because Baal worshipers believed their god was a storm-god, Elijah prayed for a three-year drought, thereby attacking Baalism at its "theological center."[90] Caught thus between "two competing worldviews," the Israelites tried to live in both and failed to commit to either.[91] Elijah therefore proposed a contest on Mount Carmel that would reveal the identity of the true God. The contrast between the two sides was unambiguous. The day-long frenetic activity of the 450 prophets of Baal resulted only in deafening silence: "[T]here was no voice. No one answered; no one paid attention" (1 Kgs 18:29). Elijah, however, simply prayed that the God of Abraham, Isaac, and Israel would answer him so "that this people may know that you, O Lord, are God, and that you have turned their hearts back" (1 Kgs 18:37). When the fire fell from heaven, the people likewise fell on their faces, acknowledging, "The Lord, he is God; the Lord, he is God" (1 Kgs 18:39).

---

89. House, *Kings*, 211.

90. Ibid., 213.

91. Ibid., 219. Meanwhile, the people of Israel continued to "limp" (*pāsaḥ*: "waver," NIV; "hesitate," HCSB, NASB) between two opinions (1 Kgs 18:21). Fretheim, *Kings*, 105–6, points out that "divided allegiances are as unfaithful as abandonment of Yahweh altogether." He elaborates: "Israel's limping with two different opinions needs to be named for what it is: It is not neutrality, tolerance, indecision, indifference, or lukewarmness. It is apostasy, pure and simple."

A bolt out of the blue had shattered their false worldview, converting them into "strict Yahwistic monotheists"—at least temporarily.[92]

The entire scenario has missional dimensions. Elijah allowed the prophets' exhaustive, desperate measures to expose the emptiness of their own beliefs: Baal could not hear or speak or act; Baal was no god at all. When Elijah's turn came, he simply called on the name of Yahweh, identifying him as the "God of Abraham, Isaac, and Israel"—a shorthand reference to the entire historical narrative of God's presence and activity among his people in the past. The phrase also recalled all the covenant promises of God's mission: to make them a people, to give them a place, to be present with them, and to bless both their descendants and all families of the earth through their offspring. God's purpose for the event was that the people would know that he alone is God.

The efficacy of Elijah's prayer depended not on the eloquence of his words, but on the power of God. As Wright points out, the biblical perspective on "conflict with the gods" is that "God fights for us, not we for him."[93] In contrast to the echoing silence that met the pagan prophets' cries, when Elijah called on God to reveal himself, Yahweh unmistakably thundered his reply. The transcendent God of Israel was not confined to the temple in Jerusalem (nor in Bethel or Dan). However, this living, active, and powerful God is also immanent. He was there—in their midst—on the heights of Mount Carmel! In sight of Sidon Yahweh proved that *he* is the God who controls lightning and rain. He not only hears but answers! The only proper response to this God is to fall down and worship, to acknowledge that he alone is God. For those who refuse to bow before him, the alternative is clear: not one escapes God's judgment. All 450 prophets of Baal were slaughtered. It is also instructive to recognize that even such a clear demonstration of God's presence and power did not convince all. As Jezebel's vow to kill Elijah shows, the miracle served only to harden recalcitrant hearts.

Unfortunately, God's mighty demonstration on Mount Carmel failed to stem the whelming tide of apostasy. In spite of the fact that God continually warned Israel and Judah through prophets who called them to repentance, the people stubbornly refused to listen (2 Kgs 17:13–14). The writer of Kings summarizes: "They went after false idols and became false, and they followed the nations that were around them, concerning whom the LORD had commanded them that they should not be like them . . ." (2 Kgs 17:15b). In other words, instead of influencing the surrounding nations, the Israelites were influenced by them. Yahweh therefore handed over the

92. House, *Kings*, 220.
93. Wright, *Mission of God*, 178.

northern kingdom to the Assyrians, who carried the survivors off into exile. Failing to be a display people, they became a displaced people. Far worse than being uprooted from the land, the people of the northern kingdom were banished from the presence of God (2 Kgs 17:18, 20).

THE TABERNACLING PRESENCE OF GOD IN THE LATTER PROPHETS

Judah tragically failed to learn from the example of Israel. Occasionally a king would try to reverse the evils of his predecessors (e.g., Hezekiah and Josiah), but the southern kingdom continued along the same painful trajectory away from God. Still, Yahweh was faithful to send prophets who warned of the extreme danger of failing to live as a people who displayed God's presence in contrast to the surrounding nations.

The Prophet Isaiah

Isaiah's Visions of God's Eschatological Presence

The book of Isaiah opens with the ugly reality of a spiritually diseased southern kingdom. Although Judah had kept up outward appearances of worship at the Jerusalem temple, Yahweh announced his disgust at their endless parade of meaningless religious activity (Isa 1). Against this backdrop Isaiah abruptly launches into a whiplash survey of the state of Judah: "from the ideal to the real and back to the ideal again."[94] The prophet reveals a startling vision of the future: one day Gentiles will stream to the temple in Jerusalem in order to learn God's ways and walk in his paths, and the God of Jacob, himself, will teach them (Isa 2:2–3). This centripetal result stems from a centrifugal message: "For out of Zion shall go the law ['instruction,' HCSB], and the word of the LORD from Jerusalem" (Isa 2:3). The prophecy is marvelously inclusive: "many peoples" from "all nations" will come. Yet there is also an unmistakable exclusivity. John Oswalt remarks, "[O]ne day it would become clear that the religion of Israel was *the* religion; that her God was *the* God."[95] The fact that Gentiles would one day worship the God of Jacob should motivate the house of Jacob to "walk in the light of the LORD" (Isa 2:5).

94. Oswalt, *Isaiah*, 113.
95. Ibid., 117; italics original.

But before this surprising revelation can begin to settle in, Isaiah pivots back to the harsh dissonance of reality. Instead of living in contrast to the surrounding culture, the people had been contaminated by it. Far from being a display people, Judah was filled with arrogance and idols; their speech and deeds defied God's glorious presence in their midst (Isa 3:8). The nation was therefore ripe for the judgment that Isaiah describes in graphic detail (Isa 3:16–26).

With his audience still recoiling from these horrific images, Isaiah unexpectedly announces a glorious future for the survivors: "In that day the branch of the LORD shall be beautiful and glorious . . . And he who is left in Zion and remains in Jerusalem will be called holy, everyone who has been recorded for life in Jerusalem" (Isa 4:2–3). The impending judgment would thus have the salutary purpose of refining a remnant. Having cleansed away the filth by a spirit of judgment, "the LORD will create over the whole site of Mount Zion and over her assemblies a cloud by day, and smoke and the shining of a flaming fire by night; for over all the glory there will be a canopy . . ." (Isa 4:5). These images clearly recall the pillar of cloud and fire of God's accompanying presence in the exodus. They not only indicate that Yahweh would remember his covenant with Israel, but they also "reaffirm that God's ultimate intention was to share his presence (the glory, Exod 40:34–38) with them as intimately as possible."[96] In contrast to the glory-filled tabernacle and temple of the past, this glory-filled, canopy-covered cloud will envelop the "whole site of Mount Zion" and shelter all who assemble there (Isa 4:5–6). The returning exiles, however, did not experience this sublime vision of God's tabernacling presence. Isaiah's glorious vision of Zion's future therefore remains to be fulfilled. Presumably, when the vision of Isa 4:2–6 comes to fruition, it will also include the "many peoples" from "all nations" who have learned to walk in the ways of the God of Jacob (Isa 2:2–3).

Isaiah's Commission

At the time of Isaiah's commission, the prophet saw a vision of the sovereign Lord, "high and lifted up," seated on a throne in the heavenly temple, the veil to the Holy of Holies evidently removed.[97] Overwhelmed in the presence of Almighty God, Isaiah concentrated his report on the periphery of the theophany: the hem of the robe filled the temple, and the seraphim covered their faces and feet with wings (Isa 6:1–2). These creatures' antiphonal praise shook the thresholds of the temple and filled it with smoke: "Holy,

96. Ibid., 148.
97. Ibid., 177.

holy, holy is the LORD of hosts; the whole earth is full of his glory!" (Isa 6:3).[98] The threefold repetition of "holy" is the strongest superlative in Hebrew; the Holy One of Israel is the *only* one who fits that description. The anthem not only proclaims the essence and character of Yahweh, but it also gives voice to his mission: God's desire is that every creature from every corner of the earth should join in the seraph-song and worship him, thus filling the earth with the knowledge of his glory.

Contemplating this perfect praise catapulted Isaiah back to the crushing reality of his own sinful condition. He was utterly undone. As a man of unclean lips living in the midst of a people similarly afflicted, Isaiah knew there was no way he could see the "King, the LORD of hosts" and live (Isa 6:5). Access to this thrice-holy God is restricted to those who are without sin. Yahweh graciously met the prophet's need with a burning coal that touched his lips: "your guilt is taken away, and your sin atoned for" (Isa 6:7). The burning ember was efficacious because it had been taken from the altar where blood sacrifices were consumed by fire.[99] Thus purified, Isaiah was able to hear and answer the ongoing missional heart cry of God—"Whom shall I send, and who will go for us?" The prophet responded, "Here am I! Send me" (Isa 6:8). As John Piper rightly observes, "[M]issions exists because worship doesn't."[100] In order for the *knowledge* of God's glory to fill the whole world, the message must go out in every generation (cf. Isa 11:9). Until the day that worship of God's glory continually fills every heart in every place, true worship should include a missional response that reflects the missional heart of God.

God's description of Isaiah's task was certainly daunting. The prophet's faithful delivery of the message would only serve to calcify the already calloused hearts of his hearers. Oswalt asks the probing question:

> What was the alternative? Perhaps if the prophet would alter the truth in certain ways the people might be more responsive and, after a fashion, be healed. Yet such a healing would be a mockery. For what can heal except God's truth? It is as though Isaiah should tell them that they did not need to see God as he did nor be cleansed as he was to be a servant of God as he was. The

---

98. Motyer, *Isaiah*, 77, observes that the shaking concentrated on the *thresholds* ". . . specifically prohibits Isaiah's entry to the divine presence, just as *smoke* forbids him to see God. The divine nature as such is an active force of total exclusion."

99. The fourth Servant Song of Isaiah 52:13–53:12 hints at the ultimate cost of this atoning sacrifice: the righteous servant of Yahweh—also "high and lifted up"—will be a guilt offering that will "make many to be accounted righteous and he shall bear their iniquities" (Isa 53:11).

100. Piper, *Let the Nations*, 11.

ultimate result would be deadly. It would confirm that generation in its syncretism and pervert the truth for all generations
to come. It would sell the future for the apparent sake of the
present. But if the truth could not save the present generation,
if it would in fact, destroy that generation, it could, faithfully
recorded, save future generations.[101]

As difficult as Isaiah must have found it to preach among those who refused
to hear, ultimately, his ministry did prove to be salvific for future generations. Isaiah's encounter with the Holy One of Israel had not only seared
his lips but also sealed his commitment. The prophet strove, therefore, to
expose the utter foolishness of putting one's trust in the frailty of another
human being or in the false hope of a man-made idol. Isaiah's experience
in the presence of "the King, the LORD of hosts" convinced him that this
transcendent and immanent God would not share his glory with another
(Isa 48:11).

Interestingly, in the passage that immediately follows, King Ahaz refused to hear the word of God through the prophet (Isa 7). Yahweh himself
therefore gave Ahaz the sign that the king had spurned: "Behold, the virgin
shall conceive and bear a son, and shall call his name Immanuel ['immānūʾēl;
'God (is) with us']" (Isa 7:14). In the initial prophetic fulfillment, the Immanuel child would be a "two-edged" reminder (both positive and negative)
of Ahaz's failure to trust in this transcendent God who was also immanent.
Oswalt explains, "The presence of a transcendent and holy God with us may
well mean weal and woe together. To the extent that we are dependent upon
him, his presence results in blessing; but to the extent that we refuse to depend upon him, his presence is an embarrassment and a curse."[102] As the
rest of the book of Isaiah attests, the presence of a holy God in their midst
was indeed two-edged, bringing both judgment and salvation.

Ultimately, however, the sign pointed to the messianic child who
would bear the same name (cf. Matt 1:23). A human child born of a young
woman in Ahaz's day could not possibly prove that God is always present.
But if the Holy Spirit should overshadow a virgin so that she would conceive
and give birth, that child would be more than "a sign of God's presence with
us. Better than that, he would be the reality of that experience."[103] Reflecting on the implications God's transcendence, Oswalt notes that humans
typically rely on their own devices in an attempt to connect with God—an

101. Oswalt, *Isaiah*, 189–90.

102. Ibid., 209.

103. Ibid., 211.

impossibility because "God is distinct from this world."[104] Therefore, the only way for them to commune with a transcendent God is by his gracious condescension to enter the realm of humanity, which is exactly the promise of the Immanuel sign—"God with us."

Isaiah's Eschatological Visions Expanded

The images of an expanded tabernacle/temple, which were introduced as small ripples in the opening chapters of Isaiah, continue to swell again and again throughout the book, growing to waves of resounding crescendos by the end of Isaiah. For example, the branch of Isa 4:2 becomes the Spirit-empowered ruler of a global Messianic kingdom where the *missio Dei* becomes reality (cf. Isa 61:1).[105] Although the book of Isaiah resounds with prophecies of judgment against the nations, it also reverberates with the missional dimensions of the global reconciliation promised in Isaiah 2. The prophet therefore exhorts the people of God to sing the particularity of the salvation song universally:

> Give thanks to the LORD,
> call upon his name,
> make known his deeds among the peoples,
> proclaim that his name is exalted.
> Sing praises to the LORD, for he has done gloriously;
> let this be made known in all the earth.
> Shout, and sing for joy, O inhabitant of Zion,
> for great in your midst is the Holy One of Israel (Isa 12:4–6).

This missional song of redemption will result in the spread of the knowledge of Yahweh throughout the entire earth.

The Egyptians and Assyrians, for example, will one day worship Yahweh together, and he will bless them all: "Blessed be Egypt my people, and Assyria the work of my hands, and Israel my inheritance" (Isa 19:25). To those "foreigners who join themselves to the LORD," who minister to him and love his name, God promises to bring them to his "holy mountain" and to make them joyful in "my house of prayer . . . for all peoples" (Isa 56:3–8). Yahweh will graciously gather people from all nations and tongues to come see his glory and worship him (Isa 66:18–19).

104. Ibid., 229.

105. Observing a marked increase in references to the Spirit in Isaiah, Greene, "Spirit," 717, argues that "[t]he increased depiction of the Spirit as God's presence is a necessary adaptation since the presence of God is no longer centered on the temple but is going throughout the world."

Indeed, by the book's end, the expansion of Yahweh's glory hinted at in Isa 4:5—from the temple precinct to "the whole of Mount Zion"—will one day fill all creation, making the temple obsolete: "Thus says the LORD: 'Heaven is my throne and the earth is my footstool; what is the house that you would build for me . . . ?'" (Isa 66:1). As G. K. Beale points out, "[S]ince God is the Creator, no particular part of his creation is big enough to contain his presence, and certainly no part of the sin-tainted old creation."[106] At the conclusion of Isaiah, therefore, Yahweh sets the stage for an entirely new creation: "For behold, I create new heavens and a new earth, and the former things shall not be remembered or come into mind"; "the new heavens and the new earth . . . [where] all flesh shall come to worship before me" (Isa 65:17; 66:22–23). Isaiah's vision of a redeemed people and a renewed worldwide sanctuary is the *missio Dei* fulfilled.

Still, this universal invitation into the majestic glory of God is restrictive: the unclean are barred from the Highway of Holiness (Isa 35). Furthermore, those who persist in rebellion against God will suffer a horrific fate: "For their worm shall not die, their fire shall not be quenched" (Isa 66:24). They will have no part in the "new heavens and a new earth" where Yahweh will rejoice in his redeemed people and his restored creation, where all creatures are reconciled to each other and to God (Isa 65).

The Prophet Jeremiah

Significantly, Yahweh's call on Jeremiah's life extended beyond Judah: "I appointed you a prophet to the nations" (Jer 1:5). The sovereign God of all the earth thus summarized the prophet's ministry: "See, I have set you this day over nations and over kingdoms to pluck up and to break down, to destroy and to overthrow, to build and to plant" (Jer 1:10). Jeremiah would proclaim judgment and restoration to the people of God—and to the nations.

God's Presence Is Not Bound to the Temple

Using imagery that echoes Isaiah's themes, Jeremiah described a day when "Jerusalem shall be called the throne of the LORD, and all nations shall gather to it, to the presence of the LORD in Jerusalem" (Jer 3:17). Yahweh's immediate presence will make even the ark of the covenant obsolete: "It shall not come to mind or be remembered or missed; it shall not be made again" (Jer 3:16; cf. Isa 65:17). This development in the mission of God is nothing short

---

106. Beale, *The Temple*, 136.

of astonishing. The ark had played a central role in the old covenant as the place where the high priest sprinkled the blood of the sacrifice on the Day of Atonement. Although the ark had served as a powerful symbol of God's presence, it would no longer be necessary: "The actual glory of God in the midst of his people will be sufficient, and therefore the typical glory will not be missed."[107] Meanwhile, however, if the Israelites return to Yahweh "in truth, in justice, and in righteousness, then the nations shall bless themselves in him, and in him shall they glory" (Jer 4:2). In other words, there is a correlation between the repentance of the display people of God and the conversion of the nations.

Tragically, the nation of Judah refused to repent in spite of the warnings of God's impending judgment. They persisted in their blatant sin and empty religious rituals, failing to comprehend that the one rendered the other absolutely meaningless. They presumed on Yahweh's faithfulness in the past, believing that because he had spared Jerusalem before, he would always. Brueggemann describes what he calls the "*royal-temple ideology of Jerusalem*": ". . . the God of Israel had made irrevocable promises to the temple and the monarchy, had taken up permanent residence in Jerusalem, and was for all time a patron and guarantor of the Jerusalem establishment."[108] In essence, the people of Judah had begun to regard the temple as a guarantee of immunity from all possible misfortune.

Standing in the gate of the temple courts, Jeremiah boldly delivered his first public sermon, in which he debunked this false theology and denounced the empty worship of his day. The prophet warned them not to trust in the temple as a religious fetish (as the Israelites had viewed the ark in Eli's day; cf. 1 Sam 4:3).[109] He rebuked the misplaced trust reflected in their incantation-like repetition: "This is the temple of the LORD, the temple of the LORD, the temple of the LORD" (Jer 7:4).[110] The citizens of Judah seemed to have forgotten that the presence of a holy God was what made the temple extraordinary. Cataloguing their sins, Jeremiah charged them with breaking several of the Ten Commandments, failing to love their neighbor, and worshiping false gods. That they then came to the temple for absolution of sins that they fully intended to commit again provoked Yahweh's utter indignation: "Will you . . . then come stand before me in this house which

107. Feinberg, "Jeremiah," 402. Feinberg explains that "the old economy was to be dissolved," yielding to another—a preview of the new covenant unveiled in Jer 31:31–34.

108. Brueggemann, *To Pluck Up*, 5–6; italics original.

109. Feinberg, "Jeremiah," 427.

110. Martens, "Jeremiah," 348, observes that the chant was likely based on Isaiah's assurance to Hezekiah that God himself would fight on behalf of Jerusalem, protecting it "like birds hovering" over the city (Isa 31:4–5).

is called by my name, and say, 'We are delivered!'—only to go on doing all these abominations?" (Jer 7:10). Essentially, they were treating the temple as robbers do their dens: "It was a temporary refuge till they sallied forth on another foray."[111] Yahweh, however, was about to destroy their refuge.

Through Jeremiah, God reminded them of the fate of Shiloh, less than twenty miles north of Jerusalem. The comparison is particularly apt. In the days of Eli the wayward Israelites had treated the ark as a talisman, and God purposefully surrendered it to the Philistines. Although the Samuel account does not record the subsequent destruction of Shiloh, Psalm 78 refers to this event: "[God] forsook his dwelling at Shiloh, the tent where he dwelt among mankind . . . . He gave his people over to the sword and vented his wrath on his heritage. Fire devoured their young men . . . . Their priests fell by the sword, and their widows made no lamentation" (Ps 78:60–64). The parallel is clear: just as the presence of the tabernacle did not grant the first cultic center immunity, neither would the presence of the temple protect the city of Jerusalem. Because the people in Jeremiah's day refused to listen, Yahweh would cast them out of his presence: ". . . I will do to the house that is called by my name and in which you trust, and to the place that I gave to you and to your fathers as I did to Shiloh. And I will cast you out of my sight, as I cast out all your kinsmen, all the offspring of Ephraim" (Jer 7:14–15).

Instead of living as contrast people who displayed the presence of God in their midst, the people of Judah had embraced their neighbors' deities and abominable practices—even child sacrifice—all the while continuing to perform empty religious rituals at the temple. Fed up with this religious syncretism, Yahweh prepared to unleash his fury on both this people—and this place. The destruction would be unimaginably thorough: "[B]ehold, my anger and my wrath will be poured out on this place, upon man and beast, upon the trees of the field and the fruit of the ground; it will burn and not be quenched" (Jer 7:20). The coming slaughter would be of such magnitude that unburied bodies would fill the Valley of Hinnom, lying exposed beneath the "sun and moon and all the host of heaven which they have loved and served," having forsaken the God of Israel (Jer 8:2).

Yahweh's patience with Judah had ended, and judgment was inescapable. The time had come to pluck up and to tear down—not only Judah, but also her "evil neighbors" (Jer 12:14). Yet still God expressed mercy: "And after I have plucked them up, I will again have compassion on them, and I will bring them again each to his heritage and each to his land" (Jer 12:15). Incredibly, God's gracious offer of restoration extended not only to Judah, but also to those surrounding nations who had led his people astray.

111. Feinberg, *Jeremiah*, 428.

Yahweh declared that if they would "diligently learn the ways of my people . . . then they shall be built up in the midst of my people. But if any nation will not listen, then I will utterly pluck it up and destroy it" (Jer 12:16–17).

Jeremiah's scathing sermon in the temple courts was not well received. In fact, Jeremiah 26 reveals that the prophet barely escaped with his life. Those who dared to speak the truth of God's word often found that countering the prevailing worldview might not only fail to produce results, but it could also be quite dangerous.[112] In the end Jeremiah's life was spared; Jerusalem and the temple were not.

The Temple Is Destroyed

The book of Jeremiah closes with destruction of Jerusalem and the temple at the hands of Nebuchadnezzar in 586 BC. Jeremiah 52 seems to have recorded every painful detail: the siege, the famine, the flight of King Zedekiah and his capture; the slaughter of his sons and the gouging out his eyes; the burning of Yahweh's house and all the houses in Jerusalem; the destruction of the walls and the exile of the people. However, although Nebuchadnezzar and the Chaldeans are the subjects of the verbs in the account, Jeremiah made it clear from the beginning that they were simply acting as agents of God: "For because of the anger of the LORD things came to the point in Jerusalem and Judah that he cast them out from his presence" (Jer 52:3). T. R. Hobbs notes, "The only remaining symbols of Yahweh's presence with his people— the temple vessels, the king, the leaders, including the priests—are newly located in Babylon . . . not because of some historical accident, but rather by the will of Yahweh."[113] Because the Israelites refused to be a holy display of the glory of God, he would make them a display of his wrath against sin.

Yet even the destruction of Jerusalem and the temple had a missional dimension. The smoldering ruins were to be a testimony to the nations. Long before the Babylonians came, Jeremiah anticipated that the inhabitants of "many nations" would pass by the destroyed city and temple, and they would ask, "Why would God deal this way with his people?" The answer given would ultimately bear witness to the identity and character of Israel's God: "Because they have forsaken the covenant of the LORD their God and worshiped other gods and served them" (Jer 22:8). In the same

---

112. Martens, "Jeremiah," 296, points out that Jeremiah's faithfulness cost him the esteem of his priestly family and set him at odds with royalty; it also "landed him in custody (37:11–16), then in a terrible dungeon (38:14–28), and eventually in court confinement (38:13, 28)."

113. Hobbs, 2 *Kings*, 369.

vein, when Yahweh would bring his people out of exile—to build and to plant them once more in the land—his actions would be a testimony to the nations. Either way, God would accomplish his mission: "behold, I will make them know . . . my power and my might, and they shall know that my name is the LORD" (Jer 16:21).

The Prophet Ezekiel

Deported in the first wave of exiles in 597 BC, Ezekiel lived with thousands of his countrymen, forcibly resettled in Babylon, radically displaced from everything that was familiar—including the temple in Jerusalem. Unable to fulfill his intended profession as a priest, Ezekiel received a call to prophetic ministry in the first of three visions that shape not only his experience, but also the message of his book.

God's Presence in Babylon

While the prophet was living among exiles by the Chebar canal in Babylon, he received a theophanic vision reminiscent of Isaiah's call: "the heavens were opened, and I saw visions of God" (Ezek 1:1). The humble detail of his location is actually quite significant because it "shatter[ed] the myth that the influence of patron deities was localized in the territory over which they were understood to have jurisdiction."[114] This first vision underscored that the God of Israel was sovereign over every place on earth. The winged creatures beneath the throne, moving about on wheels within wheels, portrayed an unhindered, spirit-directed mobility. As captivating as these details were, Ezekiel struggled to find words adequate to describe the One seated on the throne. Reduced to analogies of "likeness" or "appearance," the prophet finally realized that he was in the presence "of the likeness of the glory of the LORD" (Ezek 1:28). In response, he fell on his face. The Spirit entered him and commissioned him to go and speak to "nations of rebels"—including, ironically, the people of Israel who would be even less responsive than foreigners among whom they now lived (Ezek 2:2–3; cf. 3:5–7). Although they would refuse to heed Ezekiel's message of impending judgment, the prophet was obligated to warn them.

114. Block, *Ezekiel*, 83.

The Glory Departs the Temple

A year later Ezekiel received a second vision in which the Spirit transported him to Jerusalem, where the manifestation of the glory of God guided the prophet through four scenes of increasingly detestable abominations in the temple courts.[115] Thinking God would not notice, the Israelites had brazenly adopted the pagan practices of the surrounding culture. This defilement of the temple precincts must have been appalling to the prophet who had trained for the priesthood—and all the more so to the Owner of the house! No wonder Yahweh was ready to abandon Jerusalem, driven away by this blatant desecration of his treasured dwelling place! (Cf. Ezek 7:22; 8:6.) Before leaving, however, God gave Ezekiel an apocalyptic vision of impending judgment, in which he would make a clear distinction between the righteous and the rebellious.[116]

Then, in a tragic reversal of the tabernacle/temple dedication accounts, the glory of God's presence radiated once more in the temple before departing: "And the glory of the LORD went up from the cherub to the threshold of the house, and the house was filled with the cloud, and the court was filled with the brightness of the glory of the LORD" (Ezek 10:4). Slowly, in stages, the glory moved over the threshold, through the gate, and out of the city to the east. The time of God's judgment had come. God's presence left the temple, clearing the way for Nebuchadnezzar's army. Although the temple's destruction was unthinkable for the Israelites, the Ichabod narrative and the ruins of Shiloh should have been stern reminders of the contingent nature of God's dwelling among humanity. Block comments, "[N]othing, not even the temple, is more sacred to God than a sanctified people."[117] Once again, the glory of God departed, and Jerusalem was destroyed in 586 BC (cf. Ezek 33:21).

---

115. Blenkinsopp, *Ezekiel*, 55, outlines Ezekiel 8: 1) the idolatrous statue of the Canaanite fertility goddess Asherah standing at the entrance to the temple; 2) a dark inner room, "reminiscent of Egyptian burial chambers," filled with seventy elders offering incense to the images of animal-deities painted on the walls; 3) women weeping for Tammuz, the Sumerian god of vegetation who annually died in winter and came to life in spring; and 4) twenty-five men facing east, bowing with their backsides to the temple, in worship of the rising sun.

116. Wright, *Ezekiel*, 111, observes that when the actual battle was enjoined, the Babylonian enemies would wield the swords of slaughter. Here, however, the symbolic imagery illustrated that these human soldiers would be meting out divine justice. Yahweh summoned angelic executioners and ordered them to strike the residents of Jerusalem: "kill old men outright, young men and maidens, little children and women," sparing only those who bore a mark signifying their grief over all the abominations (Ezek 9:6).

117. Block, *Ezekiel*, 797.

The inconceivable had occurred: the temple of Yahweh was destroyed along with all Jerusalem. Undoubtedly, "the exiles suffered from intense theological shock."[118] Displaced in Babylon, they had plenty of time to ask themselves: How could such a thing have happened? Had the God of Israel abandoned them forever? Yahweh provided answers through the ministry of Ezekiel. The prophet had a key missional role to play among the exiles, who blamed God for their situation and accused him of being unfair—an attitude encapsulated in the proverb about "sour grapes and sore teeth" (Ezek 18:2). The prophet also exposed the people's sin with "passionate evangelistic persuasion," blasting them out of complacency with coarse imagery that depicted their idolatry as the lewd adultery of a faithless wife (e.g., Ezek 16, 23).[119] Ezekiel thus provided an answer to the first question—"How could this have happened?"—by showing that the temple destruction was the result of the people's iniquity: "By sinning they had defiled the sanctuary so that the Lord could no longer dwell in it."[120]

On the other hand, Ezekiel described the beauty of God's proffered grace with equal fervency. As Wright points out, in Ezekiel "the promises of God's grace are stupendous and breathtaking"; his calls to repentance are "pure gospel."[121] Significantly, Yahweh's message through Ezekiel pointed the way forward for the displaced exiles. In answer to the second question—"Has God abandoned his people forever?"—the prophet pronounced a resounding "No!" God himself would restore the remnant of his people; he would rebuild the ruined places; he would even set his Spirit within his people (Ezek 36:25–27, 36). Underscoring this truth, God gave Ezekiel an unforgettable vision of dry bones growing sinews, flesh, and skin, assembled into a vast army: "I will put my Spirit within you, and you shall live, and I will place you in your own land. Then you shall know that I am the LORD" (Ezek 37:13).

---

118. Ibid., 7. Block notes that the people of Judah had mistakenly trusted in what they considered to be an inviolable triad: "national patron deity (Yahweh), territory (land of Canaan), and people (nation of Israel)" (ibid.). Indeed, this truncated triad is a reductionistic version of the mission of God, which lies at the nexus of God's presence, people and place. The people of God had failed to remember that they must be rightly related to their God who, although he had chosen to manifest his presence in their midst, was gloriously sovereign over all his creation.

119. Wright, *Ezekiel*, 32.

120. Spatafora, *Temple of God*, 46.

121. Wright, *Ezekiel*, 33–34.

A Temple-less Sanctuary

Additionally, God introduced a new perspective on the concept of his tabernacling presence. Although Jerusalem was about to be temple-less, Yahweh poignantly declared that he *himself* had become a *sanctuary* to the temple-less exiles (Ezek 11:16). This verse indicates that God was present with the faithful remnant as "a veritable invisible temple" during their time in exile.[122] This idea challenges the understanding that the presence of God was restricted to the temple. Andreas Köstenberger notes that it also "provides an important relativization of the function of the temple, setting it in the larger context of the manifestations of Yahweh's presence to the people of Israel and the relationship he sustained with his people even prior to the Solomonic temple."[123]

Furthermore, God promised to return the purified remnant to Israel: "I will remove the heart of stone from their flesh and give them a heart of flesh . . . . And they shall be my people, and I will be their God. But as for those whose heart goes after their detestable things and their abominations, I will bring their deeds upon their own heads, declares the LORD God" (Ezek 11:19b–21). This strong contrast supports the theological concept of restrictivity. Yet there is also a hint of universality here as well. Whereas Israel had failed to display God's glory to her neighbors by her faithfulness, God determined to display his glory himself: "And I will set my glory among the nations, and all the nations shall see my judgment that I have executed, and my hand that I have laid on them" (Ezek 39:21). Likewise, when Yahweh restored his presence among the cleansed remnant, the nations would know that it is God who sanctifies his people.

This verse, Ezek 39:21, is one form of the theological "recognition formula," which occurs over seventy times in the book of Ezekiel. Block explains that these formulae are "prophetic proof sayings" whereby the observer comes to recognize Yahweh's identity and sovereign involvement in human experience.[124] Although most refer to Israel, many of the formulae specify that the nations will likewise perceive the identity and character of Yahweh, e.g., Ezek 21:4: "And all flesh shall know that I am the LORD." Wright maintains that this recognition formula is "the most significant key to a missiological reading of Ezekiel."[125] Clearly, God's activity among the Israelites—judgment and salvation, exile and restoration—unfolded on

---

122. Beale, *The Temple*, 110.

123. Köstenberger, *Theology of John's Gospel*, 63.

124. Block, *Ezekiel*, 39.

125. Wright, *Ezekiel*, 35.

center stage "in the sight of the nations" (Ezek 5:5, 8; 20:9, 14, 22, 41; 28:25; 39:21, 27). Ultimately the restoration of Israel would secure the future hope of the nations, as well.[126] Yahweh promised that one day he will restore his people as one nation under a Davidic shepherd-king; more importantly, he will set his sanctuary, his "dwelling place" (*miškān*; "tabernacle") in their midst forevermore, thus convincing the nations that he is the One who sanctifies Israel (Ezek 37:26–28).

An End-Time Temple

The book of Ezekiel closes with a vision that reverses the vision of God's glory departing the temple in chapter 10. Surely this would-be priest took great delight in recording the details of a "massive temple complex which resembled a city (40:2)."[127] As Wright points out, however, the central point of this vision is not found in the details themselves but in the fulfillment of the promised restoration of God's dwelling-place in the midst of his people.[128] Block observes that the central position of the massive altar "proclaims a glorious gospel of grace":

> [T]he altar symbolizes the delight Yahweh finds in the worship of his people. He has not returned to his temple to bask in the glory of his surroundings. He has come to have fellowship with humans. The days of wrath are far behind and he reaches out to them, offering a smile and acceptance to those who appear in his divine court.[129]

Thus, God graciously provides a way for his people to enjoy communion with him.

While the prophet's description could refer to a future temple structure, "it is just as possible, if not preferable to understand [it] as foretelling a time when the temple will be, not a physical handmade house, but God's manifest presence alone that will fill Israel (and the earth) as never before."[130] According to Craig Koester, "there is little evidence that any group with Israel attempted to put Ezekiel's vision to practice."[131] Beale suggests that the prophet's vision is of a "non-structural end-time temple," which also

126. Ibid., 38.

127. Koester, *Dwelling of God*, 19.

128. Wright, *Ezekiel*, 329.

129. Block, *Ezekiel*, 612.

130. Ibid., 111.

131. Koester, *Dwelling of God*, 19.

mirrors the garden imagery of the first temple of God's presence in Eden.[132] Ezekiel had received a glimpse of the future where the glory of God filled the temple, and Yahweh himself explained, "Son of man, this is the place of my throne and the place of the soles of my feet, where I will dwell in the midst of the people of Israel forever" (Ezek 43:4–7). The last verse in the book of Ezekiel records that, "the name of the city from that time on shall be, The LORD Is There."

The Prophet Haggai

Although the exiles returned in 537 BC, the task of rebuilding their lives soon overwhelmed them, so that the foundation of the temple lay bare until 520 BC when Yahweh sent the prophets Haggai and Zechariah to re-kindle the returned exiles' devotion. Ezekiel's vision of a massive temple did not find fulfillment in the physical temple constructed by the remnant in 520–516 BC. Yahweh acknowledged the remnant's disappointment, yet he encouraged them to work hard, assuring them, "I am with you. . . . My Spirit remains in your midst" (Hag 2:4–5). This assurance of God's presence—before the temple's completion—recalls the omnipresence of God experienced by Ezekiel.

It is also noteworthy that Scripture does not record the glory of God descending on Zerubbabel's temple as it did on Moses' tabernacle, Solomon's temple, and even on Ezekiel's end-time temple. Beale suggests, "It is quite possible that the divine presence never returned to the post-exilic temple."[133] Still, Yahweh declared that its glory would exceed that of the former temple: "I will shake all nations, so that the treasures of all nations shall come in, and I will fill this house with glory. . . . The latter glory of this house shall be greater than the former" (Hag 2:7, 9). Although this promise is fulfilled literally by the material splendor of Herod's temple renovation, its ultimate fulfillment is in Christ who came and superseded it (Matt 12:6; John 2:13–22).[134]

Reading the "shaking" in terms of cosmic upheaval, Beale argues that "Haggai 2 refers to a future time when God will enable his people to build his [eschatological] temple through the power of his Spirit."[135] Intriguingly, this passage strikes a chord of universality as God promised to shake the heavens and earth so that the *nations* would bring their treasures to fill his

132. Beale, *The Temple*, 336.

133. Ibid., 117n.

134. Baldwin, *Haggai*, 48–49.

135. Beale, *The Temple*, 304–5.

house with glory (Hag 2:6–9).[136] There is a note of restrictivity, as well, in the context of this Second Temple. Yahweh asked the priests for a ruling on clean and unclean objects in order to illustrate that the nation's disobedience had defiled the work of their hands and their offerings (Hag 2:11–14). The clean cannot purify that which is unclean; rather, the unclean contaminates that which is clean. Therefore, there must be separation of unclean from clean. The presence of God demands a clear distinction between the two.

The Prophet Zechariah

Like Haggai, Zechariah's message encouraged the exiles to rebuild the temple (Zech 1:16), but Zechariah's message "places more emphasis on the divine and human inhabitants" than the temple structure itself.[137] In his third vision, for example, Zechariah saw a man with a measuring line intent on measuring Jerusalem, presumably for the purpose of building a wall around it (Zech 2:1–5). The angel halted the young man in his tracks, revealing the remarkable news that the city would not even need a wall for two reasons: 1) a wall could not possibly contain the burgeoning multitude of people and livestock living there, and 2) Yahweh himself would protect Jerusalem: "I will be to her a wall of fire all around, declares the LORD, and I will be the glory in her midst" (Zech 2:5). Beale observes, "[T]he Shekinah presence of God, formerly sequestered in the old holy of holies, will burst forth from the heavenly sanctuary and encompass the entire future new Jerusalem."[138] Furthermore, Yahweh declared, "Sing and rejoice, O daughter of Zion, for behold, I come and I will dwell in your midst. . . . And many nations shall join themselves to the LORD in that day, and shall be my people. And I will dwell in your midst . . ." (Zech 2:10–11). The "multitude" that necessitates Jerusalem's enlargement includes not only Jews but also Gentiles whom Yahweh has incorporated into "my people"—an Old Testament term once reserved for ethnic Israel. In the latter days, God's tabernacling presence will dwell with all who trust in him.

The theme of God's presence tabernacling in Jerusalem resurfaces in Zech 8:3 in a passage which Donald Gowan calls a "combination of 'realized and futuristic eschatology'":[139] "I have returned to Zion and will dwell in

---

136. This passage finds amplification in Isa 60:5–22 and fulfillment in Rev 21:24, 26, where the kings of the nations bring their treasures to Yahweh who is the eschatological temple.

137. Boda, *Haggai, Zechariah*, 201.

138. Beale, *The Temple*, 143.

139. Gowan, *Eschatology*, 5.

the midst of Jerusalem, and Jerusalem shall be called the faithful city, and the mountain of the LORD of hosts, the holy mountain." Thus, the presence of God will transform the city so that it reflects the ethical qualities of his character, and the entire spectrum of humanity will experience abundant life (Zech 8:4–5; 14–17).[140] The land itself will experience this same renewal, and the days of painful fasting will be replaced with seasons of cheerful feasting (Zech 8:12; 19). Furthermore, the returned remnant, who had been a "byword of cursing" for the nations, will become a blessing (Zech 8:13)—a clear echo of God's promise to Abraham that in him "all the nations of the earth shall be blessed" (Gen 12:3).

Zechariah 8:20–23 gives shape to this blessing for the nations:

> Peoples shall yet come, even the inhabitants of many cities. The inhabitants of one city shall go to another, saying, "Let us go at once to entreat the favor of the LORD and to seek the LORD of hosts; I myself am going." Many peoples and strong nations shall come to seek the LORD of hosts in Jerusalem and to entreat the favor of the LORD. Thus says the LORD of hosts: In those days ten men from the nations of every tongue shall take hold of the robe of a Jew, saying, "Let us go with you, for we have heard that God is with you."

There is a sense of urgency and passion communicated here, reflected both in the Hebrew text and in the grasping of the corner of a Jew's garment. David Petersen explains, "A non-Judahite who might see a garment with tassels attached to its corners would know immediately the religious identity of its wearer. . . . [T]he skirt, though it signifies religious particularism, serves as a motif that makes a national pluralism possible, and enables the *gôyîm* to walk with the Judahites."[141] As a "well-known gesture of the ancient world," taking hold of the hem communicates submission and loyalty, signifying that the purpose of the nations is "to go to Jerusalem and acknowledge Yahweh's dominion."[142]

Carol and Eric Meyers conclude that this passage, which reveals "an ever-broadening circle of people" included in Yahweh's redemptive scheme, "makes Zechariah one of the most universalistic of all the prophets." Conveying completeness, the number "ten" highlights the universality of this pilgrimage of people who speak every language under the sun. At the same

140. Boda, *Haggai, Zechariah*, 381.

141. Petersen, *Haggai and Zechariah*, 319. According to Num 15:37–41, Moses had instructed the people of Israel throughout all generations to attach tassels to the corner of a cloak as a memory prompt to recall and obey all the commandments of Yahweh.

142. Meyers and Meyers, *Haggai, Zechariah*, 441–42.

time, Zechariah's vision "is rooted in the particularity of the geographic and sociopolitical epicenter of Yahwism."[143] There is also an implied dialogue: "the *gôyîm* [Gentiles] have been provoked to speech and movement by an expression of religious particularism, not by some universal cultural appeal."[144] Additionally, "each Judahite" emphasizes that the individual who worships Yahweh will attract those from other nations to join the worshiping community. The strong sense of movement in this passage is both centripetal and centrifugal. Not only do "[m]any peoples and strong nations" come to Jerusalem to seek Yahweh, they also go to other cities, imploring still others to join them. The oracle foresees that the good news will cover the globe, and the presence of God in the lives of his people will attract others. This passage directly links the expansion of the community of faith with a powerfully magnetic lifestyle that matches the character of the God who is vibrantly present in the midst of his people.

Similarly, the nations play a role in the coming day described in Zechariah 14. On that day Yahweh will establish his sovereign rule over all the earth, and his name will be the only name (Zech 14:9). A victorious warrior, God will subjugate the nations who wage war against Jerusalem, striking them with a horrific plague. But as Mark Boda points out, the defeat of the nations is "not an end but a means. God's desire is for the nations to worship him."[145] Indeed, the survivors of the nations will be drawn to Jerusalem to worship "the King, the LORD of Hosts" (Zech 14:16).

After the final judgment, ". . . there shall never be a decree of utter destruction [*ḥērem*]," and all will dwell in security because of the presence of the King (Zech 14:11). Yahweh's appearance on the earth will transform and renew the entire cosmos, and out of Jerusalem living waters will flow both east and west. In a glorious expansion of the theological concept of ritual purity, the title reserved for the headdress of the high priest, "Holy to the LORD" (cf. Exod 28:36–38), will be inscribed on all the utensils of Jerusalem and Judah—even on the bells of the horses, an animal formerly considered unclean. Finally the need for distinction between clean and unclean will disappear because the holiness of God will permeate every facet of life. Thus, temple and city will have merged.[146] The purifying presence of God will consecrate everything for worship, including his people (Zech 14:5): there will be no "Canaanite"—any wicked or impure person—in the house of Yahweh (Zech 14:21). God's mission will be fulfilled when he dwells in

143. Ibid., 441, 444.
144. Petersen, *Haggai and Zechariah*, 319.
145. Boda, *Haggai, Zechariah*, 532.
146. Dumbrell, *End of the Beginning*, 26.

the midst of his purified people forever. Significantly, Boda observes that two theological themes consistently surface in Zechariah 14: purity of God's community and expansion of God's rule.[147] Until the eschatological day described by the prophet, this connection between holiness and mission has significant missional implications for the people of God.

CONCLUSION

This chapter reveals several new developments in the theme of the tabernacling presence of God. The prominence of the ark in the initial conquest narratives fades from view until the debased priests parade it into battle, where it is captured by the Philistines. Ironically, when the Israelites lament "Ichabod"—"The glory has departed from Israel"—Yahweh displayed his glory in the midst of foreigners. Even when the ark returned to Israel and later entered Jerusalem, it was on God's terms.

When David later expressed a desire to build a house for God, Yahweh reminded him that he did not need a temple. Instead, Yahweh declared his covenantal intention to build David's dynastic house. Although David's son, Solomon, did eventually build the temple, he acknowledged that no house on earth could contain the Almighty. Still, God condescended to manifest his glory in the temple at its dedication. From that moment on, however, the book of Kings traces the demise of the monarchy as well as the nation, as the Israelites began a long, slow slide into apostasy. The temple receded into the background until its destruction by the Babylonians, and the exiles found themselves displaced and temple-less when once more the glory of God departed.

At this sad juncture the prophets played a crucial role in helping the Israelites understand that God was still sovereignly working out his purposes to purify a remnant. Yahweh demonstrated that he was not bound to a man-made structure in Jerusalem; rather, he himself had been their sanctuary in a distant land. The prophets not only placed the blame for the exile on the sin of the people, but they also offered hope that God would restore his people in the land, and the temple would be rebuilt. Even more importantly, the prophets sketched the outlines of not just a new covenant, but a new heaven and a new earth as well—an eschatological kingdom populated by God's purified people, both Jews and Gentiles. In this future day, the restoration will be so total that it "sublimates" the temple structure in glory,

---

147. Boda, *Haggai, Zechariah*, 533.

emphasizing instead the presence of God in the entire city, which is named "The LORD Is There."[148]

Intriguingly, many of these prophetic depictions draw not from temple imagery, but from the earlier Sinai theophanic encounters of the tabernacling presence of God (e.g., Isa 2, 4, 60, 63, 64, 65; Ezek 11; Zech 2, 14). Joseph Greene rightly concludes, "The prophetic trajectory is towards God's presence permeating ever greater portions of the world as God's true heavenly dwelling manifests itself on earth."[149] The prophet Isaiah expresses this same concept with poetic simile: ". . . for the earth shall be full of the knowledge of the LORD as the waters cover the sea" (Isa 11:9; cf. Num 14:21; Ps 72:19; Isa 6:3; Hab 2:14). God's intention is to fill the global sanctuary with worshipers from every nation who will acknowledge his glory and among whom he will dwell forever.

148. Clowney, "Final Temple," 164–65.
149. Greene, "Spirit," 721.

— 4 —

The Tabernacling Presence of God in the New Testament

This chapter chronicles a startling development in the unfolding theme of the tabernacling presence of God. The story of God's mission takes a quantum leap forward as the Gospels narrate how God came to tabernacle among his people—in a tent of human flesh. While the tabernacle and temple had served for a time as the place of the tabernacling presence of God in the midst of his people, suddenly God's presence, people, and place all converge in the incarnation of Jesus Christ. As N. T. Wright observes, the meeting place of heaven and earth was no longer somewhere, but someone—the person of Christ.[1] Even more astonishing is the realization that Jesus' mission to redeem a people in whom the Spirit of God may dwell requires a sacrifice beyond comprehension—the crucifixion and resurrection of the enfleshed Son of God.

Regarding the post-Pentecost era, R. J. McKelvey notes, "God's dwelling on earth is no longer a thing apart from his people; it is the people themselves."[2] The church as a temple of the living God is a people-as-place foreshadowing of the ultimate goal of God's mission. The closing chapters of the Bible reveal a glorious glimpse of a new heaven and earth and the New Jerusalem: God takes up permanent residence in the temple-less sanctuary of the perfected people of God, thus filling the earth with his glory.

---

1. Wright, "Opportunities," n.p.
2. McKelvey, *New Temple*, 100.

GOD'S PRESENCE UNIQUELY FULFILLED IN JESUS

The Gospel of John

The fourth Evangelist composed his Gospel for a clearly stated missional purpose: "these [signs] are written so that you may believe that Jesus is the Christ, the Son of God, and that by believing you may have life in his name" (John 20:31). With this goal in view, the prologue to the Fourth Gospel begins with an assertion of the pre-existence and deity of Christ: "In the beginning was the Word, and the Word was with God, and the Word was God. He was in the beginning with God. All things were made through him, and without him was not any thing made that was made" (John 1:1–3). Andreas Köstenberger observes, "John views creation as the first, inaugural act of salvation history and bases his account of Jesus' coming into the world . . . on this primal act." John thus presents the Word as the unique creative agent of God, the "self-expression" of God, and "an extension . . . of his own identity and deity."[3]

Jesus as Tabernacle

Having established the identity of the Word, John goes on to make the astonishing statement: "And the Word became flesh and dwelt among us, and we have seen his glory, glory as of the only Son from the Father, full of grace and truth" (John 1:14). The Evangelist uses the "forceful, almost crude" word, *sarx* (flesh), to underscore the physical reality of the Incarnation.[4] Furthermore, the incarnated Word dwelt (*eskēnōsen*) in the midst of humanity or—more literally—"tabernacled" or "pitched his tent" in their midst. Craig Koester discusses the significance of several of the Greek words in verse 14:

> Σκηνοω [*Skēnoō*] is a play on words that embraces both "flesh" and "glory." The verb resembles the noun σκήνος [*skēnos*], which can be connected with the idea of "flesh" because it often refers to the tabernacle of the human body . . . [e.g., 2 Cor 5:1, 4] as does the term σκηνώμα [*skēnōma*] (2 Pet 1:13–14). The verb σκηνοω [*skēnoō*] can also be connected with the idea of glory, for it resembles the noun σκηνη [*skēnē*], which the Greek translation of the Hebrew Bible used for the Israelite tabernacle. . . . Therefore tabernacle imagery is uniquely able to portray the

3. Köstenberger, *Theology of John's Gospel*, 179.
4. Morris, *Jesus is the Christ*, 58.

person of Jesus as the locus of God's Word and glory among humankind.[5]

God's Old Testament promises to "tabernacle" among his people (Lev 26:11; Ezek 37:27; Joel 3:17; Zech 2:10) found fulfillment when the Word of God— by whom all things were created—became flesh and lived among humans. This time the tabernacling presence of God appeared, not in a man-made structure, but in the God-man, Jesus Christ.

Similarly, the Shekinah glory that had formerly filled the tabernacle and temple now radiated in the person of Jesus Christ. As an eyewitness, John explains that he and others like him had beheld this glory—a glory that could only belong to the one and only Son of the Father. Köstenberger observes, "[T]he glory spoken of in the introduction is a *crucified* glory, a glory that shines forth initially in selected messianic 'signs' of Jesus and subsequently finds its climactic expression in the exaltation of the Son at the cross."[6] It is only by the end of John's narrative that the paradox of Jesus' glory in humility and suffering becomes fully apparent.

Significantly, John 1:14–18 contains several allusions to Exodus 33–34, where God had refused Moses' request to see his glory—no man can see the face of God and live—yet graciously revealed both his name and his character to the patriarch (Exod 33:20; 34:5–8). In contrast, the Evangelist describes the Son as displaying both the glory and character of God: "glory as of the only Son from the Father, full of grace and truth" (John 1:14).[7] Furthermore, as the only one who has been at the Father's side from the beginning, he alone has seen God, and he has revealed him (John 1:18).

John's prologue, which proclaims the tabernacling presence of God in the flesh, has several missional dimensions. Foremost among these is the exclusivity of Jesus Christ. He was with God and is God; not one thing came into being except through him. Life is in *him* alone; belief in *his* name results in spiritual birth. *He* is the dispenser of grace and truth. Because he alone has seen God, he is the ultimate Revealer of God's identity and character. There is particularity: the God of creation is the God of Israel; the grace that Jesus gives builds upon the grace given through the Law of Moses (John 1:16–17). Yet, there is also a marvelous universality: the Word is the Creator of *all* humanity; his life is their light. The purpose of the Baptizer's witness is "that *all* might believe" (John 1:7). Jesus' light "enlightens *everyone*" (John

---

5. Koester, *Dwelling of God*, 102.

6. Köstenberger, *Theology of John's Gospel*, 186. Italics original.

7. Köstenberger points out that the phrase "full of *grace* and *truth*" echoes two of the characteristics of God's self-revelation: "abounding in *steadfast love* and *faithfulness*"(ibid., Exod 34:6; italics original).

1:9). "[T]o *all* who did receive him, who believed in his name, he gave the right to become children of God," not based on lineage of the blood but by the will of God (John 1:12).[8] There is restrictivity as well: not all believed; not all who beheld his glory comprehended. Even though he came to the world he had made, the Gentile world did not know him, nor did his own people receive him. Because not all believe, all are not children of God. The mere appearance of the light does not confer automatic acceptance of the light; therefore, "the coming of the light demands a choice."[9] There is a responsibility to believe and receive, yet God is the one who wills spiritual birth. As Köstenberger points out, the prologue is thoroughly theocentric: "God's presence pervades all of salvation history and he is the source, both of the missions of the Word and of John . . . and of the life of believers."[10]

Finally, the prologue also highlights the importance of witness in the Fourth Gospel. The word "witness" surfaces four times in the seemingly parenthetical remarks about John the Baptist who came to bear witness to the Christ (John 1:6–8; 15).[11] Interestingly, the Evangelist also includes his own eyewitness testimony in both the prologue (John 1:14) and at the close of his book (John 19:35; 21:24–25). Additionally, the Son himself bears witness, revealing his intimate knowledge of the Father (John 1:18). Craig Keener observes that this repeated emphasis underscores the importance of witness: "If God was invisible till Jesus revealed him (1:18), he and Jesus would now remain invisible apart from the believing community modeling in their lives the character of Jesus (1 John 4:12; John 13:35; 17:21–23)."[12] While Keener's observation about the significant testimony of a Christlike character is certainly true, the Fourth Gospel also highlights the absolute necessity of giving a clear verbal witness as well. In John's gospel those who know God bear witness to others.

Jesus as the Lamb of God

This theme of witness continues to surface throughout the first chapter of John. When the Jews questioned John the Baptist about his identity and role, he modeled the activity of an exemplary witness, "deferring all honor

8. Italics added in this and immediately preceding verses.

9. Ridderbos, *John*, 42.

10. Köstenberger, *Theology of John's Gospel*, 184.

11. The frequent occurrence of the word "witness" in John's gospel demonstrates the centrality of the theme for the Evangelist: the verb form occurs 33 times; the noun form, 14.

12. Keener, *John*, 1:393.

to Jesus."[13] The Baptizer answered with the words of Isaiah: he was simply "the voice of one crying out in the wilderness," preparing the way for the Lord (John 1:23; cf. Isa 40:3). Likewise, when John the Baptist later saw Jesus, he proclaimed, "Behold, the Lamb of God, who takes away the sin of the world!" (John 1:29). He also bore witness that Jesus is the "Son of God" and recounted the details of the Spirit's confirmation at Jesus' baptism (John 1:32–34). Seeing Jesus yet again, John announced an abbreviated form of his earlier statement: "Behold, the Lamb of God," urging two of his own disciples to follow Jesus (John 1:35–37). This statement, twice repeated, is the distilled essence of the Baptizer's witness. Thus, the incarnate Christ is the fulfillment of both the tabernacling presence of God in their midst and the sacrificial Lamb of God who makes reconciliation possible.

Although the origin of the Baptizer's statement is a matter of debate, undoubtedly it evokes memories of the Passover lamb, the daily sacrificial lambs, and the servant lamb of Isaiah 53. Köstenberger observes, however, that in contrast to these lambs, "the Messiah is *God's* lamb, that is, the lamb provided by God himself."[14] The attendant implication is that *God's* lamb would accomplish a more efficacious removal of sin than the endless repetition of cultic sacrifices.[15] Even more astounding is the fact that the Lamb of God *is* God—in the flesh. Significantly, Jesus removes not just the sin of the Israelites, but "the sin of the world" as well, both Jews and Gentiles (John 1:29). The "Lamb of God" statement that summarizes the prophet's message is also a powerfully succinct summary of the reconciling work of Christ and the universal mission of God.

Knowledge of this good news is inherently missional. John's proclamation paved the way for two of his own disciples to follow Jesus (John 1:35). In a domino effect, one of those two, Andrew, immediately shared the good news with his brother Simon (John 1:41). The next day, when Jesus called a fourth man, Philip, to follow him, Philip in turn shared with Nathanael (John 1:45). Certainly these first followers had only a rudimentary understanding of the identity of Jesus, but they knew enough to find others in their relational circles immediately and bear witness intentionally: "We have found the Messiah"; "We have found him of whom Moses in the Law and also the prophets wrote" (John 1:41, 45). When Nathanael voiced initial skepticism, Philip simply repeated the attractional invitation of Jesus, "Come and see" (John 1:46; cf. 1:39). Keener observes, "In John's theology both the Christological witness of disciples and the personal experience of

---

13. Ibid., 1:429.

14. Köstenberger, *Theology of John's Gospel*, 189–90; italics original.

15. Ibid., 190.

Christ become necessary for adequate faith."[16] When Jesus revealed that he knew the details of Nathanael's life, the man confessed, "Rabbi, you are the Son of God! You are the King of Israel!" (John 1:49). This forthright Israelite properly acknowledged the true King of Israel. All of these first followers' descriptions of Jesus highlight the particularity of Jesus who is the fulfillment of the Old Testament promises. Although they did not know him well, their proclamations were closely tied to Scripture.

While Jesus commended Nathanael for his belief based on such meager information, he promised that he would see much greater evidence: "Truly, truly, I say to you, you will see heaven opened and the angels of God ascending and descending on the Son of Man" (John 1:51). Jesus' evaluation of Nathanael as "an Israelite indeed, in whom there is no deceit" had prompted this allusion to an event in the life of Jacob, the schemer, who became "Israel" (John 1:47; cf. Gen 28:10–22). The Old Testament patriarch had dreamed of a ladder suspended between earth and heaven, with angels ascending and descending on it. Upon awakening, Jacob named the place Bethel (House of God) because it was the "gate of heaven," and he had worshiped the God of his fathers in that sacred place (Gen 28:17). Jesus made the astonishing revelation that he, himself, is the fulfillment of Jacob's dream. The person of Christ is the exclusive place where heaven and earth meet. As the ladder between these two spheres, Jesus is therefore the only way to the Father (cf. John 14:6). Thus, the opening chapter of John presents Jesus as the fulfillment of not only the tabernacle but also the sacrifices and the temporary "sanctuaries" where the patriarchs encountered God. In the following chapter, John presents Jesus as the fulfillment of the temple as well.

Jesus as the Temple

While the Synoptic Gospels place the story of the temple clearing in the last week of Jesus' ministry, John positions it in the beginning.[17] At the time of Passover, the glory of God—present in the incarnate Christ—literally

16. Keener, *John*, 1:475.

17. Most scholars argue that there is only one such event, and that John moved it forward in his Gospel for theological reasons. However, Carson, *John*, 177–78, and Köstenberger, *Theology of John's Gospel*, 193–94, maintain that these accounts record two separate historical events because, otherwise, either John or the Synoptic writers misrepresent "the historical markers and temporal references" surrounding the narratives (Köstenberger, *Theology of John's Gospel*, 193). It is certainly conceivable that a second "clearing"—Köstenberger's term—would have been necessary since undoubtedly the religious establishment would have returned to business as usual.

crossed the threshold of the Jerusalem temple once more. What happened when the holy God-tabernacled-in-flesh Christ entered the man-made temple? Immediate judgment: Jesus cleared the temple courts by forcibly driving out the sheep, cattle, moneychangers, and animal vendors. According to Nicholas Perrin, the temple clearing was the "climactic epitome" of Jesus' career. In turning over the tables, "[Jesus] was announcing that time had expired on the regnant wicked priests, that the kingdom had come through him, and that as a result Israel could never go home again."[18] His actions were clearly restrictive: Jesus expelled those who had come to the temple with insincere or impure motives.

Jesus' disruption of the offering of sacrifices, albeit brief, demonstrated that the sacrificial purpose of the temple would no longer be necessary in light of the once-for-all sacrifice that loomed on the horizon. In fact, when the Jewish leaders questioned his authority to clear the temple, Jesus answered them, "Destroy this temple, and in three days I will raise it up" (John 2:19). Although his meaning was not readily apparent to his hearers, after Jesus' resurrection the disciples recognized that, "he was speaking about the temple of his body" (John 2:21). The Synoptic writers record that the words of Jesus were later twisted in the accusations of the two false witnesses at his trial and in the jeers by the spectators at the cross. Unknowingly, these men highlighted the truth that "[Jesus'] resurrection constitutes a rebuilding of the destroyed Temple."[19] As I. Howard Marshall points out, "Jesus himself is the true place where God's presence is revealed, both before and after his death . . . ."[20] The person and work of Christ made the physical structure obsolete, preparing the way for the destruction of the temple in AD 70. Like Solomon's temple and the Shiloh tabernacle before it, the Second Temple was only a temporary, man-made structure that was subject to judgment and destruction. "By contrast," Köstenberger notes, "God's presence in Jesus and the manifestation of God's glory in Jesus are permanent."[21]

There are hints in this pivotal story that point to the universality of the mission of God. Most likely the temple clearing took place in the outermost court of the Gentiles. Any foreigner who might have come to observe or to

---

18. Perrin, *Jesus the Temple*, 185.

19. Köstenberger, *Theology of John's Gospel*, 69.

20. Marshall, "Church and Temple," 177, observes that Jesus-as-temple is not a spiritualization of the sanctuary, but the very opposite: "It is not so much that Christ fulfills what the temple means; rather Christ is the meaning for which the temple existed."

21. Köstenberger, *Theology of John's Gospel*, 195. Jesus' fulfillment of temple symbolism is especially significant in light of Köstenberger's conclusion that John's gospel was written after the destruction of the Second Temple in AD 70 and therefore addressed the Christian response to the loss of the sanctuary (ibid., 71).

draw near to God in prayer would surely have been distracted by the din of the animals and traders. In Mark's account, Jesus declared: "Is it not written, 'My house will be called a house of prayer for all the nations'?" (Mark 11:17). Jesus was referencing Isa 56:7, a strongly universal passage that assures the foreigner and the eunuch—two categories excluded from the temple—that anyone who loves and obeys the Lord will be welcomed into his house. Jesus' concern that the Gentiles have a place to pray in the physical temple foreshadows their inclusion in the family of God. In sharp contrast to "a house of prayer for all the nations," Jesus concluded the second half of Mark 11:17: "But you have made it a den of robbers." This reference to Jer 7:11 recalls Jeremiah's warning that God would judge the Solomonic temple just as he had the sanctuary at Shiloh. Craig Evans infers from these allusions to Isa 56:7 and Jer 7:11 that ". . . Jesus' action was in part motivated by his criticism of the Temple establishment for its failure to live up to its obligations toward, among others, the Gentiles."[22] Just as God had condemned the previous two sanctuaries, Jesus pronounced judgment on the Second Temple as well.

Seeking Those Who Worship in Spirit and in Truth

Similarly, the encounters that immediately follow the temple clearing indicate that a new day is dawning. John narrates how Jesus met with three individuals one after another: a ruler of the Jews (John 3:1–15), a Samaritan woman (John 4:1–42), and a Gentile official (John 4:46–54).[23] Köstenberger observes a pattern here that may reflect Jesus' Acts 1:8 command to be witnesses in "Jerusalem and in all Judea and Samaria, and to the end of the earth."[24] Whether there is a direct correlation or not, the early church certainly found precedent for their boundary-breaking mission in the earthly mission of Jesus himself.

The first of these meetings is Jesus' encounter with Nicodemus, a Pharisee who was a ruler of the Jews (John 3:1). As religious leader, Nicodemus should have been a model of spiritual maturity and well prepared to recognize the Messiah. Unfortunately, he was not. Jesus chided him for his lack of spiritual perception and warned that only those who have been born of

22. Evans, "House of Prayer," 442.

23. Although there is nothing in the text that indicates the royal official was a Gentile, Köstenberger, John, 169, argues that the official was most likely a Gentile.

24. Ibid., 202. Speculating about John's awareness of Luke's two-volume work, Köstenberger remarks that these encounters from Jesus' mission would have indirectly validated the Gentile mission of the early church which was well underway by the time John composed his Gospel.

the Spirit may enter the kingdom of God (John 3:3, 5). Jesus also informed Nicodemus of a further restriction: "the Son of Man [must] be lifted up that whoever believes in him may have eternal life" (John 3:14–15). The verse that follows expands on this idea, summarizing the gospel in a way that would have dumbfounded Nicodemus: "For God so loved the world that he gave his only Son, that whoever believes in him should not perish but have eternal life" (John 3:16). The scope of God's love and mission is global.

This truth is demonstrated in the second encounter, where Jesus met with a Samaritan woman with a sinful reputation—the polar opposite of the Jewish religious leader. When their conversation turned to the religious differences between the Samaritans and Jews, Jesus announced "the impending obsolescence of both the Jerusalem temple and the Mount Gerizim site as definitive places of worship."[25] Jesus explained that "God is spirit, and those who worship him must worship in spirit and truth" (John 4:24). Although the woman's question regarded the proper place to worship, Leon Morris clarifies that "worship in spirit" does not mean that people can presume to approach God anytime, anywhere, in their own way. God is "a being of a different order";[26] he therefore sets his own parameters for worship. Because God is Spirit and man is flesh, "God is present in his own realm, to which man as such has no access."[27] Whereas proper worship had been centered in the locus of the Jerusalem temple, the hour had come that redefined the location: ". . . God is now to be worshiped in the place where he is present, i.e., in Him who is the truth incarnate."[28] Worship "in truth" implies that the content of worship must correspond to God's revelation of himself in the Word—in Scripture and in Jesus. It was not enough that the Samaritans were sincerely devoted to that which was not true. Salvation is particular truth: it comes through God's revelation and redemptive activity through the descendants of Abraham (John 4:22). McKelvey points out, "Christianity supersedes Judaism and Samaritanism not because it is spiritual whereas they are material but because it is centred in a person and not in a place."[29] Ultimately, God opens up the way of salvation through his own Son—the very one who encountered this Samaritan woman and revealed that he is indeed the Messiah.

25. Carson, *John*, 222.

26. Morris, *Jesus Is the Christ*, 126.

27. Hendry, *Holy Spirit*, 31.

28. Ibid., 32.

29. McKelvey, *New Temple*, 80.

Remarkably, God actively seeks those who will worship him in the proper manner.[30] Even more remarkable is the fact that his search extends far beyond his own people. As Mary Coloe observes, "Jesus' journey through Samaria is an expression of his missionary task from the Father who is seeking true worshippers."[31] Having received the spiritual truth revealed to her, the Samaritan woman immediately went to share it with others. Drawn by her testimony to "come and see," many other Samaritans came to believe that Jesus is indeed "the Savior of the world" (John 4:40). This truth is the perfect segue for the third encounter where Jesus healed the son of the royal official from a distance. Convinced by the miracle of his son's recovery, this Gentile man of means and authority believed along with his entire household (John 4:53).

It is difficult to imagine a more eclectic cluster of people than the one the Evangelist has assembled in these two chapters following the temple cleansing. They memorably demonstrate the universality of Jesus' mission and anticipate the global mission of his followers whom Jesus sends to reap the harvest (John 4:35–38). These stories also feature the particularity of election. Salvation comes through God's redemptive activity and revelation through the Jews. It rests, however, not in a tabernacle, temple, or sacrificial system. Salvation is found only in Jesus, the Savior of the world.

Significantly, questions concerning Jesus' identity—his origins and his destiny—surfaced against the backdrop of the temple and the Feast of Tabernacles (John 7–8). At this festival which celebrated the tabernacling presence of God, Jesus revealed that he was the fulfillment of the symbolism behind the water-pouring rite and ceremony of lights. On the last day of the festival, Jesus invited *anyone* who was thirsty to receive his life-giving Spirit: "*Whoever* believes in me, as the Scripture has said, 'Out of his heart will flow rivers of living water'" (John 7:38; italics added).[32] Against the backdrop of this festival, he also declared: "I am the light of the *world. Whoever* follows me . . . will have the light of life" (John 8:12; italics added). Clearly, Jesus' fulfillment of the Jewish Feast of Tabernacles would have universal implications as well.

After an extended discussion with the Jews that ended in their acrimonious accusation that Jesus had a demon, Jesus declared that Abraham himself had rejoiced in anticipation of his coming (John 8:56; cf. Gen 12:3). Jesus also boldly proclaimed his preexistence in phrasing that echoed God's

30. Morris, *Jesus Is the Christ*, 139.

31. Coloe, *God Dwells with Us*, 112.

32. John explains that Jesus spoke in reference to the Spirit, who had not yet been given (John 7:39). Interestingly, rivers also flowed from God's sanctuary presence in Gen 2:10ff, in Ezek 47:1ff, and in Rev 22:1–2.

revelation of his covenant name to Moses: "Truly, truly, I say to you, before Abraham was, *I am*" (John 8:58; emphasis added). Significantly, Jesus made this statement in the temple—"the place which previously had been the *locus* of that divine Name."[33] The new *locus* for the Name is now the person of Jesus Christ. When the enraged Jews attempted to stone him for this supposed blasphemy, "Jesus hid himself and went out of the temple" (John 8:59). Köstenberger comments, "Ominously, the glory of God, the very presence of the divine in Jesus, had hid, departing from the temple (8:59). Surely, this does not bode well for the Jewish nation and its representatives."[34] Just as when the glory departed the Shiloh tabernacle and the Solomonic temple, the incarnated glory of God left the building, clearing the way for its destruction. Jesus, however, had already pointed the way forward for his followers. In the future, believers would experience the tabernacling presence of God not in the temple, but in the living water of the Spirit.

The Promise of a Future Dwelling Place

In the Farewell Discourse (John 13–17), Jesus expounded on what would happen after he was no longer physically present with his disciples. Jesus comforted the disciples who were distraught at the revelation of his imminent departure: "In my Father's house are many rooms [*monai*; "dwelling places," HCSB]. . . . And if I go to prepare a place for you, I will come again and will take you to myself, that where I am you may be also" (John 14:2–3). The image is that of a large house with ample "subsidiary living quarters" for all his disciples.[35] As the Son, Jesus invites his followers into his Father's house.

There has been much debate surrounding the meaning of "my Father's house" (*oikia*), with most scholars identifying this expression as "a generalized description of heaven as the dwelling place of God."[36] On the other hand, others argue that the phrase refers to the temple based on the following: 1) Jesus' usage of a very similar phrase (*oikon*) referring to the temple in John 2:16; 2) frequent references in Jewish literature that depict the temple as God's house; and 3) the use of the term "place" (*topon*) in John 14:2, 3—a term that often refers to the temple—which John already used to indicate the temple (John 4:20; 11:48).[37] Jesus' reference to "my Father's house" in

33. Walker, *Jesus*, 168.
34. Köstenberger, *Theology of John's Gospel*, 223.
35. Beasley-Murray, *John*, 249.
36. Bryan, "Eschatological Temple," 193.
37. Ibid.

John 14:2 most likely refers to the heavenly dwelling place of God, which can also rightly be conceived as an eschatological heavenly sanctuary.

This passage emphasizes the comfort believers will enjoy in the presence of God: "I will come again and will take you to myself, that where I am you may be also" (John 14:3). The presupposition is that the "place" already exists; "in the context of Johannine theology, it is the going itself, via the cross and resurrection, that prepares the place for Jesus' disciples."[38] James McCaffrey contends that there is a missional dimension in this passage:

> [T]his outward missionary movement of Jesus in Jn 14, 2–3 constitutes the crowning achievement of the work of redemption. Thus there is an intrinsic element of expansion in the New Temple of the risen Jesus in Jn 14, 2–3—an outward movement of the risen Jesus to all believers. This link between the New Temple and mission highlights a significant aspect of the Christian fulfillment of the mystery of the New Temple.[39]

Jesus revealed that he is both the destination and the way: "I am the way, and the truth, and the life. No one comes to the Father except through me" (John 14:6). D. A. Carson notes, "Jesus is the truth, because he embodies the supreme revelation of God—he himself 'narrates' God (1:18) . . . . He is God's gracious self-disclosure, his 'Word,' made flesh (1:14)."[40] Jesus is also the life and the giver of eternal life (John 1:4; 4:14). Eternal life therefore is not only a place, but a Person: knowing the only true God through Jesus Christ—who is indeed one with the Father (John 17:3; cf. 14:7–11). Because of Jesus' unique identity, he alone can say, "No one comes to the Father except through me" (John 14:6b). Access to the Father's presence is restricted to those who come through Christ. As Keener points out, "[John's] exclusivity is not a claim that other ways to the Father existed and Jesus closed them off. The claim is more universal than that: given the world's alienation from God, there was no way to the Father, and Jesus provided one (3:18–19; cf. 1:10; 1 John 5:19)."[41] Likewise, Carson concludes that other religions are "ineffective in bringing people to the true God." On this basis he concludes that the exclusivity of Christ for salvation "is the necessary stance behind all fervent evangelism."[42] This claim of Christocentric exclusivity is by its very nature polemical.

---

38. Carson, *John*, 489.

39. McCaffrey, *The House*, 235.

40. Carson, *John*, 491.

41. Keener, *John*, 2:943.

42. Carson, *John*, 492.

The Indwelling Spirit

Jesus had reassured his disciples that he would return to usher them in to his Father's dwelling place. But until that time, how were his followers to experience the presence of Christ? Jesus explained that God's presence would actually take up residence in the lives of individual believers (John 14:23). The Son would ask the Father to send "another helping presence," the Spirit of truth who would dwell (*menei*) with them and in them (John 14:16–17). Jesus so closely identifies with the Spirit, that "he can say that *he himself* will return to his followers in the person of the Spirit" (John 14:18–20).[43] He clarified, "If anyone loves me, he will keep my word, and my Father will love him, and we will come to him and make our home (*monēn*) with him" (John 14:23).[44] In other words, Jesus' followers will experience a mutual indwelling that involves all three persons of the Trinity: "In that day you will know I am in my Father, and you in me, and I in you" (John 14:20; cf. 14:16, 23). Amazingly, the God who condescended to dwell in the midst of his people in the tabernacle, the temple, and the Incarnation, now promised to dwell in his people themselves through the Spirit.

Yet, as Jesus explained in John 15, this indwelling presence would require that they continue to abide in Jesus, his words, and his love just as a branch abides in the vine—a metaphor that captures their utter dependence on the indwelling Spirit. Jesus' repeated use of the word "abide" (*menō*; ten times in John 15:4–10) underscores the significance of this privilege and attendant responsibility. Morris notes that there is a "strong moral note" in connection with the work of the Holy Spirit.[45] Because the Spirit of God resides in the lives of believers, this obedience should come as the natural overflow of their love for Jesus (John 15:10; cf. 14:21).

There are many missional dimensions in the Farewell Discourse. Jesus' departure signified the completion of his earthly mission; his death and resurrection paved the way for the subsequent mission of the Spirit. Thus, Jesus told his disciples that it was actually to their advantage that he go away and send the Spirit in his place (John 16:7). This Helper, in turn, would enable the disciples in their own mission. He both teaches believers and recalls Jesus' own teaching (John 14:26). The Spirit also bears witness about Jesus and evidently is linked to believers' witness as well. Morris explains, "The thought is probably that what the Spirit does in believers forms a witness to those not yet Christian. It is part of the way the world is to be won for

43. Köstenberger, *John*, 434, italics original.

44. Köstenberger points out that this reference forms an inclusio with *monai*—the same word that is translated as "rooms" or "dwelling places" in John 14:2 (ibid., 440).

45. Morris, *Jesus Is the Christ*, 160.

Christ."[46] Believers who display the presence of the Spirit of God in their lives offer proof to those outside the faith of the existence and identity of God. Although the Spirit will bear witness, believers also have the responsibility of bearing witness, as did the apostles (John 15:26–27; "you must testify," NIV).

The one who abides in Jesus *will bear much fruit* thus bringing glory to the Father (John 15:5, 8; italics added). Not only is fruitbearing is the mark of a true disciple, but it is also the mission of a disciple: the Father chose and appointed them that they should bear fruit that will abide (John 15:16). While commentators suggest a variety of meanings for the fruit imagery, Carson argues, "This fruit is nothing less than the outcome of persevering dependence on the vine, driven by faith, embracing all of the believer's life and the product of his witness."[47] Still, the closing allusion to "fruit that will abide" rightly leads Carson to conclude that no matter how comprehensive the nature of the fruit, "the focus on evangelism and mission is truly central."[48] Just as the life of the vine pulsates through the branches, the heartbeat of Jesus' mission would soon beat in their own hearts as well. As the Father sent the Son into the world, so the Son would send his disciples into the world (John 17:18; cf. 20:21).

Based on the fact that the verb "send" (*apostellō*) occurs seven times in John 17, Lucien Legrand suggests that the "Priestly Prayer" of Jesus might also bear the title of an "apostolic" or "missionary prayer." This prayer that sums up "John's entire missionary concern" first presents Jesus as the incomparable missionary sent by the Father (John 17:1–5). Legrand calls Jesus' glorification "the founding act of mission." Receiving from his Father "authority over all flesh," Jesus is the giver of eternal life, which is knowledge of himself and his Father. In the second section (John 17:6–19), Jesus prayed for his disciples, whom he was sending into the world. Legrand observes that the sending focuses even more on "*consecration* to truth" than on "*communication* of truth." He continues, "The envoy remains before all else a 'disciple.' . . . To be sure, they are to proclaim the gospel; but more specifically, and more profoundly, they are called to be one with the truth of the Word: it is the Word that will have the initiative in the deepest heart of their mission."[49]

46. Ibid., 161.

47. Carson, *John*, 519.

48. Ibid., 523. Although Ridderbos, *John*, 522, argues against "a specifically missionary intent here," he allows that "the proclamation of the gospel in the world constitutes part of the fruitbearing of the disciples."

49. Legrand, *Unity and Plurality*, 141–42. Italics original.

Finally, in the third section (John 17:20–26), Jesus prayed for those who would come to faith in Christ through the message that his disciples would proclaim. Furthermore, he prayed, "that they may be one even as we are one, I in them and you in me . . . *so that the world may know* that you sent me and loved them even as you loved me" (John 17:20–23; italics added). The indwelling Spirit should result in a unity and glory among believers that convinces the world of God's love in sending Jesus. Their witness must focus on Jesus: "his word, his works, his death and resurrection, with all its potential for both blessing and judgment."[50] But not only must they proclaim the Word; they must also "live the Word" by reflecting the glory of God's love and unity to a world that desperately needs both to hear their message and to see it lived out.[51] Carson makes the following observation:

> That Jesus' prayer for his disciples has as its end their mission to the world demonstrates that this Gospel is not introducing an absolute cleavage between Jesus' followers and the world. Not only were they drawn from the world (15:19), but the prayer that they may be kept safe in the world and sanctified by the truth so as to engage in the mission to the world is ample evidence that they are the continuing locus of 3:16: "God so loved the world that he sent . . . ."[52]

However, because the message of God's revelation in Christ stands in sharp contrast to the prevailing worldview, the witness of believers will necessarily force a division in the world—just as it did in Jesus' ministry.

As vinedresser, the Father makes a sharp distinction between dead wood and living, fruitbearing branches.[53] If any branches do not abide in the vine or bear fruit, he will cut them off and burn them in the fire because they have no life in them (John 15:6). Keener suggests that this sober warning—"the closest image to 'hell'" in the Fourth Gospel—describes "unfruitful alleged disciples."[54] Legrand observes, "The gospel of life, light, and love is also the gospel of judgment. . . . Johannine love goes hand in hand with judgment."[55] If initial belief that fails to progress to true faith incurs eternal banishment from God's presence, how much more does outright rejection?

50. Carson, *John*, 530.

51. Legrand, *Unity and Plurality*, 143.

52. Carson, *John*, 567.

53. Ibid., 514–15.

54. Keener, *John*, 2:1000.

55. Legrand, *Unity and Plurality*, 139.

John 14:17 clearly "assigns the Spirit's presence wholly to believers in Jesus, excluding 'the world.'"[56] According to John 16:8–11, however, the Paraclete does work in the lives of unbelievers to convict them "concerning sin, and righteousness and judgment." While believers should bear witness about Jesus, they should do so in the power of the Spirit and under his direction. After all, apart from Jesus they can do nothing (John 15:5). The role of conviction, however, falls to the Spirit himself. While some will become followers of Christ, others will reject him.

Jesus cautioned his disciples that just as the world hated him without cause, they would likewise hate his followers who live in contrast to the world (John 15:18–25). Even though Christians were former citizens of the world themselves, the more they identified with Jesus, the more the world would hate them.[57] Jesus warned, "Indeed the hour is coming when whoever kills you will think he is offering service to God" (John 16:2). With these words, Jesus poignantly anticipated the events that were about to unfold: his arrest, death, and resurrection. Yet it is these very events that fulfilled the purposes of Jesus' mission. The hour had come. Paradoxically—just as the glory of God had settled on the tabernacle and temple—God would manifest his indescribable glory through the suffering of the tabernacled-in-flesh Christ (cf. John 13:31–32; 17:1–5).

After the resurrection, the disciples would understand that Jesus had indeed overcome the world (John 16:33). Just hours before the events of the cross, Jesus had informed his disciples of an enduring legacy of love, joy, and peace.[58] More importantly, however, he had made a way for them to be *with him* and to see the glory he had shared with the Father before the world existed (John 17:5, 24). Jesus assured his followers that they would continue to enjoy his abiding presence—even in his seeming absence.

The Gospel of Matthew

Craig Blomberg observes that one of the distinctive characteristics of Matthew's gospel is that although it is the most Jewish of the four Gospels, it also "foreshadows the Gentile mission as clearly as any of the other three."[59] On the one hand Matthew often cites passages from the Old Testament in

56. Keener, *John*, 2:972.

57. Carson, *John*, 525.

58. Köstenberger, *Theology of John's Gospel*, 230.

59. Blomberg, *Jesus and the Gospels*, 148. Because more than 90% of Mark's gospel is reproduced in the other Synoptics (ibid., 99), this chapter will focus on Matthew and Luke rather than Mark.

order to show how Jesus fulfills the Jewish Scripture. On the other, Matthew's gospel also relates the visit of the Gentile Magi (Matt 2:1–12), a universal judgment (25:31–32), and a global commission to make disciples of all nations (28:18–20; cf. 24:14; 26:13). Köstenberger concludes that the Gospel of Matthew gave the early church "a solid theological foundation for its mission to the Gentiles."[60] This Gospel is therefore uniquely positioned to provide significant insights on both the particularity and universality of the *missio Dei*.

The Birth of Jesus: "God with Us"

These twin themes surface immediately in the first verse of Matthew: "The book of the genealogy of Jesus Christ, the son of David, the son of Abraham" (Matt 1:1). Matthew sounds a note of particularity by tracing the Messiah's lineage back to the Father of the Israelites and to the king of Israel. At the same time, the mention of Abraham also recalls God's promise to bless all the nations of the world through the offspring of this particular man (Gen 22:18; "all the nations" [LXX: *panta ta ethnē*]); cf. Matt 28:19 (*panta ta ethnē*). In addition, Matthew highlights the universal significance of Jesus' birth by his inclusion of four Gentile women in the genealogy of the Messiah (Matt 1:3, 5–6).[61] Although commentators disagree on the author's main intention for their inclusion, these women nevertheless evoke the following subtexts: 1) the mention of these Gentiles in the Messiah's lineage foreshadows their inclusion in his kingdom; 2) the scandalous pasts of these women emphasize the role of Jesus who "will save his people from their sins" (Matt 1:21); and 3) because all four reveal the "unexpected workings of Providence in preparation for the Messiah," they pave the way for a similarly unexpected work in the life of Mary, the fifth woman in Matthew's genealogy of the Christ.[62] The above allusions underscore the desperate need for a Messiah who could save his people from their sins and the necessity that he come from God himself.

At the conclusion of the genealogy, Matthew demonstrates that Jesus of Nazareth is the Messiah based on the five scriptural proofs found

---

60. Köstenberger and O'Brien, *Salvation*, 87.

61. Carson, "Matthew," 66, suggests that because Bathsheba was married to a Hittite, she may have been regarded as a Hittite as well.

62. Ibid. While Ruth's reputation was above reproach, Carson points out that she was a Moabite, a people whose roots began in incest (Gen 19:30–37) and whose desire to curse the Israelites resulted in their own exclusion from the assembly of God down to the tenth generation (Deut 23:3).

in 1:18—2:23. R. T. France calls this section "an exercise in apologetics."[63] The Gospel writer has marshaled evidence for his clear claim that God alone is responsible for this virgin-birthed child. The application of the title "God with us" to the infant conceived by the Holy Spirit thus indicates that "[t]he presence of Jesus is the presence of God, and God's presence is saving."[64] France concludes that ". . . Matthew's overt interpretation of 'Immanuel' thus takes him close to an explicit doctrine of the incarnation such as is expressed in John 1:14."[65]

Matthew then fast-forwards to the visit of the Magi from the East, an account unique to his Gospel (Matt 2:1–12). This story contrasts the Jewish religious and political leaders in Jerusalem with these exotic visitors who travel such a great distance to see the newborn king of the Jews.[66] When Herod learned of their quest, he assembled the chief priests and scribes to inquire where the Messiah was to be born. From Micah 5:2 came the ready answer: Bethlehem, the city of King David. Herman Ridderbos notes the irony that although the definitive answer came from "the light of Israel's Holy Scriptures" and not the star, it is the Gentiles, rather than the Jewish religious leaders, who seek to worship the newborn king.[67] Herod, on the other hand, wanted only to put the child to death (Matt 2:16–18). In contrast to "Herod and all Jerusalem" who were "greatly agitated"[68] by the news, the wise men "rejoiced exceedingly with great joy" (Matt 2:10). When they found the child, "they fell down and worshiped him," offering costly gifts fit for a king (Matt 2:11). The twin poles of particularity and universality stand out clearly in Matthew's gospel. Although Jesus is the King of the Jews, born of the house and lineage of David, it is the Gentiles who recognize his identity and pay him appropriate homage.

Jesus Pronounces Judgment

Matthew's gospel continues to contrast believing Gentiles and Jewish religious leaders who reject Jesus (e.g., Matt 8:11–12; 22:1–10). This critique comes to a head in the series of woes Jesus pronounced on the scribes and Pharisees: "You serpents, you brood of vipers, how are you to escape being sentenced to hell?" (Matt 23:33). Following on the heels of this scathing

---

63. France, *Matthew*, 41–42.

64. Smith, *Matthew*, 38.

65. France, *Matthew*, 49.

66. Cf. Solomon's prayer at the temple's dedication in 1 Kgs 8:41.

67. Ridderbos, *Matthew*, 34.

68. Blomberg, *Matthew*, 63.

rebuke, however, Jesus expressed an impassioned lament for the city of Jerusalem: "O Jerusalem, Jerusalem, the city that kills the prophets and stones those who are sent to it! How often would I have gathered your children together as a hen gathers her brood under her wings, and you would not! See, your house is left to you desolate" (Matt 23:37–38). The wistful tone of the lament strikes "an important counterbalance to the sharpness of the preceding polemic."[69] Ironically, Jesus referred to the temple building as "your house" rather than "God's house." France also observes, "There is a special poignancy in the juxtaposition of 'house' (a place meant to be lived in) and *erēmos*, 'uninhabited,' which describes not so much its physical dissolution as its being deserted; its consequent destruction will merely complete the process."[70]

Immediately following this pronouncement, Jesus "left the temple and was going away" (Matt 24:1). This emphatic wording and imagery immediately recall the vision of God's glory abandoning Solomon's temple in Ezekiel 10. Similarly, Immanuel's departure from the Second Temple cleared the way for its destruction as well. Because "God-with-us" was present in their midst, Jesus had said, "I tell you, something greater than the temple is here" (Matt 12:6). Blomberg points out that the temple's role in "the unfolding plan of salvation history" was complete: "From then on no special location will be more sacred than any other; God will dwell wherever 'two or three come together' in Christ's name (18:20)."[71] The religious leaders' failure to recognize the presence of God in their midst in the person of Jesus, Immanuel, would have dire consequences.

Interestingly, the import of Jesus' words seems to have eluded the disciples who, according to the other Synoptic Gospels, marveled at the temple buildings as they departed (cf. Mark 13:1; Luke 21:5). Jesus' response made it crystal clear: "Truly, I say to you, there will not be left here one stone upon another that will not be thrown down" (Matt 24:1). Jesus' unexpected prediction of the destruction of the temple—fulfilled in AD 70—prompted a barrage of concerned questions from the disciples. In answer, Jesus explained the kinds of things that would occur before his return, including international turmoil, natural disasters, persecution, and apostasy (Matt 24–25).

At the same time, Jesus predicted: "And this gospel will be proclaimed *throughout the whole world* as a testimony *to all nations*, and then the end will come" (Matt 24:14; italics added). The global scope of God's mission is

---

69. France, *Matthew*, 883.

70. Ibid., 884.

71. Blomberg, *Matthew*, 350–51.

clear. In spite of cosmic upheaval, God's Word will spread and accomplish his mission. Until such time, Jesus' followers are to be faithful, proclaiming the gospel throughout the world until Christ returns "on the clouds of heaven with power and great glory" (Matt 24:30). The clouds symbolize God's theophanic presence; Jesus' return will thus be "universally witnessed and unmistakably plain" (cf. Matt 24:26–27, 30).[72] Because the gospel message will have circled the globe, the elect from every nation will be gathered "from one end of heaven to another" (Matt 24:31). When Jesus returns and sits on his throne, all the nations will be gathered before him for the final, universal judgment (Matt 25:32). Those whom Jesus welcomes into his kingdom will dwell in the everlasting presence of the King. As Carson notes, their inheritance "presupposes a relationship with the Father."[73] This inheritance, "prepared from the foundation of the world," is in essence the mission of God from the beginning. In contrast, those whose lives do not demonstrate evidence of a relationship with Jesus hear the worst possible judgment pronounced: "Depart from me" (Matt 25:41; cf. 7:23). Cursed, they face punishment—"the eternal fire prepared for the devil and his angels"—banished from the presence of God forever (Matt 25:41, 46; cf. 2 Thess 1:9–10).

Jesus Provides Access into God's Presence

The only way that Jesus' followers could enter into the abiding presence of God was through Jesus' substitutionary death on the cross. He bore their punishment, cursed—hanging on a tree. The Son of God, who had always known intimate oneness with the Father, faced the unimaginable—even if momentary—agony of abandonment (Matt 27:46).[74] The suffering Savior thus removed the curse from believers, securing his "brothers" admittance into his Father's kingdom. Matthew records that at the very moment when Jesus gave up his spirit, the thick temple veil—adorned with the cherubim that barred humanity from the holy of holies—was torn in two from top to bottom (Matt 27:51). Although access into the presence of God is restrictive, Jesus' death removed that barrier: his blood "poured out for many for the forgiveness of sins" had opened the way for forgiven sinners to approach a holy God (Matt 26:28). The temple and its rituals were no longer necessary. As the new temple, Jesus is now "the meeting place of God and man";

---

72. Carson, "Matthew," 506.

73. Ibid., 521. Carson also makes the observation that "[t]he reason for admission to the kingdom in this parable is more evidential than causative."

74. Ibid., 579.

therefore, the inevitable destruction of the Second Temple is a "theological necessity."[75]

Significantly, Matthew recorded the conclusive testimony to crucifixion events from the lips of a Gentile. Convinced by the witness of nature itself—the darkness, earthquake, and splitting rocks—the Roman centurion who participated in Jesus' crucifixion exclaimed, "Truly this was the Son of God!" (Matt 27:54).[76] The scope of the salvation that Jesus had just accomplished was worldwide. Matthew's mention of the Roman centurion recalls the earlier pericope where Jesus commended the exemplary faith of the centurion in Matt 8:5–13. Contrasting the faith of that Gentile soldier to the unbelieving Jews, Jesus had proclaimed the startling news: "I tell you, many will come from east and west and recline at table with Abraham, Isaac, and Jacob in the kingdom of heaven, while the sons of the kingdom will be thrown into the outer darkness. In that place there will be weeping and gnashing of teeth" (Matt 8:10–12). Later, at the conclusion of the wedding feast parable, Jesus repeated the final punch line verbatim (cf. Matt 22:13b). Similarly, Jesus' story of the eschatological banquet supports Matthew's recurring theme of the universality of the gospel. While the invitation is extended to all, not all will respond to the invitation. Those who refuse to declare "Truly this [is] the Son of God" will face judgment—regardless of their ethnic or religious background.

Jesus Commissions His Followers: "I am with you always"

In view of Matthew's recurring theme of universality, it is not surprising that Jesus' final words to his disciples contain a universal mandate. The word "all" resoundingly echoes throughout Matt 28:18–20: "*All* authority in heaven and on earth has been given to me. Go therefore and make disciples of *all* nations, baptizing them in the name of the Father and of the Son and of the Holy Spirit, teaching them to observe *all* that I have commanded you. And behold, I am with you *always*, to the end of the age" (italics added). While the Great Commission is inclusive in that it has universal scope, at the same time it is exclusive in that Jesus commands people of all nations to become disciples. As Martin Goldsmith notes, "This command disallows religious pluralism, for all are to be called to become disciples of Jesus."[77] They are to follow *him*.

75. Ibid., 581.

76. France, *Matthew*, 1085, points out that the centurion's declaration stands as a foil to the Sanhedrin who used similar language as the basis of Jesus' condemnation.

77. Goldsmith, *Matthew and Mission*, 201.

In a clear allusion to Dan 7:13–14, Jesus bases his command on the fact that the Father has given him all authority. The main verb of the command is the imperative: "make disciples." Johannes Blauw observes, "*Missions is the summons of the Lordship of Christ.*"[78] The Person of the risen Christ stands at the heart of this imperative. According to Ridderbos, the command to "make disciples" means that "by the preaching of the gospel, people must be completely won over to Christ; they must be turned into new people by what they hear and believe."[79] Following Christ entails orthopathy: a reorientation of the heart's desire and a radical shift in allegiance.

The first participle, "going," is necessary in order to fulfill the second half of Jesus' command to make disciples "of all nations." The other two participles, "baptizing" and "teaching," characterize the process of disciple-making.[80] As Carson observes, "The NT can scarcely conceive of a disciple who is not baptized or is not instructed."[81] Disciples are to be baptized "in the name of the Father and of the Son, and of the Holy Spirit." They are also baptized into a community of believers bound together by this common allegiance to this Name. Jesus' disciples are to teach these new disciples not only content—all that the Lord had commanded them—but also to *observe* all his commandments. In other words, Jesus assigned them the responsibility of passing on orthopraxy as well as orthodoxy. Since *all* that Jesus commanded includes even this Great Commission, the disciples are responsible for making disciples . . . who in turn make disciples. Jesus' command of multiplying discipleship will result in a worldwide movement that binds disciples from every nation to this community of Christ-followers.

According to Blomberg, these verses are the climax of Matthew's gospel: "Jesus is passing the torch to his disciples, even as he promises to be with them forever—spiritually, not physically—to empower them for future mission."[82] The presence of Jesus Christ himself accompanies them as they carry out *his* mission. Robert Smith explains, "He is Emmanuel, the place of the presence of God, and he continues with the community, indwelling the community wherever two or three gather in his name and lift their voices in prayer."[83] Jesus' abiding presence will thus guide and empower his disciples as they go about his mission. This promise extends to all believers, regardless of their ethnicity, geography, or generation. In light of the over-

---

78. Blauw, *Missionary Nature*, 84; italics original.

79. Ridderbos, *Matthew*, 554.

80. Carson, "Matthew," 595.

81. Ibid., 597.

82. Blomberg, *Matthew*, 431.

83. Smith, *Matthew*, 341

whelming nature of this commission, Matthew concludes his Gospel with the focus centered on Christ rather than the disciples' task.[84] After all, the mission belongs to Jesus. He will bring it to completion as he accompanies his disciples who are engaged in carrying out his global commission.

Thus, the closing sentence of Matthew brings this Gospel full circle. The author brackets his book with an inclusio: "twin promises of the presence of God and Jesus amongst people."[85] In the first chapter, the angel introduced the yet-to-be-born Jesus as Immanuel, "God with us" (Matt 1:23). In the final chapter, the resurrected Lord assured his disciples: "And behold I am with you always, to the end of the age" (Matt 28:20).[86] Just as God was present in Christ in the incarnation, Jesus will also be present in his followers to whom he has given the ministry of reconciliation. Thus, the tabernacling presence of God is the means of his mission.

The Gospel of Luke

While many commentators recognize that the structure of Acts follows the basic geographical outline of Acts 1:8, Blomberg suggests that "[t]his exact geographical sequence can be discerned in Luke's Gospel as well, only in reverse order."[87] Both volumes emphasize that Christ's followers are to be witnesses who proclaim the gospel to all nations in the power of the Holy Spirit (Luke 24:46–49; Acts 1:8). In Luke's gospel, William Dumbrell detects an additional concern in the clusters of temple references in Luke 1–2 and 19–24. Thus, Luke's arrangement suggests that he frames his Gospel to underscore the importance of the temple.[88] On the one hand, Luke presents a "ringing endorsement of the cultus"; on the other, he narrates a seismic

84. Blomberg, *Matthew*, 433.

85. Angel, "Inclusio," 527.

86. Angel also notes that Jesus' closing tagline of the Great Commission, "the end of the age," is in essence a second inclusio that echoes the judgment setting of the parables of the wheat/tares and the dragnet: "So it will be at the close of the age" (Matt 13:39, 40, 49). Thus, the Great Commission also contains a reminder that access into the kingdom of heaven is restricted: those who refuse to receive the incredible gift of salvation will face judgment at the end of the age (ibid., 527).

87. Blomberg, *Jesus and the Gospels*, 161. Blomberg, explains that Luke begins with references to Roman rulers and appointees (Luke 1:5; 2:1; 3:1), then focuses on Jesus' ministry in "Galilee of the Gentiles" (Luke 3:1–9:50) followed by Samaria (Luke 9:52; 17:11), before tracing Jesus' journey through Judea headed to Jerusalem (Luke 18:35; 19:1, 11, 28, etc.). He concludes, 161–62, that Luke designed "a two-volume chiastically structured account of the life of Jesus and the growth of the early church" that pivots on the resurrection and ascension—the heart of the kerygma for Luke.

88. Dumbrell, *End of the Beginning*, 68.

"salvation-historical shift," in which Jesus assumes a high-priestly status in preparation for a new temple.[89]

The Infancy Narratives

Luke's story begins in the temple with the birth announcement of John the Baptist by the angel Gabriel, who stands "in the presence of God" (Luke 1:19). Gabriel also delivered a second birth announcement to a virgin named Mary: "The Holy Spirit will come upon you, and the power of the Most High will overshadow you; therefore the child to be born will be called holy—the Son of God" (Luke 1:35). Darrell Bock notes the use of the term in the Septuagint: "Ἐπισκιάσει (episkiasei, shall overshadow) in the OT refers either to the Shekinah cloud that rested on the tabernacle (Exod 40:34–35; Num 9:18; 10:34) or to God's presence in protecting his people (Ps 91:4 [90:4 LXX]; 140:7 [139:8 LXX])."[90] The same glorious tabernacling presence of God that once overshadowed the Tent of Meeting between God and man now overshadowed the conception of the Son of God—the new meeting place between God and man. This latter "meeting place" would be the ultimate fulfillment of the former man-made sanctuaries.

Luke 2 opens with a study in contrasts. At first glance it appears that a simple decree of Caesar Augustus that all the world should be taxed set in motion the travel plans of a poor betrothed couple on the outer fringes of his vast empire—resulting in the birth of their firstborn son in very humble circumstances. A deeper look, however, reveals that Caesar was merely the agent God used to fulfill *his* mission: the Bethlehem birth of his Son, the long-promised Davidic heir—"a Savior, who is Christ the Lord" (Luke 2:11).[91] An angel proclaimed worldwide implications of the birth of this infant to a group of lowly shepherds: ". . . I bring you good news of great joy that will be for all the people" (Luke 2:10).[92] At the same time, "the bright Shekinah glory [of] God's majestic presence" shattered the nighttime sky.[93]

89. Perrin, *Jesus the Temple*, 62–63.

90. Bock, *Luke*, 1:122. Johnson, *Him We Proclaim*, 213, observes that the claim of a typological connection between Moses' tabernacle and Mary's womb is greatly strengthened by 1) the fact that Luke makes the same uncommon semantic choices to describe the Transfiguration—"the coincidence of radiant divine glory and an over-shadowing (*episkiazó*) cloud (*nephelē*) with the presence of Moses" and 2) the broader NT motif of the fulfillment of the sanctuary (tabernacle and temple) in Jesus.

91. Bock, *Luke*, 1:203.

92. This wording—*euangelizomai* ("to proclaim the good news/gospel")—reverberates throughout Luke's gospel: Luke 1:19; 2:10; 3:18; 4:18, 43; 7:22; 8:1; 9:6; 16:16; 20:1.

93. Bock, *Luke*, 1:214.

After the angel's pronouncement, "a multitude of the heavenly host" burst forth in praise: "Glory to God in the highest and on earth peace among those with whom he is pleased" (Luke 2:14). The angels simply could not contain such wonderful news; neither could the shepherds who first heard it. They, too, were compelled to praise God and pass along the good news that they had received (Luke 2:17–18). Bock observes a difference "between those whom Jesus comes for (all people; 2:10) and those who benefit from his coming (men of his good pleasure; 2:14)."[94] Unlike the famed—and temporary—*Pax Romana* of Augustus, the Messiah reconciles those who receive him to the God who sent him.[95]

Mary and Joseph took Jesus to the temple in fulfillment of the requirements of the Law—the presentation of a firstborn son and the purification of his parents (Luke 2:22–24). Thus, the Son of God crossed the threshold of the temple as a newborn baby cradled in his mother's arms. The couple's humble sacrifice of two doves is a decided contrast to the costly sacrifice of God's firstborn who would one day purchase the purification of not only his earthly parents, but also the whole world. The Holy Spirit underscored the significance of the occasion by directing the righteous layman, Simeon, to meet and recognize the Messiah, the object of his heart's longing (Luke 2:25–32). Simeon's speech marks the climax of the infancy narratives, "where for the first time in the Gospel Jesus' saving work is explicitly related to the Gentiles."[96] Taking the baby in his arms, Simeon praised God: "for my eyes have seen your salvation that you have prepared in the presence of all peoples, a light for revelation to the Gentiles and for glory to your people Israel" (Luke 2:30–32). While the salvation Jesus brings is for all, its roots grow out of Israel, conferring on this particular nation a special honor.[97]

But not all will recognize and receive this salvation. Simeon's prophetic word to Mary revealed that Jesus would divide the nation and face opposition that would pierce Mary's own soul with grief like a sword (Luke 2:34–35). Jesus proves to be a litmus test that exposes the thoughts of many.[98] Some will receive his salvation with joy and "rise"; others will reject him and "fall." On the heels of Simeon's testimony, Luke records a second testimony, that of the devout prophetess, Anna. Recognizing the significance of this tiny infant, the aged widow thanked God and testified of the child "to all who were waiting for the redemption of Jerusalem" (Luke 2:38). Like the

---

94. Ibid., 220.

95. Evans, *Luke*, 38.

96. Köstenberger and O'Brien, *Salvation*, 113.

97. Bock, *Luke*, 1:245.

98. Ibid., 250.

humble shepherds, Simeon and Anna draw others' attention to Jesus with their words of witness.

Finally, Luke closes his section of the childhood narratives with the transitional story of the twelve-year-old Jesus returning to the temple. When his parents expressed dismay at his absence, Jesus answered, "Did you not know that I must be in my Father's house?" (Luke 2:49). Morris comments, "The first recorded words of the Messiah are then a recognition of His unique relationship to God and of the necessity (*must*) of His being in the Father's house."[99] Although the teachers—and even Jesus' parents—do not yet grasp the full identity of this precocious child, the author certainly does. Luke's infancy narratives begin and end in the temple, or in Jesus' words, "my Father's house."

The Transfiguration

In Luke 9:28–36, God himself resolved any lingering question of Jesus' identity—a query raised in the same chapter by Herod (vv. 7–9) and by Jesus to his disciples (vv. 18–20). In the transfiguration, Jesus' face and even his clothing dazzlingly radiated the glory of God. Standing with the Messiah and sharing in his glory were Moses and Elijah, two prophets who had previously beheld the glory of God's presence and power falling on similar mountaintops (Sinai and Carmel). Luke records that the subject of Jesus' conversation with these representatives of the Law and the Prophets was none other than his looming "departure" (Greek: *exodus*), "which he was about to accomplish in Jerusalem" (Luke 9:33).

When the sleepy inner circle of disciples fully awakened, Peter awkwardly offered to prolong the moment by building three tabernacles (*skēnas*), one for each of the three figures. The trajectory of Jesus' mission, however, was not back to the tabernacle. As Joel Green notes, "the narrative of Luke-Acts situates itself against all attempts, including this one, to station the glory of God in one place."[100] Instead, the cloud of God's presence overshadowed the scene,[101] and a divine voice from the cloud stilled Peter's proposed activity: "This is my Son, my Chosen One; listen to him!" (Luke 9:35). The next day Jesus echoed this same command before predicting his impending Passion: "Let these words sink into your ears" (Luke 9:44–45; cf. 9:22). Their exodus (deliverance from enslavement to sin and the totality of evil) could only be accomplished by the Messiah's own exodus in

99. Morris, *Luke*, 92. Italics original.

100. Green, *Luke*, 383.

101. Cf. Luke 1:35; Exod 40:34–35; 1 Kgs 8:10–11.

Jerusalem—his suffering, death, and resurrection.[102] Even so, the disciples were still unable to comprehend that the mission of the Messiah included suffering.

The Journey toward Jerusalem

Having begun his account in the Jerusalem temple, Luke constructs the greater part of his Gospel as a journey of ascent toward Jerusalem. Luke's description of Jesus' triumphal entry into Jerusalem highlights the divisive nature of the Person of Christ. On the one hand, "the whole multitude of his disciples" welcomed their King with praises that echoed those of "the multitude of the heavenly host" who heralded his birth (Luke 19:38; cf. 2:14). On the other hand, the affronted Pharisees called for him to rebuke his disciples. Jesus replied that if they were silent, the very stones of Jerusalem would cry out (Luke 19:40). Evans remarks, "The inhabitants of Jerusalem may not accept their true king, but the very stones of which the city is built do."[103]

In view of the coming destruction of the city he loved so well, Jesus wept: "they will not leave one stone upon another in you, because you did not know the time of your visitation" (Luke 19:44). Tragically, the citizens of the city of Salem did not understand what—or who—would bring them peace (Luke 19:42).[104] They had failed to recognize the presence of God in their midst in the person of Jesus Christ. Having "missed the opportunity to respond to the eschatological moment" of the Messiah's visitation, the nation would therefore experience his coming judgment.[105]

Luke records that Jesus' final days in Jerusalem began with the clearing of the temple (Luke 19:45–46) and continued with his teaching daily in the temple. When the religious leaders challenged his authority for this action, Jesus told the parable of the wicked tenants who killed the beloved son of the vineyard owner. He concluded with an allusion to Ps 118:22—the rejected "cornerstone" of the temple—and a warning for those who would trip over or be crushed by this stone (Luke 20:17–18). Later, when some admired the temple's adornment with "noble stones and offerings," Jesus

---

102. At the end of Peter's life, when the disciple reflected back on this experience as an eyewitness of the "Majestic Glory," he referred to his own looming departure (*exodus*) from his body, which he twice described as a tent or tabernacle (*skēnōmati*; 2 Pet 1:13–18). Amazingly, Jesus' exodus would also make Pentecost possible, where God's glorious Spirit would indeed fill not only Peter's "tent" of flesh, but also that of all believers—in every generation and every place.

103. Evans, *Luke*, 289.

104. Ibid., 290.

105. Bock, *Luke*, 2:1564.

reiterated his prophecy that the temple, like all of Jerusalem, would be so leveled that not even one stone would remain upon another (Luke 21:5-6). Intriguingly, Luke omits the charge of temple destruction from Jesus' trial but includes the detail that the curtain of the temple was torn in two (Luke 23:45; cf. Matt 26:61; Mark 14:58).

In his post-resurrection appearances, Jesus explained from the Scriptures "everything written about [him] in the Law of Moses and the Prophets and the Psalms" (Luke 24:44; cf. 24:27). Jesus thus demonstrated that "[a global understanding of the canon as a whole] is necessary to comprehend Jesus' place within the eschatological purposes of God."[106] As Michael Goheen points out, anchoring the story of the Gospels in the larger narrative of God's purposes for the cosmos guards the universal scope of the salvation that Christ accomplished on the cross. By shouldering the sin and suffering of the world, Jesus defeated evil and secured the restoration—not only of individuals but also of the entire cosmos.[107] The disciples needed to understand the central role of Christ in the overarching mission of God before they could be sent on mission.

Luke records Jesus' commission to his followers in Luke 24:46-49: "Thus it is written, that the Christ should suffer and on the third day rise from the dead, and that repentance and forgiveness of sins should be proclaimed in his name beginning from Jerusalem . . . ." Thus, the distilled essence of Jesus' own mission is the heart of his followers' mission as well.[108] As witnesses, their task is to proclaim from Scripture 1) the necessity of Christ's suffering, 2) the truth of his resurrection, and 3) a call for repentance for the forgiveness of sins. The starting point for their commission is Jerusalem; the terminus is "the ends of the earth" (Acts 1:8). The scope is universal in that it includes all nations. Such a commission was far beyond the reach of Jesus' disciples. They needed "power from on high" for such a task. Jesus therefore instructed them to wait until he sent the promised Holy Spirit. Jesus' final instruction was that his followers were to be his witnesses to all nations (Luke 24:48; Acts 1:8). This primary task of the church is not an optional ministry.[109] The call to follow Jesus includes a missional calling to bear witness.

Luke's gospel closes with the disciples worshiping Jesus and gathering "continually in the temple blessing God" (Luke 24:53). The Evangelist's "keen interest in Israel's earthly temple with respect to its proper and improper

---

106. Köstenberger and O'Brien, *Salvation*, 123n.

107. Goheen, *Light to the Nations*, 104-5.

108. Köstenberger and O'Brien, *Salvation*, 123.

109. Larkin, *Acts*, 43.

use" surfaces once again as he closes his Gospel where he began it—in the temple.[110] Although Jesus had foretold the destruction of the temple, Luke's first volume is reticent about its replacement.[111] His second volume reveals the unexpected answer.

GOD'S PRESENCE AMONG JESUS' FOLLOWERS

The New Testament clearly teaches not only that Jesus is the new temple but also that believers themselves are somehow incorporated into this same temple. This is the obvious teaching of Paul (e.g., 1 Cor 3:16; 6:19–20) and Peter (e.g., 1 Pet 2:5). But the question arises: When exactly did the church become identified with this "new form of the end-time temple?"[112] In answer to this question, G. K. Beale concludes that the eschatological temple descended from heaven at Pentecost in Acts 2.[113] He explains, "After [Jesus'] resurrection and ascension, God's tabernacling presence descended in the form of the Spirit, making those identified with Christ into part of the temple."[114]

In the Book of Acts

The Descent of the Eschatological Temple at Pentecost

The details of the Pentecost event are reminiscent of the descent of the glory of God on the tabernacle (Exod 40:34) and on the temple (1 Kgs 8:11), and may also reflect the descent of the Spirit on Jesus at his baptism in Luke 3:22. Moreover, Beale contends that the descent of the tabernacling presence of God on the Sinai mountain-temple forms the backdrop of the Spirit's coming at Pentecost.[115] The theophany of the Spirit in Jerusalem was attended by rushing wind and flames of fire, and the Spirit filled all the believers (Acts 2:2–4). The Pentecost event demonstrated that "God's presence was among Jesus' followers in a more powerful and personal way than they had ever experienced before."[116] The indwelling Spirit was the fulfillment of Je-

---

110. Beale, *NT Biblical Theology*, 593.

111. Ibid.

112. Beale, "Descent," 83.

113. Ibid., 84.

114. Beale, *The Temple*, 388.

115. Beale, *NT Biblical Theology*, 595. See "Sinai as Temple," excursus (ibid., 608–10).

116. Lioy, *Axis of Glory*, 78.

sus' promise to make his home in his followers (John 14:17, 23). Just as he had promised, the disciples were "clothed with power from on high" (Luke 24:49).

The purpose of this outpouring of the Spirit was to empower them as witnesses beginning from Jerusalem and extending to Judea, Samaria, and ultimately, to "the end of the earth" (Acts 1:8). In some sense there was a proleptic fulfillment of this commission as the Jewish pilgrims, who had come "from every nation under heaven" to Jerusalem, heard the gospel in their own languages.[117] The people were astonished to hear "the mighty acts of God" proclaimed in their heart languages. This miracle afforded Peter the opportunity to explain how the Pentecost events were a fulfillment of Joel 2:28–32, a passage that heralded the outpouring of the Spirit on all kinds of people regardless of their age, gender, status, or ethnicity (Acts 2:17–18). John Stott rightly points out that "all flesh" does not mean "everybody irrespective of their inner readiness to receive the gift," but rather "everybody irrespective of their outward status."[118] Individuals must first meet the condition of calling on "the name of the LORD" (Joel 2:32; cf. Acts 2:21). Significantly, Peter traced this gift of the Spirit back to the name of Jesus— whom God made "both Lord and Christ" (Acts 2:36).[119] As they listened to Peter's preaching, the crowd felt great conviction and quickly responded to Peter's call for repentance and baptism. Three thousand committed to follow Christ.

Luke records that these new believers "devoted themselves to the apostles' teaching and the fellowship, to the breaking of bread and the prayers" (Acts 2:42). Signs and wonders and generosity characterized their gatherings. They were all filled with awe and joy, and "the Lord added to their number day by day" (Acts 2:47). The Spirit-filled life of the church on display in these verses undoubtedly contributed to the growth of the church. But it is God who is "the principal evangelist." Stott observes, "Those first Jerusalem Christians were not so preoccupied with learning, sharing and

---

117. Keener, *The Spirit*, 194.

118. Stott, *Acts*, 74. Stott observes that the apostolic proclamation was a fourfold message that focused on "two events (Christ's death and resurrection), as attested by two witnesses (prophets and apostles), on the basis of which God makes two promises (forgiveness and the Spirit), on two conditions (repentance and faith, with baptism). We have no liberty to amputate this apostolic gospel, by proclaiming the cross without the resurrection, or referring to the New Testament but not the Old, or offering forgiveness without the Spirit, or demanding faith without repentance. There is a wholeness about the biblical gospel. It is not enough to 'proclaim Jesus.' For there are many Jesuses being presented today. . . . We have the responsibility today to tell the story of Jesus as fact, doctrine and gospel" (ibid., 81).

119. Marshall, *Acts*, 71.

worshipping, that they forgot about witnessing. For the Holy Spirit is a missionary Spirit who created a missionary church."[120] The outpouring of the Spirit at Pentecost continued to direct and empower the faithful witness of the church as it unfolded in Acts.

Wright notes that although the early believers continued to meet in the temple in the transitional period that followed Acts 2, they had begun to discover that the temple was an "odd and contested space" and that "now heaven and earth have met somewhere else or rather in someone else"—that is to say, in Jesus.[121] The point of Acts 2 is that the glory of the Lord filled the house—just as it did in Exodus 40, in 1 Kings 8, in Isaiah 6, and in Ezekiel 43. Wright explains, "This is the living God coming back in fire and smoke and living breath to transform the hearts and lives of these early believers. The temple is being rebuilt." He concludes that the physical temple in Jerusalem had stood for a thousand years as an advance signpost that the living God ultimately does not want to live in a house made with human hands but in the midst of his people—as the human being Jesus and in the lives of millions of people. At Pentecost, God had begun to manifest his presence by pouring out his Spirit, not on a place but rather on his people. Sadly, those who had begun to idolize the signpost missed the very reality it stood for.[122]

Stephen's Sermon before the Sanhedrin

The tabernacling presence of God with his people formed the heart of Stephen's defense when he was brought before the Sanhedrin on charges of speaking against the temple and the Law. With the presence of God visibly displayed in his radiant countenance, Stephen rehearsed the history of the presence of God in the midst of his people.[123] All four of the examples Stephen cited in Acts 7 highlighted the fact that God's presence was not limited to a particular place: 1) The God of glory appeared to Abraham in Mesopotamia (v. 2); 2) God was with Joseph in Egypt (v. 9); 3) God's presence with Moses in the burning bush at Sinai made it "holy ground" (v. 33); and finally, 4) when David desired to build a temple for God, the Lord reminded him that he did not need a house, for "the most High does not

---

120. Stott, *Acts*, 86.

121. Wright, "Opportunities," n.p.

122. Ibid.

123. Larkin, *Acts*, 105, notes that this radiance "parallels the effects of Moses' standing in God's presence (Exod 34:29, 35)" as well as Jesus' transfiguration. He observes that to "a greater or lesser extent," the glory of God should be on display in the life of every Spirit-filled believer.

dwell in houses made by hands" (v. 48). Stephen clearly argued that "the God of Israel is a pilgrim God, who is not restricted to any one place. . . . [No] building can confine him. . . . If he has any home on earth, it is with his people that he lives."[124]

Stephen's historical survey also highlighted the reality that "the Temple and Jerusalem had become unfaithful to their calling and were destined to be destroyed as Jesus had predicted."[125] Tragically, many first-century Jews had placed such "an idolatrous emphasis [on] the land, the law, and the temple" that they were unable to recognize the revelation of God in Christ.[126] Charged with blasphemy against God and "this holy place" (Acts 6:11, 13), Stephen paradoxically identified his accusers as "the real blasphemers: anyone who so venerates the temple that it ceases to be a place where the transcendent God is glorified and becomes a place where self-glorying men take pride in what they have done for God."[127] Infuriated, the crowd cast him out of the city and stoned him. Even in the face of death, however, this first Christian martyr experienced the very real presence of the triune God standing with him—just like the patriarchs of old whose stories he had just recounted.[128] Providentially, Stephen's courageous testimony served to advance the mission of God. The persecution that erupted with the stoning of Stephen created "a band of missionaries, not refugees."[129] Ironically, foremost among them was the one opponent whom Luke mentions by name—Saul.

---

124. Stott, *Acts*, 139.

125. Glasser, *Announcing the Kingdom*, 316. Some commentators find a preference for the tabernacle over the temple in Stephen's sermon (e.g., Marshall, *Acts*, 146) or even a strong polemic against the temple in contrast to the tabernacle (e.g., Koester, *Dwelling of God*, 79–81). Stott, *The Message of Acts*, 138, however, argues that "Stephen is derogatory to neither." After all, God had directed Moses to construct the tabernacle according to the revealed pattern, and God had granted Solomon permission to build the temple. Solomon himself had recognized that no structure could contain the presence of the Most High God (cf. 2 Sam 7:6). But as Larkin, *Acts*, 117, points out, it was always God [who] took the initiative in revealing how he was to be approached.

126. Lioy, *Axis of Glory*, 79.

127. Larkin, *Acts*, 119.

128. Filled with the Holy Spirit, Stephen saw the glory of God, "the heavens opened, and the Son of Man standing at the right hand of God" (Acts 7:55–56).

129. Larkin, *Acts*, 124. Jesus himself testifies to his presence with his persecuted followers when he asked Saul on the road to Damascus, "Why are you persecuting *me*?" (Acts 9:4; italics added).

Paul's Address to the Areopagus

Stephen's sermon must have lingered in the mind of a young Saul who had approvingly stood guard over the witnesses' cloaks during the execution (Acts 7:58; 8:1). Years later when the former Pharisee stood before the Athenian Areopagus with the temples atop the Acropolis as his backdrop, Paul took a page from Stephen's notes and declared, "The God who made the world and everything in it, being Lord of heaven and earth, does not live in temples made by man" (Acts 17:24).

Paul had been horrified by the prolific idolatry of this "cultural capital of the world."[130] Zealous for the glory of God, Paul reasoned with the Jews in the synagogues, dialogued daily with the people in the marketplace, and conversed with the Epicurean and Stoic philosophers of the city (Acts 17:17–18). Called to give an account as a "preacher of foreign divinities" before the Areopagus, Paul respectfully began with a point of contact—their altar to an unknown God (Acts 17:23). He then proclaimed the identity of the one true God, who is "Creator, Sustainer, Ruler, Father, and Judge."[131] Moving from creation to consummation, Paul pointed out that God had made all peoples for the purpose of seeking the God whose presence is not far from them (Acts 17:26–27). The Apostle to the Gentiles acknowledged that some of their own poets had perceived that "[i]n him we live and move and have our being" and "we are indeed his offspring" (Acts 17:28). In this address to a Gentile audience, Paul provides a model of contextualization that is both culturally relevant and biblically faithful.

Although Paul clearly communicates the truth of the gospel in a way that the Athenians can comprehend, his message of the one, true, living God was inherently polemical in this context.[132] Wright observes that Paul firmly but gently unmasked the half-truths of the prevailing philosophies one by one.[133] He also did not shy away from pointing out that the Athenians'

130. Stott, *Acts*, 276.

131. Ibid., 290.

132. Schnabel, *Paul the Missionary*, 171–79, delineates five "points of contact" and eight "elements of contradiction" in Paul's speech. Schnabel explains, "For Paul, a critique of the existing religious pluralism and diversity was an essential element of his explanation of the gospel message" (ibid., 179).

133. Wright, "Opportunities," n.p. For example, Paul denounced the pantheistic worldview of the Stoics—and the concept of a divine spark within—by proclaiming a distinction between God and everything that he made; he countered the atheistic evolution worldview of the Epicureans by declaring that God had indeed created the world and that he is very near. Paul also deconstructed the "street-level paganism" that had resulted in this forest of idols by explaining that the Creator God needed neither temples nor the service of humans; on the contrary, this God sustains all creation (ibid.).

imaginative substitutes for God had not only failed to connect them to God but would also result in inescapable judgment (Acts 17:29–31). Paul boldly called for repentance and pointed to the resurrection of Christ. Although some mocked his message, others came to believe in the gospel that Paul proclaimed.

As William Larkin observes, "Human religious effort is a fact of life in almost every culture."[134] Although Paul astutely adapted his approach to address the very different concerns of his audiences in the book of Acts, whether Jews or Gentiles, both groups needed to hear that the Creator of the universe could not be confined to temples made by man. Because the preaching of the gospel challenged cherished worldviews, it often precipitated violent reaction, whether a riot over the sanctity of the temple in Jerusalem (e.g., Acts 7; 21–22) or the honor of pagan gods in Lystra and Ephesus (e.g., Acts 14, 19). Paul, who had so zealously persecuted Christians in order to defend the Jewish religion, was radically transformed by an encounter with the presence of the living Lord Jesus. This "missionary to the Gentiles" had come to realize that "[a] new temple with no geographic focus was to be centered in Jesus Christ [and that] Christ's body, the church, must now be formed into a new temple made of 'living stones' quarried out of the peoples of every tribe, tongue, and nation."[135]

The Church as Temple in the Epistles

Paul's Letters to the Corinthians

Paul developed this concept of the church as temple in several of his letters. To the Corinthians, Paul wrote that the church is God's building, constructed on the foundation of Christ alone (1 Cor 3:10–15). Indeed, "no other foundation is logically possible . . . if the building is truly to be the church of God. . . . Any other foundation would not merely make the building precarious; it would cease to exist *as that building*."[136] As the founding "missionary-pastor," Paul had been careful to lay that sure foundation; he

---

Larkin, *Acts*, 251, observes a remarkable similarity between these ancient philosophies and those that are prevalent in the post-Christian era of the West. In particular, Larkin names secular humanism's scientific empiricism and the New Age pantheistic type of postmodernism.

134. Larkin, *Acts*, 105.

135. Glasser, *Announcing the Kingdom*, 316.

136. Thiselton, *First Corinthians*, 310; italics original.

cautioned subsequent builders to be just as careful with building materials for the superstructure.[137]

Although Paul's imagery of costly metals and precious stones may have implied the building was a temple, he then states it explicitly: "Do you not know that you are God's temple and that God's Spirit dwells in you? If anyone destroys God's temple, God will destroy him. For God's temple is holy, and you are that temple" (1 Cor 3:16–17).[138] Although Paul could have used *hieron* or *oikos* to designate the temple, instead he chose *naos*, to emphasize "the state of intense holiness expected of the innermost portion of the temple."[139] Because the Spirit of God tabernacled among them corporately, they must lead holy lives. Anthony Thiselton explains, "God's presence *constitutes* the temple status of his people, and without it they are no temple."[140]

Paul uses this same imagery a few chapters later in 1 Cor 6:19–20, this time in the context of fleeing sexual immorality: "Or do you not know that your body is a temple of the Holy Spirit within you, whom you have from God? You are not your own, for you were bought with a price. So glorify God in your body." Whereas Paul refers to the corporate community as temple in 1 Cor 3:16 ("you [plural] are God's temple"), he applies the exact same imagery to the individual believer ("you" singular) in 1 Cor 6:19.[141] The Spirit unites individual Christians into the one body of Christ; therefore, "the individual interpretation derives from the collective."[142] Incredibly, as Gordon Fee observes, "God not only dwells among his people, but is himself present, by his Spirit within his people, sanctifying their present earthly existence and stamping it with his own eternity."[143] The realization that the Spirit dwells in each believer gives a sense of dignity to every aspect of life and necessarily rules out anything that is inappropriate in God's temple.[144]

---

137. Ibid., 312.

138. Blomberg, 1 *Corinthians*, 75. Wright, "Jerusalem," 70, observes that the significance of this metaphor is lost on Western Christians who anachronistically equate the temple with a cathedral. For Paul, however, the use of this imagery a mere twenty-five years after the crucifixion—while the temple still stood—carried earth-shaking significance: "The Temple had been superseded by the Church" (ibid.).

139. Gupta, "Which Body," 524.

140. Thiselton, *First Corinthians*, 317; italics original.

141. In spite of the recent shift in Pauline scholarship from the individual to the community, Gupta, "Which Body," 535, defends the individual reading of *sōma* in 1 Cor 6:19 and notes that the sovereign lordship of Christ is accomplished as both individuals and the church submit to the authority of Christ.

142. Spatafora, *Temple of God*, 117.

143. Fee, *First Corinthians*, 136.

144. Morris, 1 *Corinthians*, 99.

Just as the glory of God had filled the earthly shrines, Spirit-indwelt believers are to glorify God in this inner sanctuary.

When Paul returned to this church-as-temple imagery in 2 Cor 6:14–18, he emphasized its restrictive focus. Paul pointed out that there can be no partnership between righteousness and lawlessness, between light or darkness, between Christ and Belial, between a believer and an unbeliever, or between God's sanctuary and idols. Having stacked the deck for his argument, Paul soundly concluded, "Therefore go out from their midst, and be separate from them, says the Lord, and touch no unclean thing; then I will welcome you" (2 Cor 6:17).[145] Both corporately and as individual members, the church should be a community living in contrast to the surrounding world. As C. K. Barrett explains, "If the people of God cease to be separate in moral holiness from the rest of mankind, they cease to be the people of God."[146] Paul reminds the Corinthians that ultimately the mission of God is to tabernacle in the midst of his people—redeemed at a great price—as a father with his sons and daughters (2 Cor 6:16, 18). The presence of God living among them requires moral purity.

The tabernacling presence of God on display in the church will inevitably have a missional effect. Paul explains that if an unbeliever or outsider witnesses the Spirit-led orderly worship of the assembled church, he will hear God's Word proclaimed and come under conviction: "falling on his face, he will worship God and declare that God is really among you" (1 Cor 14:24–25).[147] Under conviction, the unbeliever comes to the profound realization that what he had "brushed aside as mere 'religious phenomena,' or 'going through the motions'" is, in fact, true. Thiselton explains, "In all reality they encounter not simply human religion which constructs or projects a god; they encounter God, who draws forth authentic worship as he is authentically active and present among the believers."[148] When the church truly functions as the temple—the meeting place of God and man—others

---

145. Harris, *Second Corinthians*, 501, points out that in view of Paul's previous instructions to the Corinthians (e.g., 1 Cor 5:9–10; 7:12–14; 9:20–23; 10:27), the apostle is not calling for complete separation from unbelievers. Rather, Paul instructs them "to avoid any public or private relationship with unbelievers that was incompatible with or would compromise Christian standards, Christian adherence to monotheism, and Christian witness."

146. Barrett, *Second Corinthians*, 201.

147. Hays, "Conversion of the Imagination," 394–95, contends that the phrasing of 1 Cor 14:25 ("God is really among you") is a *metalepsis* of Isa 45:14 and Zech 8:20–23 which teaches that the Corinthian church—"a predominantly Gentile community"— has "stepped into the role originally assigned to Israel," namely, "the eschatological conversion of outsiders."

148. Thiselton, *First Corinthians*, 1130.

will recognize the presence of God among them. They, too, will be converted as God continues to build his church.

Paul's Letter to the Ephesians

Paul employs this same church-as-temple imagery once more, in his letter to the church at Ephesus. Expounding on the glorious mystery of the gospel, Paul explained that Christ had broken down the "dividing wall of hostility" between Jews and Gentiles (Eph 2:11–18). He acknowledged that the Gentiles were formerly separated from Christ, alienated from the people of God, "without hope and without God in the world" (Eph 2:12, HCSB).[149] Christ, however, has reconciled both Jews and Gentiles to God and to each other. It is through the blood of Christ that "both have access in one Spirit to the Father" (Eph 2:18). As a result all the saints—no matter their ethnic background—are being built together into a holy sanctuary for God's Spirit to dwell in. The divide is no longer between Jew and Gentile, but rather between those who are reconciled to God and those who are not. Those who once were alienated are now members of God's household; they are part of a growing temple where God dwells. God's empowering presence among his people—corporately and individually—is what sets the church apart as a contrast community. The church should be a people who display a transcultural unity that testifies to the reconciling work God has wrought in their lives. This new community will also give credence to the message of peace that Christ preached and is still preaching through his followers who proclaim a gospel of reconciliation (cf. Eph 2:17).[150]

In this same letter Paul commanded the Ephesian believers to be filled continually (*plērousthe*, present tense) with the Spirit (Eph 5:18).[151] Fee describes this as "the ultimate imperative in the Pauline corpus: God's people so filled by/with the Spirit's own presence that they come to know God in all his fullness and reflect such in the way they live in relationship to one another and to God himself."[152] Paul delineates what the Spirit-filled life looks like in the series of participles attached to this primary imperative: speak-

---

149. Stott, *Ephesians*, 90, notes that the book of Ephesians, although composed so long ago, addresses the deep sense of alienation—from God and from one another—that is felt so keenly today. Stott also notes that "the gods of Greece and Rome entirely failed to satisfy the hunger of human hearts" (ibid., 96). In spite of this "plethora of gods," Paul refers to the people as "without God" (*atheoi*) not because they disbelieved, but because they had no knowledge of the one true God or fellowship with him.

150. Ibid., 103.

151. Köstenberger, "Be Filled with the Spirit," 233.

152. Fee, *God's Empowering Presence*, 722.

ing, singing, giving thanks and submitting to one another (Eph 5:19–21).[153] In short, worship and praise should continually well up in the lives of those who are temple-people. Amazingly, just as the glory of God's presence filled the tabernacle and the temple, the Spirit of God now fills believers, who are bound together in this new spiritual community. They should therefore focus on "living obedient Christian lives that are increasingly characterized by the Spirit's presence."[154] In light of the Old Testament teaching on the glory and presence of God, believers must live in a worthy manner.

Peter's First Epistle

Like Paul, Peter uses the imagery of the church as the temple of God: "[Y]ou yourselves like living stones are being built up as a spiritual house, to be a holy priesthood, to offer spiritual sacrifices acceptable to God through Jesus Christ" (1 Pet 2:5). Although the text does not specifically declare the nature of this "spiritual house," the mention of a priesthood and cultus clearly indicate that a temple is in view. In contrast to Paul's emphasis on the new temple as God's dwelling place, Peter uses the metaphor to highlight the new temple as a place of spiritual sacrifice.[155] These spiritual sacrifices surely include gospel witness: "But you are . . . a royal priesthood . . . *that you may proclaim* the excellencies of him who called you out of darkness into his marvelous light" (1 Pet 2:9; italics added).

Peter applies a string of Old Testament names, which once designated Israel, to this new temple-community of Jesus Christ: they are "a chosen race, a royal priesthood, a holy nation, a people for his own possession" (1 Pet 2:9). Each of these terms underscores the corporate identity of the church: those who were alienated from God and one another are now a family, a community, a nation. However, as Blauw observes, "[O]nly as a community which understands the purpose for which it has received the lovely names of Israel may it really appropriate these names. The '(in order) that' in verse 9 is the hinge on which the door turns that gives entrance to the treasures which lie piled up in these names." Blauw warns that the church dare not usurp these titles for its own use. Furthermore, he argues that "the Church of Jesus Christ has the right, solely as a *missionary Church*, to call herself 'Church' at all."[156] The world must hear that God has begun a new creation in Christ as evidenced in the lives of those who have been

---

153. Ibid., 719.

154. Köstenberger, "Be Filled with the Spirit," 240.

155. McKelvey, *New Temple*, 129.

156. Blauw, *Missionary Nature*, 128–29; italics original.

called "out of darkness into his marvelous light," or as Blauw puts it, "out of alienation into true fellowship with God and man."[157] The church receives the honor of Israel so that she may take the place of Israel in proclaiming the mighty acts of God before a watching world.

Peter further illustrates the universality of the church-as-temple when he applies Hos 2:23 to believing Gentiles: "Once you were not a people, but now you are God's people; once you had not received mercy, but now you have received mercy" (1 Pet 2:10).[158] The reminder of the transformation that God had wrought in the lives of believers would compel them to proclaim God's marvelous deeds with others. The apostle also exhorts believers to live such honorable lives that their exemplary conduct and good deeds might eventually convince their opponents to glorify God (1 Pet 2:12). Peter, however, clearly understood that Christ himself is divisive. In fact, response to Jesus determines a person's eternal destiny: those who believe in the living stone are incorporated into this living temple; those who disbelieve stumble over the cornerstone and face destruction.[159] Still, even in the face of hostility, believers have an obligation to share the reason for their hope—"with gentleness and respect" (1 Pet 3:15).

With the observation that 1 Pet 2:4–9 is a "bewildering collage of metaphors and allusions," Perrin remarks that Peter—along with other New Testament authors—"found no awkwardness in simultaneously affirming on the one side, the Christian community as temple and priesthood, and, on the other side, Christ as temple-foundation and high priest."[160] Likewise, Beale observes that the above concepts of Christ as the new temple and the church as the new temple are an "already-not yet" fulfillment of the eschatological temple. Having replaced the temple and ascended into heaven, Christ sent the Spirit to tabernacle in believers who are being built together into a sanctuary for God. Beale explains, "The Father and Son, however, still reside in the heavenly temple and not on earth. Therefore, the temple's centre of gravity during the church age is located in the heavenly realm, but it has begun to invade the earthly through the Spirit in the church."[161]

---

157. Ibid., 135. Contra those who maintain that this proclamation is only within the church, Blauw argues that it is "incomprehensible" that the declaration of God's marvelous deeds would be "confined merely to a hymn of praise behind thick church walls." True praise will spill over as a "witness in and for the world" (ibid., 132),

158. Glasser, *Announcing the Kingdom*, 317, notes that Peter had witnessed this radical paradigm shift for himself when the Holy Spirit fell on Cornelius and his Gentile household just as at Pentecost.

159. Lioy, *Axis of Glory*, 102.

160. Perrin, *Jesus the Temple*, 56.

161. Beale, *The Temple*, 389.

This "already-not yet" discussion illuminates the present situation, which is reflected in Hebrews as well.

GOD'S PRESENCE IN THE HEAVENLY TABERNACLE/ TEMPLE

The Heavenly Tabernacle in Hebrews

Peter Walker observes that Hebrews is "the New Testament document which most explicitly focuses on the Temple and its significance in light of Christ."[162] William Lane maintains that the author of Hebrews wrote to bolster the faltering faith of a small group of Jewish Christians threatened by the outbreak of persecution following the great fire of Rome in AD 64. In light of these circumstances, Lane suggests that these struggling believers must have asked, "Is God *there* [in the Jewish temple]?" to which the writer of Hebrews resoundingly answered, "No, because now he is *here* [with us]!"[163] This letter is a reminder that in spite of "*a felt absence of God*," God has revealed himself in his written Word and ultimately in his Son (Heb 1:1–2).[164]

In order to keep these believers from turning back to their former Judaism, the author sets up a series of heavenly–earthly antitheses that demonstrate the superiority of God's revelation in Christ.[165] The Old Testament shrines had merely foreshadowed the coming of Jesus Christ who is the essence of the presence of God on earth.[166] The writer of Hebrews explains that the tabernacle constructed by humans was imperfect—a mere copy and shadow of the true tabernacle which is in heaven (Heb 8:5). Jesus entered this "greater and more perfect tent (not made with hands, that is, not of this creation)" and sprinkled his own blood in the holy of holies (Heb 9:11).[167] Although Jesus' action in no way denigrates the old covenant, it does make it obsolete because he fulfilled the old covenant by his once-for-all perfect

162. Walker, *Jesus*, 201. Walker suggests that the focus on the tabernacle rather than temple allowed the author to make the theological argument that the "Tabernacle system of worship . . . had been declared redundant by God through Jesus" (ibid., 207–8). Of course, this understanding also implied that the Jerusalem temple system was likewise redundant.

163. Lane, *Hebrews*, 30; italics original.

164. Ibid., 30–31; italics original.

165. Attridge, *John and Hebrews*, 277.

166. Beale, "Eden," 19–20.

167. Spatafora, *Temple of God*, 121, points out that this language does not require that the tent is a literal sanctuary, but rather the "cultic language and temple imagery . . . speak of the transcendent."

sacrifice (Heb 10:12). Under the old covenant, "a system of barriers" stood between the worshiper and God, limiting access to "'only the high priest,' 'only once a year,' and 'never without blood.'"[168] In the new covenant Jesus is at once the high priest, the sacrifice, and the (bodily) veil which was torn so that believers might have access to the holy of holies. As Lane notes, "[Jesus'] one offering for sin secured eternal salvation and removed every barrier to the presence of God."[169]

That Jesus now sits on the throne in the presence of God declares the decisive finality of his work.[170] Through Christ's atonement believers now have unhindered access into God's presence. George Guthrie expounds on the "already-not yet" nature of this access: "Thus heaven can be experienced now because of the high-priestly sacrifice of Christ, which has won us entrance into the presence of God and will be experienced fully at the end of the age."[171] Of course, this access is restricted to those who follow their high priest, having had their hearts sprinkled with the cleansing blood of Christ (Heb 10:22). The author of Hebrews explains that "whoever would draw near to God must believe that he exists and that he rewards those who seek him" (Heb 11:6). He also warns repeatedly that a dreadful judgment awaits those who reject God's Word and spurn his Son: "It is a fearful thing to fall into the hands of the living God" (Heb 10:31).

The author of Hebrews illustrates the clear choice that lay before his readers. Because "Jesus also suffered outside the gate in order to sanctify the people through his own blood" (Heb 13:12), they must decide whether their loyalties remained "with the Temple mount or with 'the place of the skull.'"[172] The people of God must "go to [Jesus] outside the camp" (Heb 13:13); there can be no turning back to Judaism and the Second Temple. Lane explains, "[T]rue sacred space will not be found in Jerusalem, with its impermanent sanctuary and altar, but in the presence of Jesus and in the anticipation of the qualitatively different city to which they have come proleptically."[173] Meanwhile, they are to fix their eyes on Jesus, "the founder and perfecter of [their] faith," who will one day return with the heavenly Jerusalem—not a

---

168. Lane, *Hebrews*, 117–18.

169. Ibid., 121; originally italicized.

170. Ibid., 135.

171. Guthrie, *Hebrews*, 320. Guthrie notes that the author of Hebrews brackets his discourse on Christ's work as high priest with an inclusio that focuses on the exhortation: "Let us draw near to God" (Heb 4:16; 10:22) (ibid., 341).

172. Walker, *Jesus and the Holy City*, 207.

173. Lane, *Hebrews 9–13*, 546–47.

disembodied ideal, but rather the "city of the living God," a kingdom that cannot be shaken (cf. Heb 12:1–2, 22, 28).[174]

The Temple/Tabernacle in Revelation 1–20

In the book of Revelation John utilizes imagery from both the temple and the tabernacle.[175] On the one hand, by using imagery drawn from Israel's former sanctuaries, John affirms the past validity of the Jerusalem temple and its traditions. On the other hand, John assigns new meaning to these cultic images in light of Jesus' sacrificial death as the Lamb of God. In doing so, the author boldly proclaims that all that the temple had symbolized in terms of God's presence in the midst of his people is now located in Jesus.[176] A brief survey of some of these passages reveals the ultimate purposes of the mission of God.

John's initial vision is of the exalted Son of Man standing in the center of seven golden lampstands (Rev 1:10–20). These lamps represent the seven churches to whom this message was addressed, as well as "the reality of the Christian community as a whole."[177] The high Christology of the Apocalypse, which is evident in "the ascription of the titles and attributes of God to Christ," calls for worship of the glorified Lord.[178] The appropriate response in the presence of Jesus is to fall at his feet (Rev 1:17).

Jesus' presence in the midst of his churches also results in encouragement and/or reproof, depending on the status of their relationship with him. For example, five of the seven churches received a rebuke and a call to repentance (Rev 2:5, 16, 21–22; 3:3, 19). The church of Philadelphia, however, received a commendation for their patient endurance in suffering (Rev 3:10). Jesus therefore promised, "The one who conquers, I will make him a pillar in the temple of my God. Never shall he go out of it, and I will write on him the name of my God, and the name of the city of my God, the new Jerusalem, which comes down from my God out of heaven, and my own new name" (Rev 3:12). This verse introduces the concept of the people of God as the New Jerusalem—an image which presupposes the temple and the

174. Clowney, "Final Temple," 187.

175. Kistemaker, "Temple in the Apocalypse," 433, observes that some of the occurrences of temple (*naos*) refer to the persecuted church on earth (Rev 11:1, 2); some to the heavenly temple (Rev 7:15; 11:19 [2x]; 14:15, 17; 15:5, 6, 8 [2x]; 16:1, 17); and some to a temple-less New Jerusalem (Rev 3:12; 21:22 [2x]). Interestingly, tabernacle imagery appears in some of these same settings as well (e.g., Rev 7:15; 15:5; and 21:3).

176. Walker, *Jesus*, 243–45.

177. Smalley, *Revelation*, 53.

178. Mounce, *Revelation*, 58.

presence of God.[179] John, however, withholds the fulfillment of this promise until the closing chapters of the book.

The bulk of temple/tabernacle imagery in the book of Revelation describes the heavenly sanctuary. Although John does not specifically refer to temple or tabernacle in chapters 4 and 5, the mention of the altar in Rev 6:9 clearly identifies this throne room setting as the heavenly sanctuary. As Beale explains, these two chapters "introduce and overshadow all the visions in 6:1–22:5," which flow from this vision that powerfully portrays the sovereignty of God in redemption and judgment.[180] The flashes of lightning, peals of thunder, and burning fire emanating from the throne recall the theophany of God's tabernacling presence at Sinai (Rev 4:5). At the center of the cosmos is the Lamb seated on a throne, surrounded by all of his creation who praise and adore him, including the four living creatures, the twenty-four elders, myriads of angels, as well as "every creature in heaven and on earth and under the earth and in the sea, and all that is in them" (Rev 5:11–14). Their "new song" is a beautiful summary of the gospel: They worship the slain and risen Lamb who—with his very own blood—redeemed a people of God to be a kingdom of royal priests (Rev 5:9–10). This gospel message is by its very nature polemical. Those who live it and share it can expect opposition; the gospel may even cost them their own lifeblood as well (Rev 6:9–11).

John repeatedly describes the vast array of human representatives from "every tribe and language and people and nation" who were purchased by the blood of the Lamb to serve as priests in the sanctuary (Rev 5:9).[181] There is no reason to attempt to distinguish between these terms because John "is stressing the universal nature of the church and for this purpose piles up phrases for their rhetorical value. . . . [T]he church . . . recognize[s] no national, political, cultural, or racial boundaries."[182] All of the redeemed enjoy unlimited access to the Lamb, serving him as high priests day and night in the holy-of-holies. Revelation 7:15 clarifies that "he who sits on the throne will shelter them with his presence" (*skēnoō*; "spread His tabernacle over them," NASB). Sheltered in the tabernacling presence of God, the multicultural members of this multitude will experience no more hunger, thirst, or

179. McKelvey, *New Temple*, 169.

180. Beale, *Revelation*, 172. Beale notes that chapters 4 and 5 contain 17 of the 34 references to God's "throne" in Revelation.

181. These lists (Rev 5:9; 7:9; 10:11; 11:9; 13:7; 14:6; 17:15) describe not only the multicultural diversity of the redeemed, but also the sundry backgrounds of those who mock the prophets (Rev 11:9) and worship the beast (Rev 13:7). Universality, therefore, does not equate universalism.

182. Mounce, *Revelation*, 136.

scorching heat; God himself will guide them to springs of living water and wipe away their tears (Rev 7:16–17). This glorious picture of the redeemed people of God worshiping in his tabernacling presence epitomizes the goal of God's mission.

Opening with a scene of the firstfruits of humanity worshiping the Lamb before the throne, chapter 14 recounts the vision of a flying angel with "an eternal gospel to proclaim to those who dwell on earth" (Rev 14:6). The universal scope of this announcement is clear from the angel's high flight and high volume, which ensure that the message reaches "every nation and tribe and language and people."[183] Noting that Jesus had assigned the task of worldwide evangelization to the church, Keener suggests that the angel's worldwide flight may mirror the spread of the gospel through his people.[184] The imminence of the final judgment gives an even greater sense of urgency to the announcement of the gospel. The gospel is eternal in that it announces God's purpose from the beginning—that all humanity should fill the globe with worship of the Creator. The choice is clear and inevitably divisive: worship God or worship the beast (Rev 14:7, 9–10).

The verses that follow make it clear that the universal proclamation of the gospel will not result in universal repentance or salvation. Commands for two harvests emanate from the temple, the place of God's holy presence. One "like a son of man [Son of Man, HCSB, NIV]" seated on the cloud swings his sickle and reaps the harvest of grain (Rev 14:14–16); an angel likewise reaps the harvest of grapes, throwing them into "the great winepress of the wrath of God" (Rev 14:19–20). Osborne argues that the grain harvest symbolizes the redeemed and the grape harvest, the wicked.[185] Similarly, the seven bowls of wrath originate in "the sanctuary of the tent of witness in heaven" (Rev 15:5). The theophanic smoke of God's glory filling the sanctuary in this scene of penultimate judgment is reminiscent of the same filling in Exod 40:34–35 and 1 Kgs 8:10–11.[186] Even in the face of the plagues, the wicked repeatedly curse God and refuse to repent of their deeds (Rev 16:9, 10, 21). Christ's eschatological victory, however, is certain.

Revelation 20 records the final judgment where God will condemn Satan and his allies to the eternal torment of the lake of fire (Rev 20:10). The Sovereign Lord will also judge each human based on their spiritual loyalty revealed by their deeds recorded in his books.[187] Those whose names are

183. Smalley, *Revelation*, 362.

184. Keener, *Revelation*, 372.

185. Cf. Osborne, *Revelation*, 552–53.

186. Fee, *Revelation*, 207.

187. Smalley, *Revelation*, 517.

not found in the Lamb's book of life will be consigned to the same fate as the devil and his angels. Although Rev 20:15 is stated negatively to emphasize this exclusion, the converse—found in Dan 12:1—is also true: those whose names *are* found written in the Lamb's book of life will be saved by his atoning sacrifice. The contrast could not be more stark or stated more clearly: the righteous inherit the eternal kingdom prepared for them before creation, while the unrighteous are condemned to the eternal lake of fire prepared for the devil and his angels. The final judgment has set the stage for the restoration of creation.

GOD'S PRESENCE IN THE TEMPLE-LESS SANCTUARY OF THE NEW CREATION

New Jerusalem: The Perfected People of God

The theme of God's tabernacling presence culminates in the last chapters of Revelation, where John beholds the heavenly Jerusalem—hinted at in Heb 12:22 and in Rev 3:12—descending from heaven to earth in the form of a temple-city: the bride of Christ (Rev 21:2, 9; cf. 19:6–9). God's dwelling will no longer be high above his people; from now on he will literally tabernacle in their midst for all eternity (Rev 21:3). This verse is the fulfillment of God's purposes since the dawn of creation and the longings of the saints through the ages.[188] The oft-repeated promise of God finds its ultimate fulfillment: "Behold, the dwelling place [*skēnē*] of God is with man. He will dwell [*skēnōsei*] with them, and they will be his people [*laoi*; "peoples"], and God himself will be with them as their God" (Rev 21:3). Beale notes that whereas the Old Testament prophecies refer in the singular (*laos*) to the people among whom God dwells, John uses the plural (*laoi*) to highlight the inclusion of the many nations in the redeemed people of God.[189] Revelation 21:8 clarifies, however, that this is a restrictive universality: access to the glorious presence of God is denied to this list of sinners who have already inherited their share in the lake of fire.

Several similarities demonstrate that the city-temple described in Revelation 21 is the fulfillment of Ezekiel's end-time temple vision: both have twelve city gates at four compass points, a "four-cornered shape," an "illuminating glory," and "living waters flowing from the temple" past fruit trees with healing leaves.[190] The streets of gold and the perfect cubic measurement

188. Osborne, *Revelation*, 726–27.
189. Beale, *Revelation*, 1047.
190. Beale, *The Temple*, 351.

of the massive temple complex recall the holy of holies of Solomon's temple (cf. 1 Kgs 6:20): "[I]n the eschatological future God's holy of holies presence will extend out over Jerusalem and become coequal with it."[191] Therefore, there is no need for a temple because the Lord God Almighty and the Lamb *are* the temple. Whereas access to the holy of holies was limited to the high priest once a year, now all saints will have unlimited access to the unmediated presence of God. The priestly service of all Christians, which began on earth, continues and amplifies in the New Jerusalem.[192]

The symbol of a city is particularly suited to express that the New Jerusalem is the community of the redeemed people of God. Eugene Boring observes, "A city is the realization of human community, the concrete living out of interdependence as the essential nature of human life. . . . In a city . . . the beauty of life is not a solo but a symphony. As community, a city is not streets and buildings but people."[193] Thus, the believing community as a whole forms the eschatological temple where God dwells. There is thus a continuity of the church made from living stones (cf. 1 Pet 2:5) and the temple-city of the new heaven and earth. Yet there is also a discontinuity as this new dwelling of God is altogether new (cf. Rev 21:5).[194]

Although many commentators have understood that the New Jerusalem symbolizes the redeemed people of God, Robert Gundry believes that most mistakenly try to read it as the saints' abode, as well. Gundry, however, presents a strong case that the New Jerusalem is not the dwelling place of the saints at all, but rather the people themselves are the dwelling place of God. The new city, Jerusalem, is a symbol that describes "the saints in their eternal perfected state," and "and them alone." In other words, "the New Jerusalem is personal rather than topographical."[195] The abode for these perfected saints is then the new heaven and earth, which they occupy and fill with worship. Thus, God fulfills his mission to redeem both a people and a place where he might dwell in their midst.

John describes the characteristics of this new temple-city in the last two chapters of Revelation. The New Jerusalem is holy: cleansed of

191. Beale and Carson, *NT Use of the OT*, 1152–53. Kistemaker, "The Temple in the Apocalypse," 440, puts it succinctly: "The city itself has become the holy of holies."

192. McKelvey, *New Temple*, 164. John hinted at this reality in Rev 3:12 where Christ promised, "The one who conquers, I will make him a pillar in the temple of my God. Never shall he go out of it, and I will write on him the name of my God, and the name of the city of my God, the new Jerusalem which comes down from my God out of heaven, and my own new name."

193. Boring, *Revelation*, 219.

194. McKelvey, *New Temple*, 170–71.

195. Gundry, "New Jerusalem," 256–57.

impurities and "purged collectively of those non-overcomers who avoided persecution by accommodating themselves to the world" (Rev 21:8, 27). God will remove all causes of suffering and sorrow from their midst; he will satiate their deepest thirsting; he will adopt them into his family (Rev 21:4, 6, 7). The massive dimensions of the city and its wall indicate that they will be "an innumerable company of the redeemed from all nations, tribes and languages," who will know absolute, eternal security (Rev 21:15–17).[196] John's descriptors of the jeweled city anticipate that the saints will reflect the luminescent glory of the one seated on the throne (Rev 21:11, 18–21; cf. 4:3).[197] The list of precious foundation stones, which correspond to the jewels in the breastplate of the high priest, signifies that the privileges formerly reserved for the high priest alone are now freely shared by all the people of God.[198] From the throne within the city, a spring of living water wells up to eternal life and health (Rev 22:1–2; cf. John 4:14; 7:38). The final description of this new creation reflects that first primordial sanctuary in the garden of Eden; God will reverse the curse and restore his creation (Rev 22:1–4).

The essential characteristic of the city is that the redeemed saints will bask in the holy-of-holies presence of God and the Lamb.[199] Like the high priests of old, they will bear God's name on their foreheads, but unlike their predecessors, they will also see his glory and his face (Rev 21:23; 22:4). The process of transformation that began at their conversion is now complete: they rightly display the image of their Creator. Gundry compares the "reciprocal indwelling of God, the Lamb, and the saints in the *futuristic* eschatology of the New Jerusalem with the reciprocal indwelling of God, his Son, and believers in the *realized* eschatology of John 14–17."[200] The human relationship that best captures this intimate fellowship is that of marriage (Rev 19:7–9; 21:2, 9). Just as God manifested his glory in the previous earthly sanctuaries, he will fill this final temple-less sanctuary with the unfading glory of his presence.[201] As the glory of his tabernacling presence radiates throughout the city, the perfected people of God will display God's glory perfectly (Rev 21:22–23).

196. Ibid., 258, 260.

197. Beale, *Revelation*, 1066.

198. Mounce, *Revelation*, 393.

199. Ibid., 383; Osborne, *Revelation*, 726.

200. Gundry, "New Jerusalem," 262; italics original.

201. The temple-less temple was anticipated in Ezek 11:16 and foreshadowed in the Incarnation (John 1:14) and in the Spirit-filled church. Osborne, *Revelation*, 760, notes several passages that prepare the reader for the eventuality that there will be no temple: e.g., Jer 3:16–17; John 4:21; Acts 7:48–49.

New Jerusalem: Restricted Access to the Presence of God

In fulfillment of the Lord's universal purposes, the redeemed of the nations bring their glory and honor as tribute to the Lamb, and the glory of this eternal sanctuary eclipses that of all the former earthly manifestations of God's presence (cf. Hag 2:6–9). Gundry clarifies that "bringing into the city" is spatial language with non-spatial meaning: "'bring into it' has to do with the glory and honor of the saintly nations . . . that make up the city, not with unsaintly traffic from countryside into the city. . . . To enter the city is to help make it up—and there is nothing about leaving it once the glory and honor have been brought in."[202] In fulfillment of the *missio Dei*, these Jerusalem-people spread out over the face of the new earth, filling it with the knowledge of the glory of the Lord,

Gundry clarifies, "To be outside the city, then, is not to be outside it on earth. It means to be on earth not at all; rather in the lake of fire."[203] It is noteworthy that John stipulates yet again that this universality is restrictive: "But nothing unclean will ever enter it, nor anyone who does what is detestable or false, but only those who are written in the Lamb's book of life" (Rev 21:27). In fact, sober warnings of restriction reverberate like a death knell throughout these final chapters of the Bible (Rev 20:15; 21:8; 21:27; 22:11, 15, 19). The contrast between the people of God and those who reject him continues to the very end. Although the latter had been given opportunities to repent, they blatantly refused (cf. Rev 9:20–21; 16:9–11).

The book of Revelation ends with an authentication of John's message as well as a warning and an invitation for all humanity—the evil and the righteous:

> "Behold, I am coming soon, bringing my recompense with me, to repay everyone for what he has done. I am the Alpha and the Omega, the first and the last, the beginning and the end." Blessed are those who wash their robes, so that they may have the right to the tree of life and that they may enter the city by the gates. Outside are the dogs and sorcerers and the sexually immoral and murderers and idolaters, and everyone who loves and practices falsehood. "I, Jesus, have sent my angel to testify to you about these things for the churches. I am the root and the descendant of David, the bright morning star." The Spirit and the Bride say, "Come." And let the one who hears say, "Come."

---

202. Gundry, "New Jerusalem," 262. Cf. Rev 3:12; "Never shall [the overcomer] go out of it."

203. Ibid., 263.

> And let the one who is thirsty come; let the one who desires take
> the water of life without price (Rev 22:12–17).

The beautiful list of titles in this passage illustrates Christ's incomparable identity and authority to accomplish the mission of God. The invitation to come is repeated three times in verse 17, underscoring the mission theme of Revelation.[204] The Holy Spirit and the corporate church issue the first invitation. As Mounce notes, "It is the testimony of the church empowered by the Holy Spirit that constitutes the great evangelizing force of this age."[205] Second, the individual who hears the invitation should in turn share the same invitation with others.[206] This multiplying witness serves to extend the invitation until the moment Jesus returns and the opportunity to respond closes for all eternity.[207] Third, John—or possibly Jesus himself—invites those who recognize their need to come: "let him who is thirsty come; let the one who desires take the water of life without price" (Rev 22:17b). While the invitation is universal and the price is free, access to the eternal divine presence of God is restricted. This incredibly gracious invitation therefore calls for a definite response. The threefold reiteration of Christ's imminent return amplifies the urgency of both the summons and the response (Rev 22:7, 12, 20). Finally, John closes the book with a stern warning that no one has the right to add or subtract from this Revelation of Jesus Christ.

CONCLUSION

Revelation shows God's mission as a fait accompli. The Lamb has purchased a people for God from every tribe and language and people and nation, and together they are the New Jerusalem—the dwelling place of God. He dwells with and in this perfected people who are a kingdom of priests reflecting his glory. The Lord God and the Lamb are the temple of this holy city, and the new heaven and earth are filled with the glory of God. This was God's purpose from the very beginning—to create a people who would reflect his glory and a place where he might dwell in their midst. The first man and woman had enjoyed unrestricted access to the presence of God in the primordial sanctuary of Eden. When they sinned, they forfeited their priestly role, and God expelled them from his unmediated presence. Slowly the contours of God's redemptive mission began to unfold. In an intricate balance

---

204. Osborne, *Revelation*, 793.
205. Mounce, *Revelation*, 409.
206. Fee, *Revelation*, 313.
207. Mounce, *Revelation*, 409.

of universality and particularity, God promised to bless all the nations of the earth through his election of Abraham and his descendants. The series of sanctuaries where God encountered his people—the temporary patriarchal shrines, the tabernacle, and later the temple—all revealed something about the character of this holy God who tabernacled in their midst. While God graciously provided a way for his people to worship him through the mediation of blood sacrifice, access into his presence had severe restrictions. His presence demanded both a ritual cleanness and an ethical holiness among his people that stood in sharp contrast to the pagan worship of the surrounding nations. The presence of God displayed in their lives was to be a powerful testimony to their neighbors that would shatter the tenets of their false religions.

Tragically, instead of being a light to the nations, the Israelites often yielded to the allure of idolatry. When they failed repeatedly, God still declared his own glory to the surrounding nations through his punishment of the Israelites. The capture of the ark, the defeat at Shiloh, and the destruction of Solomon's temple paved the way for a new understanding: the presence of God was neither confined to a man-made structure nor to the physical descendants of Abraham. Prophets increasingly gave voice to a new covenant and a vision of an eschatological temple where true worshipers from all nations would assemble.

The New Testament opens with the astounding news that the long-promised Messiah has arrived and that he is none other than the Son of God who has come in the flesh to tabernacle among his people. Jesus Christ is the true temple that all the former sanctuaries merely anticipated. Even more amazing, he is the "Lamb of God who takes away the sin of the world" (John 1:29). The rending of the veil of his flesh opened a way for forgiven sinners to follow him, their high priest, into the holy-of-holies presence of God. With Jesus' resurrection, the reality of the eschatological temple has already begun to break into this world in the church. The redeemed from all nations are joined to Christ as a holy priesthood and living stones in the new temple that God is building. The tabernacling presence of God has already begun to dwell in them—individually and corporately—through his Holy Spirit.

Admittedly, a survey of the theme of God's tabernacling presence in the New Testament yields a tangled skein of mixed metaphors. Jesus is at once the tabernacle, the temple, the temple's foundation, the cornerstone, the high priest, the veil, and the sacrificial Lamb of God. In this already-not yet era, his redeemed people are a nation of priests, stones of the temple, the temple, and the dwelling place of the Spirit of God. In the age to come the perfected people of God will be the bride of Christ and the New Jerusalem where God will dwell in their midst and be their temple forever. Although it may be impossible to untangle each strand, the cumulative effect communicates the mysteriously mutual and intimate indwelling of the glorious presence of God in the midst of his people. Human language ultimately fails to articulate the indescribable fulfillment of the mission of God. The only proper response of the multicultural assembly gathered before the throne is to fall to their knees before his glory and offer worship in every tongue of every tribe.

Although this multihued cultural mosaic fulfills God's purposes for creation and showcases his glorious grace, its universality does not equate universalism. The consistent testimony of Scripture reveals that access to the presence of God is only for those who have washed their garments in the blood of the Lamb and whose names are written in his book of life. Those who reject God's gracious gift will be excluded for all eternity. Until that final day, the mission of the church is to be the temple of God, so filled with his presence that it continually expands the knowledge of God's glory globally as it carries out Jesus' command to make disciples of all nations. Likewise, the power for this task and the hope of every generation of believers is the enduring promise of Jesus' abiding presence in the midst of his people—until that day when at last the tabernacling presence of God pervades every corner of the new creation. Then in unbroken, intimate fellowship for all eternity, the perfected bride of Christ will worship in the unmediated presence of the King of Glory.

— 5 —

The Current Canadian Context

The book of Acts records the expansion of the kingdom as the good news of Jesus crossed cultural boundaries in fulfillment of the Great Commission. Paul demonstrates the sensitivity needed to communicate the gospel in various cultural contexts as he adroitly adapted the way he shared this message depending on whether he was addressing Jews or Gentiles. For example, at the synagogue in Pisidian Antioch, Paul started with Old Testament passages to point the Jews to Christ (Acts 13). Before the Areopagus in Athens, however, the Apostle to the Gentiles began with the pagan altar to an unknown god as a point of contact and then proceeded to explain the identity of the one true God. Paul even used the Greeks' own cultural texts to lead into his proclamation of the gospel: "As even some of your own poets have said . . ." (Acts 17:28).

Today, as in Paul's day, those who share the gospel must be able to exegete not only the Scripture, but also the culture in order to communicate the truth of the gospel in a particular context. Admittedly, describing an entire nation with broad brushstrokes is only a starting point, but understanding some of the basic themes that characterize today's Canadian culture prepares the canvas for the more detailed exegesis of a specific cultural setting. This chapter therefore begins with an introduction to some broad cultural themes that impact all Canadians and then follows with a sample exegesis of a particular cultural text written by one of Canada's own poets. While much of the information shared in this chapter is specific to Canada, it will no doubt sound familiar to Americans, whose nation appears to be a few steps behind but on a similar trajectory.

CANADA AT A GLANCE

"From Sea to Sea to Sea"— the motto of Canada—hints at the vastness of the landmass that forms this nation. Bordered on three sides by the Atlantic, Pacific, and Arctic Oceans, Canada is the second largest nation in the world in landmass, covering almost ten million square kilometers. That huge geographic expanse contains richly diverse regions, including the majestic Rocky Mountains, seemingly endless prairies, coastal fishing villages, and frigid arctic tundra. Canada's massive size, combined with its relatively small population (thirty-seventh in world ranking),[1] makes it one of the most sparsely populated countries in the world. The vast majority of its thirty-three million residents, however, live within three hundred kilometers of the southern border that it shares with the United States.

An Urban Population

Four out of five Canadians live in metropolitan areas. In light of Canada's rapidly growing urban population, it is surprising to realize that just over one hundred years ago, the nation was basically a rural society. In 1867, at the time of the Canadian Confederation, less than 20 percent of citizens lived in towns with a population of one thousand or more. Glenn Smith observes, "Now there are over 140 urban centres, occupying less than 3 per cent of the land. In the three largest urban centres—Vancouver, Toronto and Montreal—we find 35 per cent of the population occupying 0.8 per cent of the land."[2]

The growth of these megacities over the last century has been phenomenal. For example, Toronto's population has swelled from 208,000 in 1901, to 5.8 million in 2011.[3] More than eight million people—one-quarter of the entire population of Canada—live in the "Greater Golden Horseshoe" area surrounding Toronto. In addition, more than half the population of Canada resides in the narrow corridor that stretches between Windsor, Ontario and Quebec City—an urban axis which includes the Greater Golden Horseshoe

---

1. "Country Comparison: Population," n.p.
2. Smith, "Canadian Urban Ministry," 84.
3. Hiller, *Urban Canada*, 31. Cf. Statistics Canada "2011 Census of Population," n.p.

area. Not surprisingly, Canadians refer to this region as "the main street of Canada."[4]

Living in the city has a profound impact on the nature of human relationships. Ironically, surrounded by millions and wired for constant electronic communication, people often lose a sense of belonging to a people or a place.[5] David Wells explains the psychological impact of urban living and globalization: "Loneliness is the modern plague. This is the plague of being disconnected, of not being rooted, of not belonging anywhere . . . . It is the affliction of being alone, of being unnoticed, of being carried along by an indifferent universe."[6] People often search to fill this longing for identity and community in small groups. Whereas in the past those living in the same geographic community had a common bond, now people look beyond their residence for meaningful social ties with others who share similar affinities, such as "[r]eligious or political values, hobbies, occupational interests, sports," etc.[7] A sense of rootlessness in the modern city has thus created a crisis of *atopia*, or placelessness.[8] Another social reality is increasing urban inequality, as families fall through the cracks of social safety nets. There is therefore a great need for the advancement of urban social justice in Canadian cities.[9]

A quick glance also reveals that the nation's population is shrinking. Canada is aging. The fastest growing segment of the population is seniors over the age of eighty, and projections show their numbers will rise to 1.3 million within the decade. The fertility rate (the average number of children a woman bears in her lifetime; 3.9 in 1959) has steadily declined to the present rate of 1.5, far below the replacement rate of 2.1. The *Canadian Atlas* reports, "If present trends continue, natural increase (births minus deaths) will be at zero in 2030, and immigration will be the only way the population

4. Hiller, *Urban Canada*, 28.

5. Bedard, "Faith Today Interview," 22, records Leonard Sweet's observation that while social media promises connections, it only tickles the appetite for relationships: "People [remain] ravenous for the real thing."

6. Wells, "Supremacy of Christ," 33.

7. Hiller, *Urban Canada*, 85.

8. Bartholomew, *Where Mortals Dwell*, 4.

9. Hiller, *Urban Canada*, 126. Although there are obvious commonalities shared by cities north and south of the Canada–U.S. border, there are noteworthy differences, as well. Smith, "Canadian Urban Ministry," 87, enumerates "Seven Startling Differences between Canadian and American Cities." He observes that Canadian cities are more compact, denser in population, more reliant on public transportation, and more ethnically diverse. They have higher incomes, more "traditional family" units, and radically different urban government, as well. Canadian cities are also safer and more stable than cities in America.

can grow."[10] Canada is therefore dependent on an influx of immigrants to maintain its population.

A Pluralistic Society

Immigration has always played a significant role in the history of Canada and has resulted in a plurality of ethnicities, cultures, religions, and world-views. Arrivals from France and England fueled the population growth of the early seventeenth century, and early decades of the last century (1911–1931) witnessed large numbers of immigrants as well.[11] Since the 1960s, however, the origin of Canadian immigrants has shifted from Europe to Asia and other Third World countries.

A Cultural Mosaic

In 1971, Canada became the first country to adopt an official policy of multiculturalism. The Canadian Charter of Rights and Freedoms (1982) recognized this ideal of cherished pluralism[12] as a distinctly Canadian value, and the Canadian Multiculturalism Act (1988) formalized the policy that was "designed to preserve and enhance the multicultural heritage of Canadians while working to achieve the equality of all Canadians."[13]

In contrast to the concept of American society as a "melting pot," Canadians consider their society to be a "cultural mosaic," where ethnic diversity enriches the lives of all Canadians—at least in theory. In actuality, a 2012 Angus Reid Public Opinion poll shows that Canadian buy-in of the "mosaic" (30%) versus the "melting pot" (58%) is evaporating. While the majority of Canadians still believe multiculturalism has been good for Canada (62%), the nation is equally divided on the question of immigration: 39 percent of respondents report immigration has a positive effect; 39 percent, a negative effect.[14] John Stackhouse Jr. opines that while "the policy of multiculturalism intends to build stronger, richer communities

10. "Who We Are," n.p.

11. Belanger and Malenfant, "Ethnocultural Diversity," 19.

12. Carson, *Gagging of God*, 13–22, makes the following distinctions between three types of pluralism: 1) Empirical pluralism is the mere fact of plurality or diversity; 2) Cherished pluralism values and celebrates this plurality; and 3) Philosophical pluralism maintains that in light of plurality no single option can be pronounced superior to another.

13. Bibby, "Canada's Mythical Religious Mosaic," 235.

14. "Canadians Are Divided on the Actual Effect of Immigration," n.p.

and countries," ironically it has resulted in "a multiplicity of cultures that strains the unity of the society that comprises them."[15]

Although the promise of mutual enrichment may have failed to materialize convincingly, the 2011 National Household Survey reveals the undeniable fruit of Canada's policies of cherished pluralism. The proportion of foreign-born population (6,775,800) represented 20.6 percent of the total population, "the highest proportion among the G8 countries."[16] Between 2006 and 2011, Canada's population grew by 5.9 percent, and immigrants were responsible for two-thirds of that increase.[17] Of the 1.2 million recent immigrants, 57 percent came from Asia. Most recent immigrants gravitate toward Canada's largest census metropolitan areas—Toronto, Vancouver, and Montreal. In 2011, these three cities were home to 63 percent of Canada's foreign-born population, while being home to only 35.2 percent of the country's Canadian-born population. Additionally, one in five Canadians belongs to a visible minority group.[18] Not surprisingly, Statistics Canada predicts that the Canadian trend toward empirical pluralism will only increase.[19]

A Religious Mosaic?

The nation of Canada has seen significant shifts in religious affiliation in the last few decades as well. Although the numbers claiming Roman Catholic and Protestant affiliation held steady over the past decade, their percentages decreased as the overall population of Canada grew. Between 2001 and 2011, Roman Catholics fell from 43 percent to 39 percent of the general population; Protestants, from 29 percent to 27 percent.[20] Within Protestant ranks, the mainline denominations have plummeted from a high of 50 percent in 1931, to a current 15 percent.[21] The proportion of evangelicals, which had consistently remained at 8 percent from 1871 to 2001, has increased

---

15. Stackhouse, *Humble Apologetics*, 35.

16. Statistics Canada, "2011 National Household Survey," 1.

17. Martel and Chagnon, "Canadian Population in 2011," 4.

18. Chui and Sanders, "Immigration," 7–14. The percentage of foreign-born in Toronto is 46%; Vancouver, 40% (ibid., 10).

19. Belanger and Malenfant, "Ethnocultural Diversity," 21.

20. Statistics Canada, "2011 National Household Survey," 2.

21. According to Miner, "Predeceased by their Churches," n.p., the United Church, Canada's largest Protestant denomination, has shut more than 400 churches in the past decade and is currently closing about one church a week.

over the past decade to 11 percent of the population.[22] In this same time period, those with religious affiliation other than Christianity have seen substantial gains. Consistent with the increased immigration from Asia and the Middle East, those reporting affiliation with the Muslim, Hindu, Sikh, Buddhist, and Jewish religions increased from 4.9 percent to 7.2 percent of the total population.[23] Finally, the "religious" group that increased the most substantially in the last decade—from 16.5 percent to 24 percent of the total population—was the category of "Nones." In 2011, approximately one in four Canadians claimed to have "No Religion."[24]

Somewhat surprisingly, recent immigration has actually resulted in an infusion of Christians into Canada. According to the 2010 General Social Survey, in the years 2005–2010, five out of ten immigrants arrived as Catholics (30%) or Protestants (21%), while about three in ten identified with other major religions (34%), with the remaining 15 percent reporting "No religion."[25] Additionally, immigrants' level of monthly attendance of religious services (44%) tended to be much higher than that of people born in Canada (24%).[26] Church historian Bruce Guenther observes, "Few Christian traditions in Canada have benefited as much during the twentieth century from immigration and the intentional promotion of multiculturalism, as have evangelical Protestants."[27]

Sociologist Reginald Bibby therefore challenges the "widely-held assumption ... that the cultural diversity of Canadians is translating into increasing religious diversity, as people arriving from other countries bring with them an array of different religions."[28] Although religions such as Islam, Buddhism, Hinduism and Sikhism are growing in Canada, their

---

22. Although Statistics Canada does not track evangelicals as a group, Bibby, *New Day*, 33, reports this surprisingly consistent percentage over the past century, as well as the recent uptick (ibid., 30). Reimer, "A Demographic Look at Evangelical Congregations," 3, points out that historians have not given much attention to Canadian denominations in general, and evangelicals in particular. Estimates of the evangelical population are therefore disparate, depending on definitions of "evangelical."

23. This 7.2% breaks down as follows: Muslim 3.2%, Hindu 1.5%, Sikh 1.4%, Buddhist 1.1% and Jewish 1.0%. Statistics Canada, "2011 National Household Survey," 2.

24. Ibid., 3.

25. Bibby, *New Day*, 33.

26. Ibid., 15.

27. Guenther, "Ethnicity," 398. Guenther also points out that "the Chinese [represent] the fastest growing and most dynamic component of the increasingly diverse world of evangelical Protestantism in Canada" (366). In the same volume, Beyer, "Appendix," 440, estimates that in 2001, 17% of evangelicals were immigrants with over 70% of those arriving after 1971.

28. Bibby, "Canada's Mythical Religious Mosaic," 235.

adherents are primarily immigrants from the Middle East and Asia. These religions are making very few inroads among the general Canadian populace: "less than 2% of Canadians of British, French, German, and Italian origins combined are identifying with religions other than Christianity."[29] Additionally, there is evidence that the gains these other religions receive from increased immigration are often neutralized through assimilation, particularly through intermarriage where "the inclination is for the ensuing offspring to be raised as Catholics or Protestants—or No Religion."[30] Bibby concludes that although the population is increasingly multicultural, the perception that Canada is a religious mosaic is, in fact, a myth. Guenther concurs: "[T]he entry of recent immigrants has resulted not so much in the de-Christianization of Canadian society, but in the de-Europeanization of Canadian Christianity."[31]

Still, there is no denying that there has been a dramatic shift in the religious makeup of Canada. The Center for the Study of Global Christianity reports that the Christian share of the Canadian population has fallen from 94 percent in 1970 to 69 percent in 2010. Contra Bibby, this 2013 study observes that in actuality, "[t]he presence of nine religions each with at least 1% of the total population makes Canada one of the most religiously diverse countries in the world."[32] One of the study's key findings is that 20 percent of non-Christians in North America do not even know a single Christian personally. When atheists/agnostics are removed from the calculation, this number skyrockets to 60 percent.[33] Christians may still dominate the religious mosaic in Canada, but their numbers are dropping, and evidently many appear to be content to stick together and keep their faith to themselves. While other religions may only represent a few tiles in Canada's religious mosaic, no one can ignore the burgeoning segment of religiously unaffiliated—which is "a major change in the religious demographics of the region."[34]

Philosophical Pluralism

Undoubtedly, Canada's policy of multiculturalism has had a significant impact on the society as a whole. In 1990, Bibby reviewed the initial results

29. Ibid., 237.

30. Ibid., 239.

31. Guenther, "Ethnicity," 367.

32. "Christianity in Its Global Context, 62–63.

33. Ibid., 8.

34. Ibid., 63.

of Canada's "experiment" with multiculturalism and voiced his concern: "[Canada now has] . . . not only a cultural mosaic but also a moral mosaic, a meaning system mosaic, a family structure mosaic, a sexual mosaic. And that's just the shortlist. Pluralism has come to pervade Canadian minds and Canadian institutions."[35] In this context pluralism is no longer just a descriptive term for sheer diversity, but rather is a policy that legitimizes diversity.

Initially, the emphases that accompany individualism and pluralism— freedom, tolerance, respect, appreciation for diversity—sound like welcome correctives to a group-oriented society that had failed to recognize the rights of "lesser" members.[36] As Canada has discovered, however, pluralism walks hand-in-hand with relativism: "Pluralism establishes choices; relativism declares the choices valid."[37] Bibby concludes, "In Canada, truth has become little more than personal opinion. 'It's all relative,' declare Canadians from British Columbia to Newfoundland. . . . Relativism has slain moral consensus . . ." leaving Canadians bereft of ethical and moral guidelines.[38] The data from the 2010 ISSP Religious Survey confirm his appraisal. Almost three in four Canadians agree that "Everything's relative," while over half agree that "What's right or wrong is a matter of personal opinion." Ironically, a large majority of respondents agree with the statement: "In general, values in Canada have been changing for the worse" (72%).[39]

The irony is that a large number of these survey respondents unwittingly rendered a value judgment when they had just stated it was improper to do so. Yet the attempt to ground values in truth claims is anathema in a culture committed to tolerance as its highest value.[40] If society decrees

35. Bibby, *Mosaic Madness*, 9.

36. Bibby explores the marginalization of women and cultural minorities in pre-1960s Canada in chapter 2, "How We Got into All This," in *Mosaic Madness*, 16–36.

37. Ibid., 10.

38. Ibid., 13–14.

39. International Social Survey, n.p. A recent survey shows the results of such relativistic thinking as reported in "Americans More Morally Conservative," n.p. Greater percentages of Canadians than Americans found the following issues morally acceptable: sexual relations between unmarried men and women, 83% (U.S. 59%); having a baby outside of marriage, 78% (U.S. 53%); doctor-assisted suicide, 65% (U.S. 35%); abortion, 60% (U.S. 36%); and prostitution, 41% (U.S. 23%).

40. Carson, *Intolerance of Tolerance*, 12, quotes Leslie Amour, professor emeritus of philosophy at the University of Ottawa as saying, "Our idea is that to be a virtuous [Canadian] citizen is to be one who tolerates everything except intolerance." Carson explains: "The *old* tolerance is the willingness to put up with, allow, or endure people and ideas with whom we disagree; in its purest form, the *new* tolerance is the social commitment to treat all ideas and people as equally right, save for those people who disagree with this view of tolerance" (ibid., 98; italics added).

"that an educated, enlightened, sophisticated Canadian is a person who tolerates almost everything and seldom takes a position on anything," then Canadians will frown upon a faith that is committed to the truths of the Bible.[41] Most consider the very idea of sharing one's faith with others simply incomprehensible. Bibby explains:

> Frankly, evangelism is not very Canadian; it smacks of intolerance, even bigotry. It also is a violation of privacy. And when it's directed at new arrivals, the poor, the young, and the aged, it borders on imperialism and exploitation. Some say it may even violate the Charter of Rights and Freedoms. . . . The person who bucks the pluralistic and relativistic norms of the day and goes public with private views and beliefs pays a fairly sizable bill.[42]

He also observes, "[Canadian] culture permits Jesus to be one way, but it gasps at any suggestion that he is the *only* way."[43] In such an environment, the temptation is strong to remain quiet or even to adopt the philosophical pluralism of the culture. Indeed, many religious groups have drifted from their theological moorings of earlier decades.

The Project Canada survey responses also illustrate an excessive individualism: 75 percent of respondents agreed that "[m]ost of the time people are just looking out for themselves."[44] In contrast to the American concept of "rugged individualism," Canadian society has historically had a group-orientation. Intriguingly, Bibby argues, "[T]he accelerated emphasis on individualism in the Western world is a far greater threat to social solidarity in Canada than it is in the United States."[45] The sociologist explains that the creed that has historically bound Americans together balances strong individualism with collectivity: "we the people." Americans' patriotism, celebration of heroes, and passion for high school and university sports demonstrate a shared ideology that is simply missing in Canada. Although Bibby is not as pessimistic as political scientist Gad Horowitz who considers multiculturalism "the masochistic celebration of Canadian nothingness,"[46] he does conclude that a "tenuous willingness to coexist" is hardly a rallying cry for the future of the nation.[47]

---

41. Bibby, *Mosaic Madness*, 100.

42. Ibid., 142, 145.

43. Ibid., 88; italics original.

44. Bibby, "Project Canada 1995," n.p.

45. Bibby, *Mosaic Madness*, 96.

46. Horowitz, "Mosaics and Identity," 473, as quoted in Bibby, *Mosaic Madness*, 92.

47. Bibby, *Mosaic Madness*, 94–95.

Certainly not all share Bibby's concern. John Ibbitson, for example, is positively sanguine about the role of pluralism in Canada's future. He writes:

> We have discovered the golden secret of the third millennia: They who don't simply tolerate diversity, but embrace it, thrive. . . . [B]ecause Canada and Canadians have largely mastered the art of getting along, the twenty-first century will be Canada's century. We shall be an example, a template, a lesson. Canada should, and hopefully will, be known throughout the world as the exemplar of what can be achieved when chauvinism gives way to accommodation, when the obsessions with shared race, shared blood, shared history are transcended by an infinity of permutations.[48]

The reality is likely somewhere in between the polar ends of the spectrum represented by Horowitz and Ibbitson. What is certain is that Canada's experiment with empirical and cherished pluralism that began in the 1970s has resulted in a deeply entrenched philosophical pluralism that characterizes Canada today.

A Postmodern Society

Canada's experiment with pluralism over the last four decades has coincided with the advent of postmodernism. This recent cultural phenomenon dovetails with philosophical pluralism and provides the intellectual underpinnings for the relativism that both hold in common. This new era is characterized by an intellectual outlook and cultural expressions that are a radical break from the epoch of modernity that held sway for centuries following the Enlightenment.[49] Although harbingers of postmodernism surfaced as early as the 1930s, it was a 1979 Canadian government report that "put postmodernism on the intellectual map." In that year the Conseil des Universités of Quebec asked Jean-Francois Lyotard to write a report on "knowledge in the most highly developed societies." His brief report, *The Postmodern Condition: A Report on Knowledge*, described the theoretical and philosophical basis of the cultural sea-change that was already under-

48. Ibbitson, *Polite Revolution*, 4. Ibbitson's unbridled enthusiasm seems a bit over-optimistic, especially in light of the significant deterioration of economic outcomes of immigrants in comparison to native-born Canadians in the last few decades. See Ferrer et al., "New Directions in Immigration," 1–36.

49. Grenz, *Primer on Postmodernism*, 13. For an in-depth academic analysis of postmodernism, see Fredric Jameson, *Postmodernism, or, The Cultural Logic of Late Capitalism* (1991); and Perry Anderson, *The Origins of Postmodernity* (1998).

way.[50] While acknowledging that postmodernism defies definitive description, Stanley Grenz explains that it is an epistemological revolution that rejects a unified worldview: There is "no transcendent center to reality as a whole."[51]

Some Postmodern Philosophers

Grenz awards Friedrich Nietzsche (1844–1900) the dubious title "patron saint of postmodern philosophy." Observing that Western civilization had distanced itself from the transcendent, Nietzsche announced "the death of God," thus fragmenting any divine foundation for truth, values, and morality. Advocating an "aesthetic nihilism," Nietzsche called for humans ". . . to become the artists of our own existence, inventing a world suited to our being."[52] Having lobbed the first volley in the attack on modernity, Nietzsche paved the way for all of the postmodern thinkers who followed him.[53]

Nietzsche's "truest disciple," Michel Foucault (1926–1984) rejected the Enlightenment assumption that objective truth exists and can be discovered by a disinterested knower.[54] Instead, he claimed that so-called knowledge is constituted through social, political, and economic networks of power. In order to expose power, Foucault traced the development of a body of knowledge to unmask the conditions that led to its formation.[55] In a similar vein, Jacques Derrida (1930–2004) argued that because of the limitations of language, one cannot assume to know anything with certainty. For Derrida, language has no fixed meaning; it is not connected to a fixed reality; it does not reveal definitive truth. Derrida also objected to the "metaphysics of presence," which assumes that at the foundation of language there is a "presence" of being or a "transcendental signifier" that is "the infinite understanding that God possesses."[56]

According to Derrida, it is naïve for readers to think they can "step out of [their] skins" to discover the meaning behind the text: "*there is nothing outside context.*"[57] He therefore "deconstructed" the values of a given interpretive community in order to expose the ideological lens through

50. Grenz, *Primer on Postmodernism*, 39.

51. Ibid., 6.

52. Ibid., 95.

53. Ibid., 88.

54. Ibid., 131.

55. Smith, *Who's Afraid*, 134–35.

56. Grenz, *Primer on Postmodernism*, 142.

57. Derrida, *Limited Inc*, 136, in Smith, *Who's Afraid*, 52; Smith's italics.

which they read the text. Following Derrida's lead, subsequent postmodern philosophers have applied his theory of literary deconstruction not only to texts but also to the world as a whole. Grenz points out the consequences: "This means that there is no one meaning of the world, no transcendent center to reality as a whole."[58] Reality itself is left open to myriad interpretations.

Jean-Francois Lyotard (1924–1998) summarized his findings on knowledge in *The Postmodern Condition*: "Simplifying to the extreme, I define *postmodern* as incredulity toward metanarratives."[59] Having divested themselves of such metanarratives, postmoderns still perceive life itself as drama. Now, however, they focus on "fabricating stories that can define personal identity and give purpose and shape to social existence."[60] Against a backdrop of global pluralism with its multiplicity of worldviews, these local stories prove useful in constructing "truth" that is, of course, relative to the community who shares it.

Characteristics of Postmodernity

Grenz notes several characteristics of this new era of postmodernity. Gone are the buoyant optimism and the naïve belief that progress is inevitable; in their place is a pervasive, gnawing pessimism. Life on earth is fragile, and humanity is unlikely to solve the problems facing the planet. Because truth is relative to the community that constructs it, there is also a communal focus to postmodern society.[61]

Mark Liederbach and Alvin Reid delineate some of the challenges posed by postmodernism. The denial of a transcendent presence leads to a moral and ethical relativism, which reduces morality to a social construct that is "relevant only to individuals and particular communities."[62] The authors observe, "In a postmodern worldview *tolerance* becomes the supreme virtue while *conviction* becomes a vice." Imbued with a deep distrust of authority, "[postmoderns] vehemently oppose external, objective

---

58. Grenz, *Primer on Postmodernism*, 6.

59. Lyotard, *Postmodern Condition*, xxiv. Smith, *Who's Afraid*, 63, observes, "The French term (curiously) translated by 'metanarratives' is '*grand récits*,' big stories" (italics original). Smith nuances that Lyotard does not reject the scope of unified grand narrative per se, but rather he rejects the attempt "to legitimate or prove the story's claim by an appeal to universal reason" (65). Thus, according to Lyotard, scientific knowledge masquerades as a universal truth but fails to own up to its mythic grounding in a narrative of progress (67–69).

60. Grenz, *Primer on Postmodernism*, 46.

61. Ibid., 7–8.

62. Liederbach and Reid, *Convergent Church*, 58.

truth claims."[63] While Grenz stresses the significance of community for postmoderns, Liederbach and Reid point out that in actuality the autonomous self is just as central as it was in modernity, but now it is cloaked in communal language. Whatever a person believes is irrelevant as long as one is authentic or true to oneself. Because postmodernism has erased the claim that humans share a basic human nature, the self is merely a social construction. In a fragmented world it is left to the individual to do the exhausting work of creating and re-creating one's own identity in the context of one's narrative.[64]

In this environment Christianity has lost its influence, and biblical literacy is evaporating. According to the recent Canadian Bible Engagement Study conducted by Angus Reid, weekly Bible reading has dropped by half since 1996, both among the general population (21% to 11%) and among Canadian Christians (27% to 14%). Fully 80 percent of Canadians (74% of Canadian Christians) report that they seldom or never read the Bible. Not surprisingly then, the majority of Canadians agree that "the scriptures of all major world religions teach essentially the same things" (64%; 60% of Canadian Christians.) Although 51 percent of Evangelicals read the Bible weekly, 36 percent seldom or never do and 38 percent agree that all religions teach the same things.[65] Clearly, the decades that have seen a rise in postmodernism have also seen a decline in Canadians' engagement with the Bible.

Not everyone agrees on the extent of postmodernism's hold on society. Although the cultural transition from modernity to postmodernity is still underway, its influence is steadily seeping from the intellectual fringes of society into the everyday life of North Americans. Gene Veith Jr. observes, "Postmodernism shapes our lifestyles, the way we make a living, how we educate our children, and how we approach our personal problems and those of society."[66] On the other hand, while Christian apologist William Lane Craig does not deny that postmodern ideas have influenced Western society, he argues, "The idea that we live in a postmodern world is a myth."[67] He contends that living in a postmodern world is impossible because it is an "unlivable world." He points out that when treating a headache, even postmoderns choose a bottle labeled "aspirin" rather than "rat poison" because "texts have objective meaning." Craig maintains that people today still operate in a modern world of meaning, particularly in the fields of science,

63. Ibid., 59; italics original.

64. Ibid., 64–67.

65. Hiemstra, "Confidence," 5.

66. Veith, *Postmodern Times*, 175.

67. Craig, *Reasonable Faith*, 18.

technology, and engineering. It is in the areas of religion and ethics where the relativistic and pluralistic concepts of postmodernism have had their greatest influence. Interestingly, Stackhouse observes that this fluid shifting between modernity and postmodernity leads to phrases like "your truth" and "my reality." He remarks, "[T]his strainless switching among various and even contradictory values and cognitive styles . . . is one of the most striking characteristics of the postmodern mind."[68]

Consumer Spirituality

Undoubtedly, both philosophical pluralism and postmodernism have contributed to the spiritual confusion that characterizes today's society. The idea of creating one's own identity highlights a consumer mentality that, ironically, flourishes in both modern and postmodern environments. In the latter, Stackhouse explains, "The bewildering anarchy and anomie of postmodernity typically produce a self that is fragmented and thus it takes its cues from various and ever-changing social forces and contexts."[69] In such an environment where self is the final arbiter, "[r]ightness, of course, is entirely in the eye of the consumer."[70] Religion itself becomes a buffet to be picked over. Individuals feel free to peruse the choice parts of various religious traditions, selecting an eclectic mix that best satisfies their own desires and needs. Stackhouse describes the attitude behind this pervasive consumerism: "I pick the gods I want; I pick the rules I want to live by; I pick the rituals that suit me best. No higher authority and no higher power tells [sic] me what to do."[71] When there are no absolute truths, "[a]esthetic criteria replace rational criteria."[72] People simply look within themselves to construct a god who meets their needs. Not surprisingly, this consumerism ". . . yields a God who is familiar, safe, accommodating, but also very small."[73] The resulting designer-deity resembles its human creator more than the transcendent Creator of the universe.

68. Stackhouse, *Humble Apologetics*, 32.

69. Ibid., 57.

70. Ibid., 59.

71. Ibid., 62.

72. Veith, *Postmodern Times*, 193. Veith points out that people today discuss religion in terms of preference: for example, "I really like that church," and "I really like the Bible passage that says, 'God is love'" (193–94). Similarly, if one dislikes a particular biblical teaching—like hell—one simply chooses not to believe it, and Christians seeking to avoid offense seldom mention it.

73. Wells, *Courage to Be Protestant*, 120. Wells explains that postmoderns emphasize God's immanence over his transcendence: the "inside God" over the "outside God."

Left with the relativistic perception that one religion is as good as another, most Canadians have bought in to this consumerist approach to religious beliefs. Data from the 2010 ISSP Religion Survey show that Canadians have adopted an eclectic approach to religion. Survey respondents reported their belief in ESP—extra-sensory perception (57%), heaven (51%), miracles (50%), hell (32%), reincarnation (27%), supernatural powers of deceased ancestors (25%), and nirvana (13%).[74] These polls reveal that while Canadians continue to hold on to some vestiges of Christian belief, they are becoming increasingly syncretistic. In a pluralistic society, the lines between religions inevitably tend to blur—especially in a postmodern mind.[75] Increasingly empty pews across Canada testify to the widespread impact of philosophical pluralism and postmodernism.

A Polarized Society

"Canada's Great Religious Recession"[76]

According to the 1945 Gallup Poll of Canada—the first such national survey—65 percent of Canadians attended church in a three-week period as compared to 58 percent of Americans in a similar survey.[77] Although these numbers held steady through the 1950s, by 1965, weekly attendance slipped to 55 percent.[78] From 1975 to 2010, weekly attendance fell precipitously from 41 percent to 19 percent. During that same time frame, the number of Canadians reporting that they *never* attend a religious service doubled from about 20 percent to 42 percent.[79]

A pattern of increasing secularization holds true for Canadian youth as well. *Hemorrhaging Faith* is the title of a recent research project commissioned by the Evangelical Fellowship of Canada—the first of its kind in Canada. The survey queried over two thousand Canadians aged eighteen to thirty-four about their spiritual lives and church attendance as children, teens, and young adults. This 2011 survey shows the drop-off in church attendance is more pronounced in Catholic and mainline traditions, where

74. International Social Survey, n.p. Roberts, *Recent Social Trends*, 451, cites another survey that shows belief in the "Devil" has doubled from 21% in 1969 to 40% in 1995.

75. Wells, "Supremacy of Christ," 26.

76. Bibby, *Beyond the Gods*, 15.

77. Ibid., 10. In Roman Catholic Quebec, attendance was 90%. This paragraph discusses attendance rather than affiliation, which was the subject of the previous section, "Religious Mosaic?"

78. Ibid., 16.

79. Bibby, *New Day*, 9.

only one in ten respondents raised in church now report attending weekly, as compared to four in ten evangelicals. In light of stereotypes, the drop-off in attendance was surprisingly greater between childhood and adolescence than the decline between adolescence and young adulthood.[80] The survey also reported attrition of affiliation: mainline traditions lost about two-thirds of their childhood affiliates; Catholics, one half; and evangelicals, one-third. The majority of those who stopped affiliating with the tradition of their childhood have not re-affiliated with another Christian tradition, but now identify themselves as atheist, agnostic, spiritual, or "None."[81] Consequently, the percentage of teens who never attend services nearly doubled between 1984 and 2008: presently fully half of Canadian teens never attend church.[82] Based on the face-to-face interviews, the study reports, "Despite being unable to explain what God's presence feels like, many young adults seem to be certain of what it means to experience his absence." Young people evidently expect to encounter the presence of God in church. When they do, they stick around; when they do not, they are willing to walk away from faith.[83]

While the drop in attendance is more pronounced among younger generations, the rates in attendance have declined in all generational cohorts.[84] There has been a decided "religious recession" among all generations across Canada. Mark Noll summarizes the dramatic changes in church attendance in Canada vis-à-vis the United States:

> Put generally, in 1950 Canadian church attendance as a proportion of the total population exceeded church attendance in the United States by one-third to one-half, and church attendance in Quebec may have been the highest in the world. Today church attendance in the United States is probably one-half to two-thirds greater than in Canada, and attendance in Quebec is the lowest of any state or province in North America. Over the course of only half a century, these figures represent a dramatic inversion.[85]

Noll observes, "... Canada's exchange of traditional Christian anchorage for an alternative compass of ideological multiculturalism ... remains a

---

80. Penner et al., *Hemorrhaging Faith*, 21–22.
81. Ibid., 25.
82. Bibby, *A New Day*, 7.
83. Penner et al., *Hemorrhaging Faith*, 50.
84. "Canada's Changing Religious Landscape," n.p.
85. Noll, "What Happened to Christian Canada?," 249.

considerable puzzle for historical analysis."[86] Undoubtedly, there are many factors that have contributed to religious decline in Canada.

Secularization or Polarization?

This intergenerational drop-off in attendance seems to lend credence to the claims of a growing secularization of Canada. Bibby has tracked this steady decline for over three decades and has recorded his findings in more than a dozen books. At times his voice joined those who predicted the demise of religion in Canada; at other times he reported results that hinted at a possible renaissance. In his 2011 book, *Beyond the Gods and Back: The Demise and Rise of Religion and Why It Matters*, Bibby announced that he was closer to solving the puzzle: the appropriate description of the religion situation in Canada is neither secularization nor revitalization—but rather, religious polarization.

At the same time that Catholics and mainline Protestants experienced such a steep decline in church participation, weekly church attendance among evangelicals actually stood at 58 percent in 2000, a robust percentage that—according to Sam Reimer—"if anything, has only increased over time."[87] Bibby explains how this evidence influenced the development of his determination that increasing polarization characterizes Canada:

> A fairly stable core of people continues to value and participate in organized religion. That stability led me to think that a measure of revitalization . . . could be taking place. At the same time, the proportion of Canadians who do not value or participate in religious groups has been increasing—seemingly consistent with the secularization thesis. What has been largely missed in all this is the fact that the two inclinations are co-existing, while the size of "the ambivalent middle" has been shrinking. Put another way, Canadians increasingly embrace or reject religion.[88]

86. Ibid., 271. Noll attempts just such an analysis in this article, which is also published in a book by the same title.

87. Reimer and Wilkinson, "Demographic Look at Evangelical Congregations," 1. This high attendance rate is one of the reasons that evangelicals account for one-third of the approximately thirty thousand Canadian congregations even though they make up only about 10% of the population (5). The authors list several reasons behind evangelicals' strength: They are a distinctive subculture with a high view of Scripture, slightly larger families, and an emphasis on making disciples; they plant new churches, train new leaders, and attract new immigrants; and their "[s]maller congregations allow for more institutional diversity within a geographic area" (20–21).

88. Bibby, "Continuing the Conversation on Canada," 837.

Appraising the religious situation in Canada in 2012, Bibby estimates that approximately one-third of Canadians are in the ambivalent middle while the remaining two-thirds are split equally between the polar ends of the spectrum.[89]

Similarly, Kurt Bowen divides the religious spectrum into four categories: the Very Committed (attend weekly and say religion is important; 20 percent), the Less Committed (attend less regularly and say religion is important; 10–12 percent), Seekers (rarely attend but say religion is important; 28 percent) and the Non Religious (never attend and say religion is not important; 41 percent).[90] Movement along "the polarization continuum" will likely continue in the future with both ends becoming increasingly entrenched.[91]

When Worldviews and Rights Collide

D. A. Carson suggests that one of the tenets of postmodernism is that "[n]o religion has the right to pronounce itself as right or true, and the others false."[92] Therefore, if the viewpoints and lifestyles of every individual are equally valid, inevitably conflicting rights will collide. In such a world, Christianity in particular draws fire.

Recent headlines across Canada have recorded just such a collision of rights in the controversy surrounding the proposed law school of Trinity Western University (TWU), British Columbia. The privately funded Christian institution now finds itself embroiled in court battles to shut the school down as discriminatory. The outrage against TWU centers around one statement in a five-page belief and behavioral covenant that asks students to "limit sexual activity to the Biblical definition of marriage; 'between a man and a woman.'"[93] Although the B. C. Education Ministry granted approval to the law school in December 2013, one year later the government of British Columbia revoked its prior approval.[94] This reversal came on the heels of a vote of the B. C. Law Society, whose members voted 3,210 to 968 to reject the school, following the example of law societies in Ontario and Nova Scotia who voted against accrediting students from the school.[95]

89. Bibby, "Why Bother with Organized Religion?," 91.

90. Bowen, *Christians in a Secular World*, 50.

91. Bibby, *Beyond the Gods*, 56.

92. Carson, *Gagging of God*, 19.

93. Dueck, "Trinity Western," n.p.

94. "Trinity Western law school," n.p.

95. Canada Press, "Lawyers vote," n.p.

Meanwhile, Toronto civil rights lawyer Clayton Ruby has approached Vancouver's gay community and found a British Columbia plaintiff, Trevor Loke. Ruby explains how the proposed law school violated his rights:

> Mr. Loke had never heard of TWU, but when he heard there was a law school that was off limits to him in any meaningful way, that was an anathema, it was hateful. . . . Within the confines of religion, the most inane nonsense can be believed and practiced and passed on to one's children. That's freedom of religion, have a nice time. But when you go to the government and say I want your approval for this, I want tax status for this, then it's beyond mere freedom of religion, there has to be a primacy for the right to equality.[96]

However, director of the proposed law school, Earl Phillips, clarifies that in asking for compliance with the community covenant, the school is "not making it a term of acceptance that you not be gay, or deny that identity." Canadian students actually choose TWU and willingly sign its covenant because it reflects *their* identity.[97]

Both sides are gearing up to defend their rights in a case that may well make it to the Supreme Court of Canada. Ironically, Trinity Western has already been there when it went through a similar contest when opening a school of education in 2001. Last time the Supreme Court ruled in favor of TWU over the B. C. College of Teachers. This time round, however, the university's opponents are hoping for a different outcome since in the interim Canada has legalized same-sex marriage.[98]

Not surprisingly, the fractured Canadian family is certainly a casualty of the excesses of individualism and relativism. In 2011, the number of married-couple families dropped to 67 percent of all census families (down from 91.6% in 1961),[99] while common-law families increased to 16.7 percent, and lone-parent families rose to 16.3 percent. Nearly two out of ten children in Canada live with lone parents. Same-sex couples now represent 0.8 percent of all couples: "[Their] number . . . nearly tripled between 2006

---

96. Dueck, "Trinity Western," n.p.

97. Ibid.

98. Clemenger, "Organizations Free to Maintain Religious Identity," n.p., reports that on January 28, 2015, TWU won a favorable ruling from the Supreme Court of Nova Scotia. Challenges to the law societies in Ontario and British Columbia are still pending.

99. Statistics Canada, "Fifty Years," 1.

and 2011, reflecting the first full five-year period for which same-sex marriage has been legal across the country."[100]

In response to the mounting evidence of fractured families, the Statistics Canada website proffers this dubious advice: "[A]s social norms crumble . . . couples must negotiate new, mutually acceptable standards of behavior."[101] Sociologist Pamela Young expresses this same relativism as she challenges churches to reflect Canadian culture:

> Views of sexuality are changing among Canadians, so that even those churches most opposed to "non-traditional" expressions of sexuality might well have to shift their rhetoric so that they will not be seen as speaking negatively about Canadians whose sexual expression does not accord with their specific church views. . . . Relationships come in many forms. Religious traditions will have to grapple with these social changes if they want to remain relevant to the vast majority of Canadians.[102]

It is noteworthy that Young singles out churches and not mosques or venues of other religions, whose presence precipitated the allowances for pluralism. In this environment where relativism rules the day, tolerance becomes the chief virtue.

Ironically, Canadians appear to bend over backwards to accommodate other belief systems, yet often fail to extend the same tolerance to the faith of the majority. Associate professor of journalism and contemporary studies at Wilfrid Laurier, David Haskell carefully researched several years of Canadian media coverage of evangelicals. He concludes that journalists often forsake objectivity to slant their reporting against perceived ideological opponents, and he offers many examples that show a bias against Christians seems to extend beyond reporters as well. According to Haskell, "Christianity has become a faith *non grata* in terms of public discourse and practice."[103]

Haskell proffers several examples, reaching as far back as the 1998 memorial service for the 229 victims of the Swiss Air Flight 111 crash, where Protestant and Catholic ministers were instructed that they could not say "Jesus" or refer to the Bible. Haskell notes that while ". . . a rabbi was allowed to read from the Torah, a Muslim from the Koran, and a native Canadian was allowed to speak of the Great Spirit; only the Christian clergy were censored." A few years later, at the federal government public memorial service following the tragic attacks of September 11, 2001, references to God,

100. Statistics Canada, "2011 Census of Population," 1–2.

101. Clark and Crompton. "Till Death Do Us Part?," 23.

102. Young, "Two by Two," 100–101.

103. Haskell, *Through a Lens Darkly*, 43.

the Bible, and prayer were conspicuously absent. At the 2003 swearing-in ceremony for the incoming Prime Minister, the only religious observance was a cleansing ceremony conducted by a native elder, who "fann[ed] sage smoke . . . with an eagle feather" over Paul Martin, a devout Catholic.[104]

In a culture that champions excessive pluralism, there is scant room left for claims grounded in truth. Religious truth loses importance in a setting where "[p]luralism has declared its quest inappropriate; relativism has declared it futile."[105] Reimer notes that "[t]he pragmatic solution to this tension [between commitment to civic pluralism and religious commitments] is not necessarily a diminished belief in God or general secularization, but a softening of the exclusive and absolutist claims of religion."[106] Apparently, most Canadians agree. According to the ISSP 2010 survey, 74 percent of respondents agreed with both of the following statements: "Religions bring conflict" and "Religious people are too intolerant"; less than 4 percent agreed that "there is truth in only one religion."[107] Given the present cultural milieu, Stackhouse observes, "[G]enuine religions are a threat to the values and order of consumerism. They are an enemy to the consumerist ethos. . . . They are literally countercultural."[108] Ibbitson exemplifies this attitude in the preface to his book entitled, ironically, *The Polite Revolution*:

> The Christian evangelist who condemns homosexual unions and the imam who would limit the full participation in society both represent, for this writer, deeply obnoxious beliefs that must be confronted and condemned. But the liberal democratic traditions of Canadian society are remarkably robust, and can easily handle such challenges.[109]

Obviously, this mindset presents unique challenges for believers wanting to communicate a gospel witness to those who are entrenched in philosophical pluralism.

---

104. Ibid., 43–44.

105. Young, "Two by Two," 87.

106. Reimer, "Does Religion Matter?," 122.

107. International Social Survey, "Religion III," n.p.

108. Stackhouse, *Humble Apologetics*, 62.

109. Ibbitson, *Polite Revolution*, xii–xiii. This is the same author quoted previously in this chapter as declaring that Canadians have discovered "the golden secret of the third millennia": the art of learning to get along.

The Future of Faith in Canada

Spiritual Openness?

Even though many have left the church in the last few decades, Canadians still express a strong interest in spirituality.[110] The 2010 ISSP survey reports that 68 percent of respondents said that spirituality is important to them, and 42 percent claim to have experienced God's presence.[111] Likewise, Bibby's research shows that "[a]cross the country, some seven in ten adults and more than five in ten teens explicitly indicate that they have spiritual needs."[112] Along these same lines, William Stahl observes, "In everyday discourse it is not uncommon to hear people say that they are 'spiritual' but not religious."[113]

Survey responses about belief in God further illustrate this ambiguity. A majority of the 2010 ISSP respondents reported belief in God, but only the polar opposites seem to have nailed down their beliefs: 30 percent do not doubt that God exists; 7 percent are sure he does not. Closer examination of the responses in the middle, however, reveals enormous uncertainty: "While I have doubts, I feel there is a God" (20%); "I find myself believing in God some of the time, but not at others" (10%); "I don't believe in a personal God, but I do believe in a higher power" (20%); "I don't know whether there is a god and I don't believe there is a way to find out" (11%). Over half agreed with the statement: "I have my own way of connecting with God." Additionally, while three in four agreed that "religious people are too intolerant," the same percentage also believed that "religion helps people find inner peace," and an even higher number affirmed that "religion helps people gain comfort."[114]

While many religious groups read all these statistics as opportunity, a word of caution is in order. Wells warns that this less conventional "spirituality" is postmodern—and pagan—to the core: "It is deeply subjective, nonmoral in its understanding, highly individualistic, completely relativistic, and insistently therapeutic."[115] Drawing a distinction between biblical spirituality and contemporary spirituality, Wells argues that they are not variations on the same theme, but rather they are stark alternatives. He explains, "In the one, God reaches down in grace; in the other, the sinner reaches up

---

110. Roberts, *Recent Social Trends*, 452.

111. International Social Survey, "Religion III," n.p.

112. Bibby, *Beyond the Gods*, 122.

113. Stahl, "Is Anyone in Canada Secular?," 64.

114. International Social Survey, "Religion III," n.p.

115. Wells, *Courage to Be Protestant*, 123.

(or in) in self-sufficiency."[116] While religion makes public truth claims about God, contemporary spirituality is private. It is an internal exploration to find spiritual secrets that will unlock the meaning of life.[117] Survey results lend support for this observation: While only 20 percent of Canadians agree that "Life is meaningful because God exists," three times as many agree that "Life is meaningful because you provide meaning for yourself."[118] Openness to spirituality in Canada does not necessarily translate to openness to religion, much less to biblical faith.

Openness to Religion?

While the polarized ends of the spectrum seem to be fixed, there is evidence that large numbers of both adults and teens in the ambivalent middle have not yet closed the door on religion: among those who attend less than once a month, 62 percent of adults and 40 percent of teenagers indicated they would be receptive to greater involvement *if* they can find it to be worthwhile.[119] Surprisingly, these numbers represent 40 percent of the national population![120] According to Stahl, even many of the "Nones" report a lingering openness to religion: "40 percent say they believe in God; a third engage in private religious practices, and two-thirds eventually reaffiliate with a church."[121]

When Bibby asked "religiously undecided" Canadians what would make their involvement in church worthwhile, only 6 percent mentioned explicit emphases on God and spirituality. Similarly, when "Insiders" (those who attend services at least once a month), answered the question—"*What is the main thing your religious involvement adds to your life?*"—only 21 percent mentioned *God and spirituality*.[122] George Barna's research reveals that these responses are not out of line with what Christians actually experience in worship services. Barna reports, "Eight out of every ten believers do not feel they have entered into the presence of God, or experienced a connection with Him, during the worship service"; half report they have not

116. Ibid., 177.

117. Ibid., 185.

118. International Social Survey, "Religion III," n.p. Only 4% indicated "Life does not serve any purpose."

119. Bibby, *New Day*, 19.

120. Bibby, "Why Bother with Organized Religion?," 99.

121. Stahl, "Is Anyone in Canada Secular?," 70.

122. Bibby, "Why Bother with Organized Religion?," 97–99; italics original. The majority of answers cited *personal enrichment* and *people*.

experienced God's presence in a worship service over the past year; and by their own admission, most do not worship God outside of church services.[123] Tragically, even those who regularly attend church may not do so because they value a relationship with God.

An Angus Reid Public Opinion Poll reveals insights into what Canadians do value most in life. "Having enough free time to do what I want," ranked highest (96%), followed by career success (89%), volunteering (72%), having children (72%), and getting married (55%). Canadians ranked "following my religious beliefs" as least important (46%).[124] While religion may contribute to a person's quality of life, Canadians evidently find the same benefits outside of religion as well. In the area of personal well-being, both religious and non-religious Canadians report roughly the same levels of happiness and meaning/purpose in life.[125] The fact that Canada ranks third in the world in measures of well-being suggests that most Canadians are not likely to look to religion out of a sense of need to improve their lives.[126]

Life after Death?

Research suggests that the one area where religion makes a unique contribution concerns the ultimate question on which science has remained mute: Is there life after death? Those who attend services weekly are five times more likely than those who never attend to indicate that their primary response to the reality of death is hope (45% vs. 9%). This finding is particularly significant because Canadians are clearly intrigued by the question. More than nine out of ten Canadians—regardless of age—say they have wondered about life after death. When asked for specifics, four in ten "believe there must be something beyond death," but admit that they "have no idea what it may be like"; three in ten think "there is probably no such thing"; one in ten believe in reincarnation; and the remaining two in ten believe that life after death involves "some combination of rewards and punishments."[127] The 2010 ISSP poll indicates that while half of Canadians believe in heaven, only a third believe in hell.[128]

Intriguingly, the topics of heaven and hell are making the headlines in Canada. The nation's weekly news magazine *Maclean's* acknowledges

123. Barna, *Revolution*, 31–32.

124. "Having Enough Time," n.p.

125. Bibby, *Beyond the Gods*, 104.

126. "OECD Better Life Index," 15.

127. Bibby, *Beyond the Gods*, 174–75.

128. International Social Survey, "Religion III," n.p.

Canadians' increasing interest in the issue of life after death with a recent article entitled "Why so many people–including scientists–suddenly believe in an afterlife: Heaven is hot again, and hell is colder than ever." The author, Brian Bethune, peruses some of the numerous afterlife books that have continued "to pour down the publishing pike" in response to "the extraordinary popularity of heaven tourism" spawned by Don Piper's 90 *Minutes in Heaven*. Almost all of these books that recount near-death experiences (NDEs) describe heaven as "the presence of unconditional love and the absence of judgment." In contrast, Bill Weiss's volume, 23 *Minutes in Hell*, has failed to generate the same popularity or imitations. Bethune offers the following commentary on Canada:

> We seem to be moving inexorably from a society where organized religion dominates issues of morality—and mortality—but not to the secular promised land of reason. Rather, we are orienting ourselves to a more personal spirituality, at once vague and autonomous. Ordinary sinners increasingly don't believe that they deserve judgment, let alone hell. Theists and atheists alike dispute any earthly authority's right to judge, and both feel NDEs give them reason to hope for something beyond the grave. And many believers confidently expect that God isn't judgmental either.[129]

This increasing discomfort with hell generates a perceived need to erase, soften, or ignore the biblical teaching on the subject.

In October 2012, Canadian filmmaker Kevin Miller released a movie entitled *Hellbound?* Intended to provoke a conversation about hell, the film contains interviews with more than 25 representatives from both sides of this contentious issue. Miller claims that the process of making the movie has been transformative, laying to rest his own fears about hell that have haunted him since he became a Christian at Bible camp at age nine. He explains that the film has made him an evangelist of sorts: "[T]he good news is not . . . 'you don't have to go to hell when you die.' The good news is that death is not the end. This death-driven, fear-driven culture that we find ourselves in isn't all there is. There really is a way out of it—there really is a path toward freedom."[130] The fact that Miller's conclusion does not align with biblical teaching does not seem to concern him. In a postmodern setting if a biblical doctrine like hell is uncomfortable, one can simply choose not to believe it. Likewise, in a polarized society, the temptation is strong for those Christians who do believe in hell to avoid offense by failing to mention it.

129. Bethune, "Heaven Is Hot Again," n.p.
130. Epp, "Hellbound," 24.

Oddly, at a time when North Americans are asking questions about life after death, Christians are either reticent or offer the answer they believe society wants to hear.

Bibby predicts that in an increasingly polarized society, the life-after-death question will continue to surface. He observes, "Reflective people *have to* raise it—and not answer it prematurely. There is too much at stake. . . . [W]ithout religion, hope will be hard to find."[131] Thus, Christians have a unique opportunity—and responsibility—to address truthfully the life and death questions that people are asking. In a polarized society, how can Christians overcome their fear of offending others? How can they do more than pay empty lip service to the gospel in a Canadian cultural context that is characterized by plurality and relativism? Perhaps one of the first steps is learning to see and love the individuals behind the statistics.

IN THEIR OWN WORDS

Across the Generations

Without a doubt, scores of statistics numb the mind to the very real people the numbers represent. In order to put a face on—or at least give a voice to—those who actually live in this culture, this section offers excerpts from ethnographic interviews with a cross-generational sampling of Canadians, arranged in descending order of age.[132] The following comments open a window to listen in on conversations with individual Canadians about the topic of religion.

A tall, soft-spoken gentleman in his early seventies, George is a retired engineer. Recounting his own religious experience, George said that he was baptized in the United Church, attended as a child, and even helped with the youth group in the 1960s. As an adult, however, he saw some of the negative aspects of organized religion, and has since stopped going to church. He explained, "The Jesus I learned about as a kid is different from the Jesus others talk about today. He was loving and forgiving, and not all this other stuff people say today." George believes that the basis of any belief system is the Golden Rule and that is what he tries to live by. He still feels at home in the United Church if he goes there for funerals. He admitted that one day he could see himself going back to religion: "A crisis might draw me back in."

131. Bibby, *Beyond the Gods*, 185.

132. Although these original interviews (October 2011) covered a wide variety of subjects, the following excerpts all relate to the topic of religion. The identities have been altered to protect privacy.

In her sixties, Grace is a spunky, bright-eyed nutritionist who is also a cancer survivor. Unhappy with her childhood experience in a Catholic school, Grace left the Church and was "nothing for a while" until she married and attended the United Church with her husband. Grace says she enjoyed the freedom: "They have no strict dogma. I like that they have a buffet approach. They lay out all the beliefs and say, 'Here it is. You can choose what to believe and what not to believe.' I like that." After a time though, Grace became disenchanted and left organized religion. Grace firmly outlined her beliefs:

> I have a very strong faith in God. It is tremendously important to me. I've seen miracles happen. There is no question in my mind that God is important, but there is no need to belong to a particular religious organization. All the new immigrants in Canada are bringing in religions with them. They are all like the rivers of the world flowing together to get to the same destination—the ocean. They all have the same goal. There is an *Energy*, and I know that when I'm done here, I will go and be a part of it there. It does not matter what they worship or whether their moral rules are right or wrong. I may not agree with them, but we must respect one another, honor their specific days and the history behind all that. It's all good. We're all doing good in our hearts.

Pausing to take a breath, Grace reflected that she felt sorry for anyone who doesn't have faith in something because you need a place to go when all else fails.[133]

Diane is a quintessential homemaker in her mid-fifties. Speaking of her own beliefs, Diane said that she believes there is a Creator and that there is a spiritual aspect in daily life. She explained, "It's a really personal thing. I just do it. There is no necessity to be in a group." She was, however, in a meditation group that has since broken up when the couple who led it moved away. It was a huge part of her life, and she misses it. Diane summarized her ideas briefly:

> I believe in past lives and future lives and in other worlds. I believe there are other dimensions right beside us. I have been following the Mayan calendar rather closely and am interested to see what 2012 brings. I believe it will be a new world full

133. Grace did happen to mention, however, that in spite of her optimism about the good in humans, she found the hockey riots in Vancouver very disturbing. Six months after the interview, Grace's cancer returned as did the chemotherapy. A year after the interview—on the heels of one of several gospel conversations—Grace placed her faith in the reconciling work of Christ. She is now in hospice care.

of peace and contentment, equality and love—the way it might
have been before. It will be a greater cause and a greater thing
yet to happen. But we need to look with loving eyes instead of
fear.

Not interested in reading the Bible, Diane said she gets her understanding of
religion from New Age books and "angel readings."

Johnny came to Canada as a refugee from Southeast Asia almost thirty
years ago. He says his family has maintained their own culture, but he wor-
ries that might change when his children enter high school. He and his wife
run a restaurant, work six days a week, and commute three hours a day.
Johnny explained that he never has time to go to the Buddhist temple, so
instead they offer food and burn incense twice a month at home. He believes
there is nothing after death, and he practices his religion because "you don't
want to make your parents cry." Back home, Christians were mostly poor
people who needed help from the church. Buddhists, like Johnny's family,
did not need help. When asked if any Christians in Canada had ever talked
to him about Jesus or invited him to church, Johnny said one local pastor
had, but he was not interested—"No time!"

Thirty-five-year-old James worked for ten years as an insurance claims
adjuster in Toronto before recently transplanting to Alberta. Although his
parents did not attend church, James's dad wanted a good life for his sons,
so he allowed them to go to the Salvation Army Church on the bus. James's
subsequent commitment to follow the Lord at age twelve has had a huge
impact on the trajectory of his life. He explained that for most Canadians,
"Religion is like where you like to shop or what shampoo you use. It's a
matter of personal preference. It's all good as long as you're not in my space
about it. But where your fist reaches my nose, your rights end." James underscored his intention to raise his children with a very different worldview
than the one he grew up with as a child.

Maria, a "temporary foreign worker" from Southeast Asia, arrived in
Canada about a year ago in order to fulfill her vision of a good life. Unfortunately, the Canadian dream has evaporated for the twenty-seven-year-old.
Because she barely gets enough work to pay her own bills, she cannot send
money to family back home. Raised as a nominal Catholic, Maria shyly explained that several years ago she received a Bible as a gift, but she left it in
cellophane and told it, "I'm not ready for you yet." Desperate for hope in her
current circumstances, Maria recently responded to the gospel with tears
and repentance. Later she described the difference Jesus makes in her life:
"Now I don't wake up angry every day. Instead, I thank God for being there
with me even in the hard times."

"I'm with You": A Cultural Text[134]

The youthful voice of millennials comes through most clearly in the medium that is as familiar to them as their own skin. In place of an interview with a millennial, the following is a brief cultural exegesis of the music video "I'm with You," written and performed by one of Canada's own poet-musicians, Avril Lavigne. Although the song is not about faith, it reveals a plaintive heart-cry that contains fading echoes of the *missio Dei*. For this reason, it may prove to be a useful contact point for sharing the gospel as modeled by Paul in Acts 17: "As one of your own poets has said . . . ."

The World behind the Text

Avril Lavigne was born in 1984 and grew up in Napanee, Ontario (pop. 5,000). Cynthia Fuchs writes, "As a child in a solid middle-class family, [Avril] didn't actually need to rebel, she wasn't into punk, and she didn't learn to skateboard until the 10th grade. Still, she would stand on her bed and sing, 'visualizing thousands of people surrounding me.'"[135] The sixteen-year-old songwriter's dreams came true when she landed a million-dollar-plus contract. The next year her debut album catapulted her to stardom, selling over 6.8 million copies. Her success is in large measure a result of her ability to articulate the full range of teenage emotions, "from sadness and loneliness to exultation and defiance."[136] In some sense, Lavigne—or at least the skate-punk identity she has carefully crafted for herself—speaks on behalf of her entire generation.

---

134. Vanhoozer, *Everyday Theology*, 26, explains that culture is a *work* that produces *cultural texts*—i.e., products, "from the Sears Tower . . . to soccer moms, *The Simpsons*, and shaving cream"—that express a particular worldview and invite others to dwell in that world. Vanhoozer argues convincingly that Christians who want to become competent proclaimers of the gospel must learn to read and interpret both the Bible and culture. In general, this section will follow Vanhoozer's model of cultural interpretation by 1) examining *the world behind the text, the world of the text*, and *the world in front of the text*; 2) locating the cultural text in terms of the presence of God and the fourfold biblical plotline (*Creation, Fall, Rescue, Restoration*); and 3) reflecting on how the gospel addresses the cultural world of the text (35).

135. Fuchs, "A Chick with Edge," n.p.

136. Ibid.

The World of the Text

Lavigne's first album featured a song she wrote called "I'm with You." Following the lyrics—written below—is a description of the music video by the same title, which graphically portrays the world of this text.[137]

> I'm standin' on the bridge
> I'm waitin' in the dark
> I thought that you'd be here by now
> There's nothing but the rain
> No footsteps on the ground
> I'm listening but there's no sound
>
> (chorus) Isn't anyone tryin' to find me?
> Won't somebody come take me home?
> It's a damn cold night
> Tryin' to figure out this life
> Won't you take me by the hand?
> Take me somewhere new
> I don't know who you are
> But I, I'm with you, I'm with you
>
> I'm lookin' for a place
> I'm searching for a face
> Is anybody here I know?
> 'Cause nothing's going right
> And everything's a mess
> And no one likes to be alone (chorus)
>
> Oh, why is everything so confusing?
> Maybe I'm just out of my mind
> Yea eee yeah, yea eee yeah . . . (chorus)
>
> Take me by the hand
> Take me somewhere new
> I don't know who you are
> But I, I'm with you, I'm with you.

The music video of this song begins with the melancholy sound of a bow slowly gliding over cello strings in a minor key. The plaintive notes perfectly capture a profound sense of loneliness that is out of sync with

---

137. Avril Lavigne, "I'm with You," from the Album, *Let Go* (Arista Records, 2002). The "I'm with You" music video directed by David LaChapelle is available online: http://www.youtube.com/watch ?v=dGR65RWwzg8. The YouTube view counts prior to Mar 10, 2010 (pre-VEVO) were at 23,850,982. As of February 2, 2015, the view counts had almost doubled to 46,832,675.

Lavigne's surroundings. Entering a seedy club, the teen forks over some cash, gets her hand stamped, and joins the party scene in front of her—but not really. Dressed in a tank top, black cutoff cargo pants, and black boots, Lavigne looks like a tough, edgy teen, but her kohl-blacked eyes belie a deep vulnerability as she searches the crowd for someone. Everybody else jumps and pulsates in slow motion to inaudible rock music while Lavigne sings her ballad to the beat of a—literally—different drummer.[138] Although she is surrounded by dozens of people, she is utterly alone. Oblivious to her, guys slam into her again and again, as if she is invisible. When one finally notices and dumps his date to make a move, Lavigne angrily shoves him away and exits the club, continuing her search into the night.

The video constantly switches back and forth between the cramped, soundless party and urban scenes of Lavigne walking down the center of an empty street, or standing in front of massive piles of snow. The singer is dead center in the camera frame for the entirety of the video—a technique that is challenging to produce and is obviously intentional.[139] Thus, the focus is on Lavigne and her pain rather than the object of her search. She and the camera are constantly on the move. In the few times that Lavigne pauses, the music reaches a crescendo, and her song morphs into a gut-clenching, bent-double, primal yell that exposes the full extent of her desperation. By the video's end, the volume softens, the music fades, and Lavigne utters one last "I'm with you." But despite her repeated affirmations of relationship, there is no resolution: the song ends and she is alone on the city street, still searching, surrounded by silence.

The lyrics of "I'm with You" reveal a root metaphor of painful absence. The first stanza perfectly captures the loneliness: "There's nothing but the rain / No footsteps on the ground / I'm listening but there's no sound." The opening line—"I'm standing on a bridge"—raises at least the hint of suicidal desperation. Who did she expect would "be here by now"? In the context of the video—and the entire album—it seems likely that the teen is speaking of a relationship with a guy. The second stanza, however, broadens the scope: "Isn't *anyone* tryin' to find me? Won't *somebody* come take me home?" The

138. The director brilliantly creates this sense of an almost alternate reality by shooting the scene much faster than normal and speeding up the music so that when the rate of speed slows down for the final video, the artist's lips are in sync with the music.

139. The only exception is the footage of individual members of the band who are also on the streets, playing alone. Interestingly, these scenes reinforce the sense of movement and search. The drum-less drummer beats the air with sticks; a guitarist plays by an empty phone box; another sits on a bench while a bus passes behind him. The vocalist Lavigne walks down the street passing over the painted letters "Wait Here." When she stands in front of the snow, a train passes behind her below the bridge in the background.

girl longs to find someone who is, in fact, searching for her. She feels this absence so deeply that she declares, "I don't know who you are / But I, I'm with you." The fact that she is surrounded by people does little to assuage her loneliness. They are a crowd, not a community. Although "no one likes to be alone," even the members of the so-called "band" play in ironic solitude. Not only is Lavigne "searching for a *face*," she is also looking for a *place*, "somewhere new." Her world is "a damn cold night" where "nothin's going right," "everything's a mess," and "everything [is] so confusing." Maybe she is "out of [her] mind," but her attempts to "figure out this life" come up empty. In spite of her (eleven) cries of "I'm with you," the video ends and she is still very much alone.

The World in front of the Text

Undoubtedly, many of the 6.8 million fans who have purchased the album have also bought into the worldview of this cultural text. Life is all about them. The world can be cold and hard and it is up to them to figure it out. The self-absorbed search for a meaningful relationship is often painful and may very well come up empty. The great majority of Lavigne's other songs alternately celebrate or lament a seemingly endless cycle of boyfriend-girlfriend startups, betrayals, and breakups. The decade that has elapsed since this recording reveals that Lavigne has personally continued to dwell in the world of this cultural text. Her first marriage lasted only three years. Not surprisingly, Lavigne channeled her pain over the dissolved relationship into her album "Goodbye Lullaby," which she calls "the most raw and vulnerable track I've ever written and recorded."[140]

But apparently Lavigne has not given up the search. On July 1, 2013, the twenty-eight-year-old songwriter married again, this time in a French castle in a ceremony complete with Canada Day festivities. Lavigne described the event: "My body was overtaken by emotion. I saw him and he was so calm and happy. He had a tear coming down and he wiped it away. I felt so good walking to him. It made me feel like a complete woman."[141] For now, Lavigne can say "I'm with you," but it remains to be seen if this latest relationship succeeds in filling her profound sense of absence. Time alone will tell if she continues to dwell in the world depicted in her cultural text.

140. See "Avril Lavigne's Bio," http://www.avrillavigne.com/ca/bio.
141. Ryan, "Avril Lavigne," n.p.

"I'm with You": In View of the Biblical Narrative

Lavigne may not be aware of it, but the lyrics of her ballad reverberate with echoes of the overarching story of the Bible: Creation, Fall, Rescue, and Restoration. Although the world depicted in her text seems far removed from God's good Creation, there are faint memories that things were not always this way. Lavigne intuitively senses that she was created for relationship. In her own words, she is "looking for a *place*, searching for a *face*." Unknowingly, the seventeen-year-old poet penned an expression of the very purposes of God from the beginning: the creation of a people who would worship him and a place where he might dwell in their midst.

But instead of recognizing the presence of a God who walks with her, Lavigne only senses a gnawing sense of profound absence: "There's nothin' but the rain / No footsteps on the ground / I'm listening but there's no sound." Odd details in the video offer glimpses of the "home" she has lost: a phone box stands empty; the painted fruit-and-vegetable stand is inaccessible behind locked bars; and a broken-down oven sits abandoned on the sidewalk. The world of the cultural text is the broken world of the Fall, and Lavigne summarizes its curse: "It's a damn cold night" where "nothing's going right / And everything's a mess." Despite the fact that "no one likes to be alone," her aching desire for community fails to find fulfillment. The relationship Lavigne craves finds no satisfaction in a crowd where everyone ignores her and people rudely shove past. The world should make sense, but the girl's fruitless attempts to understand lead her to question her own sanity. For all her introspection, she fails to see that she contributes to the brokenness. By casting her "self" as the main character of her narrative, the songwriter has wrested the focus away from the God who made her. Usurping his rightful place, she can no longer hear the voice of God or sense his presence. No matter where she searches, her quest is futile.

Lavigne intuitively knows that this desperate situation calls for a Rescue—someone who will come take her by the hand and take her home. Sensing she is lost, she pleads, "Isn't anyone trying to find me?" The one who is searching desperately hopes someone is searching for her. Feeling displaced, Lavigne also senses the need for a place—somewhere new—where things are put right. Most of all, she craves a meaningful relationship with another human being. Convinced of the possibility of Restoration, even in her hopeless circumstances, she cries out repeatedly, "I don't know who you are, but I'm with you! I'm with you!" Tragically, the teen seems ignorant of the presence of the One who made her for that very purpose.

"I AM with you": A Reflection on the Gospel

The young woman in the music video needs to hear that someone is indeed searching for her, but he is not the one she expects to find. The truth is, even if she finds a meaningful human relationship, it will ultimately disappoint because no one can fill the absence that she senses. That longing exists because she was created for a purpose—to live in the presence of the holy, loving, Almighty God. She is not the main character of the story; HE is. He fashioned the world to be a sanctuary, a place where he would dwell with the people he created. Made in his image, they are designed to fill it with worship—with perfect poems of praise that reflect his glory.

The confused teen needs to know that she is not "out of [her] mind"; life should make sense. Her intuitions—though distorted—point toward the truth. Something is dreadfully wrong: the world is broken, and she has lost a home. She needs to hear the biblical metanarrative that explains there is an alternate reality to the cultural world she is submerged in. God has launched a rescue mission to restore both the people and the place he created. She needs to listen to the hundred-fold echo of God's promise to his people through the ages—"I AM with you." For God so loved the world that he sent his Son, Jesus, who stepped into this sinful world as Immanuel—"God with us"—dwelling in the midst of his creation in a tent of flesh. His love, as great as his justice, paid for her sin by his death on the cross; his power, as great as his mercy, raised him from the dead.

Jesus is now preparing a dwelling place for all who will receive him, and he will "come and take [them] home." Meanwhile, he will never forsake them; the Spirit will indwell them as a temple—both individually and corporately. Jesus' already-not-yet kingdom has begun, and soon the risen King will come take his redeemed bride home to "somewhere new"—a newly redeemed creation. There, in the new heaven and earth, God will dwell in the midst of his purified people forever.

Tragically, it seems as if this young poet does not recognize that the face and place she is searching for—"I don't know who you are"—are found in Jesus. Until someone loves the Avrils of the world enough to share with them this good news, they will restlessly try to fill this dreadful absence with somebody or something else. They need to hear that the presence of God, in fact, already surrounds them; they belong to him and are accountable to him. His incredibly gracious rescue comes at the unimaginable cost of the life of his Son. Jesus' all-out sacrifice calls for a reciprocal all-in surrender: "I'm with *you*." Those who repent and place their trust in him find abundant life in his tabernacling presence—both in this life and in the life to come. If, however, they reject his unfathomable love and mercy, they must resign themselves to an even more unfathomable Absence—banishment for all eternity from the presence of God.

Long before Avril voiced her heart-cry in song, a Hebrew poet penned a similar stanza from a biblical worldview:

> Nevertheless, I am continually with you;
> you hold my right hand.
> You guide me with your counsel,
> and afterward you will receive me to glory.
> Whom have I in heaven but you?
> And there is nothing on earth that I desire besides you.
> My flesh and my heart may fail,
> but God is the strength of my heart and my portion forever.
> For behold, those who are far from you shall perish;
> you put an end to everyone who is unfaithful to you.
> But for me it is good to be near God;
> I have made the Lord God my refuge,
> that *I may tell of all your works* (Ps 73:23–28; italics added).

One who has found shelter in the tabernacling presence of God has the responsibility and privilege of pointing out the way for others through a worshipful witness.

— 6 —

Implications for Gospel Witness

Reading the story of the Bible through a missional lens in chapters 2–4 helped bring into focus several missional dimensions in both the Old and New Testaments. Briefly surveying the current Canadian context in chapter 5 highlighted certain cultural characteristics that shape today's society, including pluralism, postmodernism, increasing polarization, and an urban population. This chapter now triangulates these two previous sections in order to discern implications for mission and gospel witness. The goal of this practical reflection is the development of a practice of evangelism that is at the same time biblically grounded and culturally relevant.

ADDRESSING THE CHALLENGE OF CULTURAL PLURALISM

Pluralism is not a new cultural phenomenon. In the Old Testament, for example, the nation of Israel naturally rubbed shoulders with the surrounding cultures and international travelers who streamed through her ancient thoroughfares. The people of God were thus constantly exposed to the localized deities who populated their neighbors' pantheons. Similarly, in the New Testament era the gospel circulated in a cultural milieu where religious diversity included a panoply of Greek and Roman gods and goddesses, mystery religions, and various competing philosophies. Undoubtedly, exclusive claims about the one true God in any pluralistic culture have provoked

193

scorn or even antagonism. How then do Christians sharing their faith today address charges of ethnocentrism?

In a culture that cherishes pluralism, it is important to emphasize that God himself created and cherishes diversity. As the one true God, he is the universal God of all humankind. He created every human being from the very first man and woman; therefore, all humanity shares a common source, dignity, and unity. Because every human bears the image of their Creator—even though tragically marred by the fall—every person should reflect his glory and worship him. The diversity of his creation magnifies the greatness of his glory. In Genesis 10, the Table of Nations exemplifies this variety in the genealogy of Noah's descendants "by their clans, their languages, their lands, and their nations" (Gen 10:5, 20, 31). Likewise, the multitude of redeemed worshipers assembled around the throne in Revelation magnificently illustrates God's purpose for this diversity as representatives from "every tribe and language and people and nation" worship God (Rev 5:9). But how does God accomplish his mission to redeem this culturally diverse throng in the time that elapses between these two passages?

Twin Poles of Mission: Universality and Particularity

Even the limited survey of Scripture presented in chapters 2–4 reveals that God's plan involves an intricate balance between the twin poles of mission: universality and particularity. In a departure from the universal setting of Genesis 1–11, the biblical story turns to a particular man, Abraham, whom God promised to bless with land and descendants. Significantly, God also made the universal promise that in Abraham ". . . all the families of the earth shall be blessed" (Gen 12:3). The rest of the Bible traces the descendants of this particular family—the Israelites—up to the birth of the promised Messiah, who would reconcile the world to God. Clearly, God elected Abraham and his descendants for his own name's sake and for the sake of the nations.

As the story of the Israelites unfolds, the pattern in Scripture shows that God has always had the nations in view. Many times God's powerful displays of his sovereignty among the nations resulted in the deliverance of his people and the proclamation of his name in all the earth. Some of those who heard of his fame chose to fear God and to cast their lot with the people of God. When the Israelites disobeyed and failed to display his glory, God handed them over to the surrounding nations, declaring his sovereignty even through their failure. The prophets show an increasing awareness that the nations would one day stream to Jerusalem and praise the God of Abraham, Isaac, and Jacob.

The intimations of universality in the Old Testament become bold declarations in the New Testament. The Gospels declare that Jesus is "the true light, which enlightens everyone," "the Lamb of God, who takes away the sin of the world" (John 1:9, 29). Yet even the most inclusive statements also clearly articulate particularity: "For God so loved the world, that he gave his only Son, that whoever believes in him should not perish but have eternal life" (John 3:16). God's gracious gift of salvation rests in the selfless sacrifice of the tabernacled-in-flesh Son of God and descendant of Abraham. After his resurrection, Jesus' commission to his followers was breathtaking in its universal scope, yet particular in its content: "[M]ake disciples of all nations, baptizing them in the name of the Father and of the Son and of the Holy Spirit . . ." (Matt 28:19); "repentance and forgiveness of sins should be proclaimed in his name to all nations" (Luke 24:47); "you will be my witnesses in Jerusalem and in all Judea and Samaria, and to the end of the earth" (Acts 1:8). The book of Acts then chronicles the spread of the gospel across geographical borders and cultural barriers.

Paul describes the resulting multicultural miracle of the early church as a unified sanctuary, the dwelling place of God:

> [H]e himself is our peace, who has made us both one and has broken down in his flesh the dividing wall of hostility . . . . For through him we both have access in one Spirit to the Father. So then you are no longer strangers and aliens, but you are fellow citizens with the saints and members of the household of God. . . . [T]he whole structure, being joined together, grows into a holy temple in the Lord. In him you also are being built together into a dwelling place for God by the Spirit (Eph 2:14–22).

Peter also uses a temple metaphor to describe the church whom God assembles "like living stones" into a spiritual house. The apostle explains how God has incorporated all believers into the family of God: "[Y]ou are a chosen race, a royal priesthood, a holy nation, a people for his own possession that you may proclaim the excellencies of him who called you out of darkness into his marvelous light. Once you were not a people, but now you are God's people; once you had not received mercy, but now you have received mercy" (1 Pet 2:9–10). God forges even former enemies—Jews and Gentiles—into one new people, a holy nation.

The Bible closes with a glimpse of God's mission fulfilled in the gloriously diverse multitude that stand before the throne of God—their voices blending in multilingual harmony to the praise of the one who by his own blood ransomed a people for God from every corner of the world: "Therefore they are before the throne of God, and serve him day and night in his

temple; and he who sits on the throne will shelter them with his presence"
(Rev 7:15).

A Reflection on Canada's Cultural Mosaic

The concept of a "cultural mosaic" has become a root metaphor for the
nation of Canada. Over the last four decades Canadians have cherished
the concept of a cultural mosaic and enshrined it in law. But although the
majority believe that multiculturalism has been good for Canada, buy-in
to the concept of a mosaic society has dropped to 30 percent. There are
those who think that Canada's policy of multiculturalism strains the unity
of the nation. Unfortunately, this noble ideal seems easier to envision than
to achieve.

The root metaphor of a cultural mosaic affords an excellent opportunity for gospel witness. Christians need to applaud the concept and explain
that the ideal of a multicultural mosaic stems from the very heart of God.
Canadians need to hear that far from being ethnocentric, the Christian
faith results in a true cultural mosaic that beautifully depicts the fulfillment of God's mission from the beginning of time. Because sin dwells in
human hearts, however, the ideal of a multicultural mosaic can only be
fully achieved as people repent, believe, and receive the Spirit of Christ who
transforms human hearts and takes up residence there. Redeemed believers
retain those marvelous aspects of cultural diversity that bring God glory, yet
they are joined together by more than mere geography and a willingness to
coexist. As brothers and sisters in Christ, they are truly family. Together they
form a new people, a holy nation, united in their devotion and allegiance
to a common King. *This* cultural mosaic is not an ephemeral "golden secret
of the third millennium"[1] but the far better mystery of the ages: "[God's]
purpose, which he set forth in Christ as a plan for the fullness of time, to
unite all things in him, things in heaven and things on earth" (Eph 1:9–10).
Perhaps an even better metaphor for this mystery is a beautiful stained-
glass window, in which the multicolored hues of the whole redeemed people
of God are gloriously transformed by the presence of the light of Christ
in their midst. Affirming the value of multiculturalism as part of a biblical
worldview will go a long way toward defusing the charge that Christianity
is ethnocentric.

As an outpost of the kingdom of God, the church should resemble
this perfected transcultural mosaic more and more—especially as communities in Canada become more culturally diverse. The increasing cultural

1. Ibbitson, *Polite Revolution*, 4.

pluralism is a wonderful opportunity for believers who have a global commission to make disciples of all the nations. No longer does one have to board an airplane to reach out to the peoples of the world. The nations have arrived in droves on our very doorstep.[2] Of all people, believers should embody the ideal of a cultural mosaic by welcoming immigrants into their churches, into their homes, and into their hearts. Churches can demonstrate love by meeting practical needs such as helping immigrants navigate the obstacles of educational, medical, and legal systems. After all, God has always instructed his people to show special concern for "the foreigners" living in their midst (e.g., Lev 19:34).

This same compassion should extend to visible minorities as well. On the surface it may seem as if Canada has escaped some of the deep racial fault lines that threaten its southern neighbor from time to time. But an honest look beneath the surface reveals that Canada has its own fissures— notably those that separate First Nations from the rest of society. And although the cultural differences between English and French-speaking Canadians are not visibly obvious, the historical animosity between these two cultures threaten the actual physical unity of Canada. These are just a few of the areas where Canadian Christians should demonstrate the universal love of Christ for all peoples. Genuine care for immigrants and minorities will in itself be a powerful witness to a lost world that followers of Christ are not self-centered exclusivists. In addition, as God adds diversity to his living sanctuary, the church should display the love and unity that are the authenticating marks of the indwelling Spirit (cf. John 13:35; 17:21–23). The world should recognize that this is something only God can do.

Focusing on the Uniqueness of Christ

Just as demonstrating the genuine love of Christ goes far beyond mere tolerance, it also goes beyond meeting immediate needs. God calls his people to be a kingdom of priests through whom he will bless the nations of the world. In context, God's promise to bless all the families of the earth through Abraham's descendants was ultimately fulfilled in the person and work of Jesus Christ. This universality, however, does not mean universalism. Scripture clearly teaches that the gloriously diverse assembly of those who worship the Lamb of God for all eternity does not include everyone. Therefore, the greatest love a follower of Christ can show another person—regardless of

---

2. Of course this local opportunity does not negate the responsibility of making disciples in the far-flung corners of the earth that remain unreached and unengaged. The church must renew its commitment to taking the gospel to the ends of the earth.

their ethnicity or cultural background—is at the point of his or her greatest need. While believers must share the gospel visibly in deeds, they must also share the gospel verbally in words.

Most newcomers will experience varying degrees of displacement for a period of time. This transition may very well be a window of openness to new relationships and new ideas. In sharing the gospel with newcomers, believers must be sure to differentiate between Western cultural Christianity and a biblical understanding of what it means to follow Jesus. As the preexistent second person of the Trinity, he is the Creator and Sustainer of *all* things. He has *all* authority in heaven and on earth. Christ is the culmination of *all* the sanctuaries; he is the meeting place between God and humanity (2 Cor 5:19). Jesus is the tabernacle, the temple, the high priest, and the sacrificial Lamb of God who takes away the sin of the *world*. Because the risen Christ sits on the judgment seat, *every* person who has ever lived will face him before entering a final destiny (Matt 25:31–46). Jesus is the *only* way to the Father; his is the *only* name under heaven for salvation (John 14:6; Acts 4:12). Commissioned as ambassadors and compelled by the love of Christ, Christians have the responsibility and privilege of delivering the message of reconciliation that people of every culture desperately need to hear (2 Cor 5:14–21). Even in today's cultural context, followers of Christ dare not shrink back for fear of being called ethnocentric. The good news of the gospel is for everyone.

ADDRESSING THE CHALLENGES OF POSTMODERNISM

Unmasking Relativism and Consumerism

The missional dimensions identified in the study of God's tabernacling presence address the challenges of philosophical pluralism and postmodernism as well. Like pluralism, relativism is not new. In some sense, relativism lay at the root of the first sin in the garden of Eden. Adam and Eve usurped the place of God, rebelling against his authority, because they wanted to be able to determine right and wrong for themselves. In the days of the Judges, relativism was certainly in vogue as "Everyone did what was right in his own eyes" (Judg 17:6; 21:25). In twenty-first-century Canada, this same axiom shows up in statements such as "Everything's relative" and "Right and wrong are a matter of opinion." In a fallen world where the final arbiter is oneself, people often assume the right to fabricate truth, morals, ethics, and even identity according to their own individual tastes.

As discussed in chapter 5, today's pervasive consumerism extends to the area of religion, as well. Although humanity's perception of reality is now distorted, people retain broken shards that hint at vestigial truths: the utter senselessness of life without meaning; an unquenchable longing for an absent Other; and lingering whispers of an eternity planted in their hearts. Without a transcendent center, however, the responsibility falls to the individual to piece these bits of truth together, filling in entire sections with a sort of homemade spiritual putty. The result is an eclectic spirituality that relativism asserts is just as valid as any other religion. Tragically, the resulting designer worldview falls far short of God's purpose for creation.

The opening phrase of the Bible, however, sweeps away any such pretensions of inventing one's own truth system or religion or purpose for life. God's revelation begins with an audacious statement of centeredness: "In the beginning God . . ." (Gen 1:1).[3] In spite of postmodern assertions to the contrary, the Bible affirms there *is* a transcendent being who was present before it all began. As the main character in the story of the world, he designed the heavens and the earth, and he populated it with people. He is a God on mission, directing the trajectory of human history to his desired end: God will dwell in the sanctuary of his creation in the midst of a people who perfectly reflect his glory. Only a shift in worldview will enable postmoderns to see that someone other than themselves is at the center of reality.

Dismantling Worldviews

A study of the tabernacling presence of God reveals different ways of dealing with rival worldviews. At times in the Bible God himself deconstructed the distorted worldviews of Israel's neighbors in a powerful display of his

---

3. In view of postmodernists' objection to logocentrism—the idea that language is the carrier of meaning—it is intriguing that the Fourth Gospel expresses the Creation account as follows: "In the beginning was the Word, and the Word was with God, and the Word was God" (John 1:1). This same Word who brought all things into being, became flesh, tabernacled among his people, and revealed his heavenly Father to them (John 1:14, 18). In spite of postmoderns' claim that the limitations of language prohibit a knower from knowing anything with certainty, they fail to acknowledge that God has communicated truth in both the written and living Word of God. Although Derrida is in some sense correct in saying that readers cannot "step out of [their] skins" to discover meaning, the Second Person of the Trinity has stepped *into* skin as Truth Incarnate. Admittedly, a believer's cultural context colors his understanding of revealed truth, and absolutely no human can claim to know a transcendent God fully. Still, God's revelation of himself is sufficient for salvation. Although the Bible is a unified grand narrative—or metanarrative—its legitimacy is not based on an appeal to universal reason, but rather on God's gracious revelation of himself and his mission.

sovereignty. The plagues, for example, obliterated the Egyptians' pagan pantheon; the mere presence of the ark of testimony felled the Philistines' idol to Dagon; and the fire from heaven that consumed Elijah's altar brought the Baal worshipers to their knees. At other times, however, God used prophetic voices to expose the emptiness of religiosity. Isaiah laid bare the impotency of man-made idols; Jesus condemned the self-righteousness of the Pharisees; and Paul exposed the ignorance of the Athenians. While God may still choose to display his sovereign power visibly on occasion, the use of apologetics today falls more in line with the prophets of old.[4]

Most Canadians have a worldview that is radically different from a biblical worldview. But how can they discover that their worldview misses the mark? Situations where people are not willing to give the biblical worldview a hearing may initially call for the use of apologetics to help them realize the deficiencies in their own personal worldview. While cultural pluralism makes the expression of differing worldviews legitimate, it should not lead to mindless acceptance of all viewpoints as equally true. For example, the same survey that shows that more than 50 percent of Canadians claim right and wrong are relative, also reports that over 70 percent believe Canadian values are changing for the worse. The inconsistency is obvious.

Apologist Francis Schaeffer believed that it is impossible for people to live out the inconsistencies of their worldview. He observed that people typically build a protective roof over the most vulnerable point of their worldview. Schaeffer, therefore, adopted an evangelistic strategy that pushed people to examine the conclusion of living out of their presuppositions, in essence, "taking the roof off," in order to expose them to an avalanche of reality. As Schaeffer points out, even a committed relativist will object to having boiling tea poured on his head because he is unwilling to live with the world created by his presuppositions.[5] Schaeffer observes, "When the roof is off, each man must stand naked and wounded before the truth of

4. Craig, *Reasonable Faith*, 21, writes that John Stackhouse once described Craig's apologetic debates on university campuses as "a Westernized version of what missiologists call a 'power encounter.'" Intriguingly, Penner, *End of Apologetics*, also describes an apologist as a prophet/apostle who appeals to revelation from God—as opposed to a genius/expert who appeals to reason like the modern apologist Craig, whom Penner strongly critiques. While Penner calls for a major shift to a postmodern apologetic paradigm (12), he does clarify that he is not against apologetics *simpliciter*: "pointing out where a given challenge to Christian belief is flawed or highlighting how it is that Christianity makes good sense of the world" (7). Meanwhile, Craig, *Reasonable Faith*, 18–19, argues that because a postmodern world is unlivable and therefore a myth, people remain deeply modernist; thus, apologetics remains a strategic tool even in a culture influenced by postmodernism. Obviously, this is a transitional era for the field of apologetics, a full discussion of which is beyond the scope of this book.

5. Schaeffer, *The God Who Is There*, 110.

what is."[6] Across the board, people prefer to be treated as those made in the image of God rather than as a random collection of atoms—regardless of their worldview.

Canadian apologist John Stackhouse Jr. allows that there may be occasion for such extreme measures, but only when one is absolutely confident of the Holy Spirit's leading. Instead, Stackhouse maintains that the majority of believers are more likely to "dislodge a shingle or two, or offer a concerned opinion about the structural integrity of the roof rather than undertake its wholesale demolition."[7] He cautions that the downside of using strong tactics is that although the apologist may win the argument, he or she may lose the battle amidst charges of arrogance or triumphalism.[8] Obviously, the intended audience is a major factor in choosing a strategy, whether it is a debate in a public forum or a private conversation among friends. In a kind, loving manner, Christians need to listen carefully and then help others recognize the inconsistencies within their worldviews.

For example, religious pluralists often say that just as there are many roads to the top of a mountain, all religions lead to the same destination. Believers should point out in response that all religions have mutually exclusive truth claims, not just Christianity. Muslims believe in one god; Hindus believe in many gods; formal Buddhists do not believe in god; and Christians believe that God is a unity of three persons. Who then will be on top of the mountain? Because the possible answers are mutually exclusive, they cannot all be true. Similarly, when someone insists that all religions are the same, an effective way to question the veracity of the statement is a simple question: "Really?"[9] A follow-up question would be to ask if there is no difference between infant baptism and infant sacrifice.[10] Most people would quickly admit there is indeed a difference.

Likewise, when relativists speculate that God and heaven are whatever anyone believes them to be, it may be helpful to point out that does not work with persons. If a Christian tells his middle-aged pluralist neighbor that he believes her father is an eighteen-year-old marine who loves ballet, she will surely protest. If he tells her he is going to visit her dad who lives with Bono

6. Ibid., 141.

7. Stackhouse, *Humble Apologetics*, 187.

8. Ibid., xvi. Stackhouse's humble, dialogical approach will likely resonate with most Canadians. Cf. chapter 10, "Guidelines for Apologetic Conversation," 161–205.

9. Newman, *Questioning Evangelism*, 58–59. This kind of gentle prodding exposes the untenable nature of statements like the following from the ethnographic interviews: "It does not matter what they worship or whether their moral rules are right or wrong. . . . It's all good. We're all doing good in our hearts."

10. Stackhouse, *Humble Apologetics*, 6.

in a trailer park in Nunavut, she will correct him. After all, her dad has an identity. In the same way, God is a person who has revealed his identity and character in the Bible; the only way to meet the Father is through Jesus Christ; and eternal life is to know him, the only true God, and Jesus Christ, whom he has sent. Many truths, like gravity, are narrow, but that in no way proves them false. Faith must rest in a trustworthy object. Saving faith must rest in the unique person of Jesus Christ. Telling his story is essential to establishing a biblical worldview.

Reclaiming the Biblical Metanarrative

The tabernacling presence of God study reveals that the biblical narrative itself confronts rival worldviews. For example, although the creation story does not specifically mention a rival worldview, the simple narration of Genesis 1 counters every other possible cosmology. The orderly biblical account of the one sovereign, living God, who created the world from nothing and made humanity in his image, underscores the sharp dissimilarities between the God revealed in Scripture and the anthropomorphic deities that populated ancient Near Eastern myths. The same is true of the biblical account of the flood as well. By nature, the biblical metanarrative is a missional polemic.

Recounting the story of Scripture is central to developing a biblical worldview. Moses adjured the Israelites to rehearse the mighty acts and commands of God continually in the daily *Shema*, the annual Passover meal, the yearly festivals, and the stone memorials. The psalmists and prophets repeatedly recall the biblical narrative. The New Testament shows that Jesus used the overarching biblical framework to explain the gospel to the two disciples on the road to Emmaus. Even though these two had witnessed the events of the first Easter weekend, Jesus elucidated the gospel, "beginning with Moses and all the Scriptures" (Luke 24:27; cf. Luke 24:44). In Acts, Stephen traced God's tabernacling presence across the biblical metanarrative at his defense (Acts 7). Likewise, Paul underscored the biblical framework that is the basis of his own gospel witness: "For I delivered to you as of first importance what I also received: that Christ died for our sins *in accordance with the Scriptures*, that he was buried, that he was raised on the third day *in accordance with the Scriptures . . .*" (1 Cor 15:3–4; italics added). Throughout the canon, God's revelation of himself is wedded to the biblical narrative.

Unfortunately, today's evangelistic strategies often rely on gospel presentations that were developed sixty years ago when biblical literacy was high. Even worse, many Christians who are dissatisfied with these presentations do not share their faith at all. The decline in biblical literacy mentioned in the previous chapter should significantly impact the way believers share the gospel. In this setting one must be cautious about leading someone to pray a "sinner's prayer" after a five-minute gospel presentation. In a pluralistic setting, even the mention of the word "God" carries very different meaning for different people. Anchoring a gospel witness to the biblical narrative is therefore crucial in a Canadian context.[11]

As part of a process that leads to a sweeping worldview change, it is important that a Christian witness build a biblical framework and worldview for the message of the gospel. There is certainly a need for resources to equip believers to witness in this changing context. Timothy Keller explains: "In general, I don't think we've done a good job at developing ways of communicating the gospel that include both salvation from wrath by propitiation and the restoration of all things. Today, writing accessible presentations of the gospel should not be the work of marketers but the work of our best theologians."[12] D. A. Carson concurs, suggesting that training new believers for effective witness in today's setting calls for the development of "a short gospel presentation that weds biblical theology and systematic theology and tells the storyline of the Bible."[13] The church needs to equip believers to communicate the story of the gospel clearly in today's cultural context.

A significant opportunity for gospel witness also lies in postmoderns' fondness for narrative. Studying the example of Jesus, a marvelous storyteller, believers can learn to tell stories from the Scripture—and tell them well. Christians need to be ready to share their own faith story and communicate how it connects to the biblical metanarrative. Importantly, believers should ask others to share their life stories and listen well. This may open doors to overlay the person's story with the template of the biblical narrative, pointing out where it connects with their story as well as where it confronts.

Building a Biblical Framework

The tabernacling presence of God and the mission of God play a significant role in building a biblical framework as a foundation for the gospel. This is especially important when sharing the gospel in a culture where biblical

11. A fairly strong caveat is in order here. The importance of the biblical metanarrative does *not* mean that new believers must wait until they know everything before sharing. Anyone who has had a life-transforming encounter with Jesus can—like the blind man—declare, "One thing I do know, that though I was blind, now I see" (John 9:25).

12. Keller, "The Gospel," 111.

13. Taylor, "Conversations," 166–67.

literacy is in steep decline. One way to communicate the overarching story of God's activity and mission is the fourfold plotline of the biblical meta-narrative: Creation, Fall, Redemption, and Restoration.[14] This plotline also answers basic worldview questions that are universal: Who am I? Why am I here? What is wrong with the world? What is the solution? What does the future hold? Additionally, any one of the four elements may be the springboard for a gospel conversation. For instance, a friend's lament that the world is a mess may prompt observations that refer to either Creation or Restoration: "You're exactly right, but it wasn't always like this," or "That's true, but it won't always be this way." Depending on the friend's openness, the conversation may evolve into the full narrative or simply address one of the four elements at that time.

THE FOURFOLD PLOTLINE IN TERMS OF PRESENCE

While the witness will want to use the biblical narrative to tell the story of the four main events, at the same time it may be helpful to conceptualize the fourfold plotline in terms of the tabernacling presence of God and his mission. For example, Figure 1 in the appendix illustrates the original purposes for creation in Genesis 1–2.[15] God made people in his image in order that they might perfectly display his glory in worship, and he created the earth as a place where he might dwell in their midst. Figure 1A shows how God placed the first couple in Eden as a sanctuary where they might enjoy communion in the unmediated presence of God. He commissioned them to be fruitful and multiply and to fill the earth with worshipers. Figure 1B pictures the intended future consummation of this first great commission, as the sanctuary of Eden expands to fill the whole world with worship of a glorious God.

Figure 2, however, illustrates the mission of God after the story of the fall narrated in Genesis 3. While Figure 2A "Creation" is still the same as 1A, Figure 2B "Fall" shows the globally catastrophic results of sin: humanity's relationships with God, with one another, and with creation were irrevocably broken, and there is nothing humanity can do to recapture that perfect communion. God expelled Adam and Eve from Eden and barred them and their descendants from having access to his unmediated presence in this

14. "The Story" by Spread Truth Publishing, 2011, is a brief gospel summary that follows the fourfold biblical plotline of Creation, Fall, Rescue, Restoration.

15. This figure and all subsequent figures are located in the appendix. The triangle shape illustrates the essence of the mission of God which lies at the nexus of God, people, and place. Others have also used a triangle shape to illustrate the triadic configuration of God, people, and land. See chapter 2, page 53, footnote 175.

sanctuary. Figure 2C "Redemption" illustrates God's gracious mission to redeem humanity and restore creation. This rescue mission—to reconcile the world to God through Jesus Christ—spans the bulk of Scripture, from Genesis 3 all the way to Revelation 20. Because this third element in the plotline covers such a lengthy chronological period, Figure 2C, which represents it, is actually three-dimensional. The witness can expand this part of the gospel as time allows and the Spirit leads (as explained in the following paragraphs). Figure 2D "Restoration" expresses the fulfillment of God's mission as he dwells with and in his redeemed people in the new heavens and earth described in Revelation 21–22. Ultimately, God will fulfill his intended purpose as expressed in Figure 1B: He will fill both people and place with his unmediated presence, and all of the new-creation sanctuary will delight in the worship and glory of God.

A Study of the Tabernacling Presence of God

While an explanation of the gospel based on the fourfold plotline of the Bible is an excellent starting point, most gospel presentations still tend to jump somewhat abruptly from the fall directly to the cross. Unfortunately, this approach seems to devalue the entire Old Testament and may leave seekers with many more questions. The witness may want to include at least a basic summary of the preparation for the Messiah.[16] If time and interest allow, however, perhaps the best way to build a biblical worldview is through a study of the Bible over several weeks in community with others who are living out this worldview. A more thorough and process-oriented approach would also build a much more comprehensive biblical framework for the gospel.

Figure 3, for example, illustrates how an in-depth study of the tabernacling presence of God could expand Figure 2C in greater detail. Imagine that Figure 2C is actually three-dimensional—a three-sided pyramid emerging from the paper with the cross at its pinnacle. The left-hand portion of Figure 3 is this same three-sided pyramid rotated for viewing from a side-angle. This "prism" represents the *missio Dei* in the Old Testament timespan after the fall with its global consequences. In anticipation of the promised deliverer, the prism narrows as it traces the lineage of Abraham's descendants

---

16. For example, it may be helpful to explain that even after the fall, God graciously allowed repentant sinners to worship him as long as they met his requirements for worship, including animal sacrifice. As part of his unfolding rescue mission, God chose one man, Abraham, and promised to bless all the nations through his descendants. Over time, God continued to meet with his people in the tabernacle and temple. All of this prepared them for the coming of the promised deliverer as foretold by the prophets.

and their placement in the Promised Land—up to the pinnacle where God, people, and place converge in the Incarnation. The cross in Figure 3 represents the entirety of Jesus' earthly life—from the announcements of his birth to his ascension. Of course, the cross also symbolizes the heart of the gospel: Jesus' death, burial, and resurrection. The left-hand prism is mirrored by a second prism on the right-hand side that represents the *missio Dei* in the New Testament era of expansion. The right-hand prism begins at the pinnacle where God, people, and place converge at Pentecost and expands globally as the church—the temple of the Holy Spirit—makes disciples from Jerusalem to the ends of the earth. The dashes and arrows indicate that this missional expansion continues in every age until some moment in the future when Jesus returns and ushers in the restoration where the holy-of-holies presence of God fills both people and place as a new-creation sanctuary. The central focal point of Figure 3 is the heart of the biblical narrative and the nexus of the mission of God—where God, people, and place meet in Jesus Christ, the God-tabernacled-in-human-flesh sanctuary.

A study of the tabernacling presence of God would begin by tracing the dotted line on the left side, examining each of the various sanctuaries where God met with his people across the biblical metanarrative. This study would be thoroughly Christocentric because it would reveal that the person/work of Christ is not merely the culmination of all these sanctuaries, but that as the true temple, Jesus is the basis for their very existence. The presentation of the gospel would follow in its proper biblical context. The study would then trace the tabernacling presence of God along the right-hand side of Figure 3 as the Spirit poured out at Pentecost expanded the mission of the early church. The Spirit continues to indwell the church in every place, in every generation, empowering them to fulfill Christ's commission until the day when Jesus returns and consummates the restoration. At that time God will tabernacle in the midst of his redeemed people and restored creation, and he will be their temple-less sanctuary—forever.

CONTRASTING WORLDVIEWS

Whether one uses the basic fourfold plotline or a more in-depth study of the biblical narrative, both approaches need to communicate that coming to faith in Christ entails adopting an entirely new worldview. Just as the previous study in chapters 2–4 attests, God's people throughout the ages have found that a biblical worldview inevitably clashes with the prevailing worldviews of the surrounding culture. Presenting the gospel in terms of exchanging worldviews helps to ensure that a person understands the ramifications of making a commitment to Christ. Knowing that conversion involves a transfer of allegiance to the King and his kingdom is also important for discipleship in that it helps prepare a new disciple for both spiritual growth and spiritual battle.

The graphics in Figure 4 illustrate the contrast between worldviews. Figure 4A represents a natural person's worldview.[17] According to the research in chapter 5, some believe that there is nothing beyond the visible material world of people and place; the inner gray triangle is all that exists. The majority, on the other hand, believe that there are forces and/or beings outside of the visible world, whether good (light) and/or evil (dark) in varying degrees according to the particular worldview. In Figure 4A the dashed lines of the inner gray triangle suggest the majority's mistaken understanding that they can connect to God in their own way.

Figure 4B shows the life of natural persons from the perspective of a biblical worldview. While hints of God's common grace may make them vaguely aware of God's presence, they cannot connect with him on their own terms—thus the solid line on the inner triangle's right side. A compulsion to worship drives them to fill that void with a god of their own making. Their lives are therefore oriented away from God rather than toward God. Although they are likely unaware of it, as a result of the fall, all people are members of the kingdom of darkness by default.

In contrast, Figure 4C illustrates Christ-followers who have been transferred out of the kingdom of darkness into the kingdom of light. Under conviction, they have repented of their sin, turning away from it and turning toward God. They have believed that Jesus, the Son of God, paid the penalty for their sin in his death on the cross. By faith, they have trusted in the resurrected Lord and have received his life-giving Spirit. The Holy Spirit dwells in them and helps them to understand the things of God. Believers who have died to self and the things of this world are to "[fix their] eyes on Jesus, the pioneer and perfecter of faith" (Heb 12:2). Like their forefathers in the faith, they recognize that "here [they] have no lasting city, but seek the city that is to come" (Heb 13:14). Having declared allegiance to the King, they have already begun to experience his rule and presence in their lives even though they remain in the world. The white dots in the gray triangle represent the in-breaking of the kingdom of light both in the lives of individual believers and in the gathered church. Kingdom citizens are called to be a holy sanctuary, display people living out kingdom principles in contrast to the surrounding world, so that others will recognize God's presence in

17. Paul describes such a person in 1 Cor 2:14: "The natural person does not accept the things of the Spirit of God, for they are folly to him, and he is not able to understand them because they are spiritually discerned."

their midst: "God really is among you!" They are still vulnerable to temptations and assaults from the kingdom of darkness, but when they are filled with the tabernacling presence of the indwelling Spirit, they begin to know his peace and power, his fellowship and fruitfulness. For now, the citizens of the two kingdoms exist in this world side by side (like the wheat and weeds of Matthew 13; the sheep and goats of Matthew 25), but a day of judgment awaits them all.

THE GREAT DIVIDE

In "The Great Divide," Figure 5A pictures a final day when Jesus returns, and God rends the two kingdoms asunder. He deposes the rulers of the kingdom of darkness and casts them into the lake of fire (Rev 20:10). In the end, the kingdom of darkness is no kingdom at all, as represented by the dashed lines (Figure 5B, left). There is no community among its former citizens—only a gnawing isolation; there is no place of belonging—only an empty homelessness. And most grievous of all, there is no sense of the intimate presence of God—only a profound absence.

In stark contrast, God will gather all those who are already citizens of the kingdom of light into the eternal sanctuary of his unmediated presence (Figure 5B, right). This future reality has been God's intention since the dawn of creation and the ultimate goal of his redemptive mission (cf. Figures 1B and 2D). In the kingdom of heaven there will be no pain or grief or tears, and the redeemed people of God will know intimate communion as the purified bride of Christ. In the restored heaven and earth, they will experience only eternal security and abundant provision. This new creation is an actual place populated by believers in resurrected bodies, not an immaterial spiritual existence in the clouds of heaven. Best of all, the pale shades of mutual indwelling that believers experience in part in this life—the love, joy, glory, and unity of John 15 and 17—will radiate with unimaginable vibrancy when God dwells with and in his people.

Not surprisingly, given the contrast, Paul describes this day in sobering terms:

> This will happen when the Lord Jesus is revealed from heaven with his mighty angels in flaming fire, inflicting vengeance on those who do not know God and on those who do not obey *the gospel of our Lord Jesus.* They will suffer the punishment of eternal destruction away from the presence of the Lord and from the glory of his might, when he comes on that day to be glorified in his saints and to be marveled at among all who have believed,

because our testimony to you was believed (2 Thess 1:8–10; italics added).

The distinction between these two outcomes is unambiguous: "eternal destruction away from the presence of the Lord" or eternal worship in the glory of his tabernacling presence. As highlighted by the italics above, the way that a person gains access into God's eternal presence is by hearing and believing the testimony of Christ-followers, and by obeying the gospel of Jesus.

Benefits of a Biblical Framework for Witness

Sharing the gospel from this biblical framework has many advantages. This approach is especially appropriate for people who are not very familiar with the Bible. Like the pattern of God's revelation of himself in Scripture, this approach grounds propositions about God in the biblical narrative and in biblical theology.[18] The gospel begins with *this* God and *his* story; *he* is the main character. Starting with God and his purposes for creation before mentioning human needs sets the tone for a God-centered understanding that leads to a commitment to Christ.[19]

This presentation of the gospel is also missional from the very beginning because it explains God's purposes for creation in terms of God's mission. Therefore, a person who commits to follow Christ will already have a rudimentary understanding of the mission of God and his or her role in it. Developing materials that trace the singular theme of God's tabernacling presence could make this missional study reproducible. The repeated focus on God's dwelling in the midst of his people also helps the hearer understand that the Christian faith really is a relationship and not religiosity or simple assent to certain doctrinal statements. Truly, the greatest commandment is to love God. This biblical framework also anchors biblical imperatives to biblical indicatives—just as God gave his covenant law in the context of his mighty deliverance of the Israelites. This is especially important for those who mistakenly believe Christianity is "just a list of rules."[20]

18. Although tracts like "Four Spiritual Laws" and "Steps to Peace with God"—written sixty years ago—have been used effectively in the past, truncated gospel presentations like these are not as appropriate in contexts with low biblical literacy.

19. In contrast, a man-centered approach may produce adherents of Moralistic Therapeutic Deism—the growing belief that a distant God exists to meet people's needs, make them happy, and help them get along with others. See Smith and Denton, *Soul Searching*, for a thorough explanation of Moralistic Therapeutic Deism.

20. Some approaches to evangelism begin by asking people whether or not they

Another benefit is that this approach challenges those who may mistakenly think they are Christians. The very first steps of discipleship begin with understanding the framework of Scripture and the difference between a biblical worldview and a natural worldview. It also gives hearers an understanding of the kingdom of darkness and the kingdom of light, and that commitment to Christ involves declaring allegiance to a King. Thus, it also teaches the "already-not yet" nature of the kingdom.

A comprehensive explanation of the gospel also shows not only what followers of Christ are saved *from* but also what they are saved *for*. Salvation is not merely that the individual believer can escape hell—although that is significant and should be mentioned. The Spirit of God makes his home in believers now, both individually and corporately. The new creation begins now for the person who is in Christ and the transformation continues. The Christian, however, also has the incredible hope that God will also redeem the entire cosmos. The new heaven and earth will be a real world—but one without sin and without sorrow. The redeemed people of God will have perfect communion with each other and with God. God himself will dwell with and in them for all eternity. The centrality of the community of faith also helps guard against the temptation to try and live out one's faith independently from the church.

Furthermore, sharing the gospel from a biblical framework strengthens believers. Meditating on the gospel-centered metanarrative of the Bible helps believers renew their minds according to a biblical worldview. Reclaiming the biblical metanarrative is also essential for capturing the hearts of the next generation. The Lord repeatedly instructed the Israelites to review his mighty acts and commands before their children. Sadly, the book of Judges recounts their failure to do so and the resulting tragedy of a generation who did not know the Lord of their forefathers. This teaching is extremely important in the teen years when youth are crystalizing their worldview and developing their identity. As research shows, however, it is just as critical for the transition between childhood and teen years when so many drop out of church and eventually walk away from faith. Making disciples of all nations must not neglect the innermost concentric circle of evangelism—members of the immediate family.

But sharing the gospel obviously does not stop there. Believers need to be intentional about praying for God to use them to share the good news

---

have kept each of the Ten Commandments. This method may actually reinforce the idea that Christianity is only a code of conduct. While this approach may work among those with a religious, moralist background, it has serious drawbacks for those who have little understanding of the identity and character of God and do not readily accept the authority of Christian Scripture.

of Jesus in all their circles of influence. Knowledge of the Lord and these biblical truths is inherently missional. Believers should testify and share the truth of the gospel—even in a culture that finds the topic uncomfortable. A final advantage of sharing the metanarrative is that some of the more difficult teachings grow out of the framework of the Bible as a whole where they find balance with other themes such as the universality of the gospel.

The Biblical Metanarrative and Restrictivity

The biblical metanarrative not only helps to build a framework for sharing the gospel, but it also helps to answer some of the objections people have to restrictivity. A study of the tabernacling presence reveals that God has restricted access into his presence since the third chapter of the Bible all the way through to its last page. When the first human couple sinned, God expelled them from his unmediated presence. From that moment on, God in his mercy still receives worship—but only from those who meet his parameters for worship. God graciously condescended to dwell among his people in the tabernacle, but strict cleanliness laws and gradations of holiness were necessary to protect the people from the inherent dangers of living in close proximity to a holy God. At Isaiah's commission, for example, the prophet experienced both the overwhelming majestic presence of a thrice-holy God and the terrifying realization that he was a sinner in desperate need of atonement—which God graciously provided.

The endless parade of animal sacrifices offered at both tabernacle and temple anticipated the final, once-for-all sacrifice of the very Son of God who by his own blood opened a way through the curtain of his flesh, gaining access for purified worshipers to enter into the holy-of-holies presence of God. While Jesus' offer of salvation is universal, the consistent testimony of Scripture reveals that access into the glorious presence of God is only for those who have washed their garments in the blood of the Lamb and whose names are written in his book of life. All others will be permanently excluded for all eternity. Knowledge of these two final realities—hell and the kingdom of heaven—is inherently missional. The believer who comprehends the metanarrative of the Bible will be compelled to testify and share it with others.

As research in the previous chapter shows, Christians have the unique opportunity to speak to the nearly universal question of life after death. Those who know what Christ has in store for believers have a wonderful message of hope to communicate to the 90 percent of Canadians of all ages who wonder about this question. The entire cosmos awaits redemption, and one day Christ will return and put all things right as he creates a new heaven and earth. There will be no more pain or suffering for those who have washed their garments white in the blood of the Lamb (Rev 7:14). As the bride of Christ, the redeemed people of God will bask in his presence for all eternity, and eternal life begins the moment they come to know God the Father thorough Jesus the Son (John 17:3). Christians need to lead with this glorious message of hope when they share the gospel.

But when some refuse to receive Jesus' great-exchange offer—his righteousness in exchange for their sin (2 Cor 5:21)—they need to hear the flip side of hope. Rejection of Jesus carries unimaginable consequences: eternal separation from God's presence. Even so, a Christian witness should communicate the message with a concern that matches the compassion of Jesus who—just days before his crucifixion—longed to gather the citizens of Jerusalem under his wings, but they were unwilling (Matt 23:37).

ADDRESSING THE CHALLENGE OF POLARIZATION

Answering Canadians' Objections to Restrictivity

Sharing the exclusive claims of Christ is not always welcome. Canadians see themselves as extremely polite, civilized, and inclusive. They enjoy their reputation as global peacekeepers and pride themselves on a system of socialized medicine that leaves no one behind. There is, however, one thing that Canadians do not tolerate well, and that is perceived intolerance. They simply cannot imagine that some people would be excluded from the presence of God in heaven. Most would admit that a few—like Hitler—might deserve such a fate. The average Canadian then tries to imagine other categories that Christians would exclude from heaven—say, homosexuals or Buddhists. He or she takes up their offense and declares, "How dare Christians be so unbelievably narrow-minded?"

Perhaps the best option is to agree. Christianity is, in fact, so narrow that *all* are excluded: gays and gossips, Buddhists and Baptists, murderers and Mother Teresa. Their ranks include both the average Canadian and certainly the Christian trying to witness to him. No one who has ever sinned can enter the presence of a holy God—and that includes absolutely everyone. This shocking truth results not in a level playing field, but rather, a leveled playing field. No one is left standing. Sin condemns them all—equally: "None is righteous, no, not one" (Rom 3:10).

It is in light of this dreadfully bad news that the gospel becomes marvelously good news indeed: "For our sake he made him to be sin who knew no sin, so that in him we might become the righteousness of God" (2 Cor 5:21). As the canonical study of previous chapters demonstrates repeatedly, the mission of God is actually radically inclusive. Not wishing that any should perish, God desires that *all* come to repentance (2 Pet 3:9; italics added here and below). Paul expands on this same theme in 1 Tim 2:4–7:

> [God] desires *all* people to be saved and to come to the knowledge of the truth. For there is one God, and there is one mediator between God and men, the man Christ Jesus, who gave himself as a ransom for *all*, which is the testimony given at the proper time. For this I was appointed a preacher and an apostle . . . a teacher of the Gentiles in faith and truth.

Although the offer of salvation is universal, the above verses show that it calls for repentance and knowledge of the truth of Jesus' atoning sacrifice. This "knowledge of the truth" is intrinsically missional: those who know of this salvation share it with others.

The following analogy may help Canadians understand restricted access into the presence of God. Those persons who desire to become Canadian citizens must submit to a lengthy and costly process in which they must provide proof of the following: financial stability, innocence of any criminal activity, general good health, and freedom from any communicable diseases. Then, after passing residency requirements, language exams, and a citizenship test, they must declare by oath that they will be loyal to the Queen, that they will obey Canada's laws and customs, and that they will fulfill the duties of a Canadian citizen. After all, even as inclusive as Canada is, it would be foolish to admit people who would be a threat to the nation or its citizens.

In comparison, the kingdom of heaven is, in some ways, much more inclusive. God grants access to those who freely admit their spiritual bankruptcy, who confess their treasonous guilt, and who acknowledge that they are not only infected with sin but are, in fact, spiritually dead and in need of resurrection. The one thing required of all who desire to enter the kingdom of heaven is that they transfer their allegiance to the King. In response, God transfers repentant sinners from the domain of darkness into the kingdom of his beloved Son, who has purchased their redemption at the cost of his own life's blood (Col 1:13–14). He lavishes his love on those who believed in him when they heard the gospel of their salvation and guarantees their future inheritance with the seal of his Holy Spirit who dwells in their midst (Eph 1:13–14). In gratitude, they enjoy not only the privileges and responsibilities of kingdom citizenship now but also communion with the King who dwells with and in his redeemed people. Undoubtedly, no matter how well the witness explains or defends the gospel, not all will embrace it. As the survey of Scripture in chapters 2–4 repeatedly demonstrates, the good news of God's gracious activity is divisive: while some receive it gladly, others will reject it outright.

A Biblical Perspective on Polarization

Christians should not be surprised at the increasing polarization in Canada. After all, Jesus cautioned his disciples that just as the world hated him, their Master, the world would also hate his followers. He warned them that persecution would come to them as well because they bear his name. Even in the face of persecution, however, followers of Christ can have peace because Jesus promised them, "I am with you always, to the end of the age" (Matt 28:20). He encouraged his disciples that the presence of the Spirit would come and remain with them (John 15:18–27).

The book of Acts records the fulfillment of Jesus' words. When Stephen was stoned to death after proclaiming that the presence of God was independent of man-made structures, he was comforted by the presence of the Spirit and a vision of Jesus standing with him—literally. With his last breath, Stephen followed Jesus' example, praying that God would forgive his tormentors (Acts 7:54–60). Later, both Peter and the author of Hebrews encouraged their readers undergoing persecution by reminding them of the tabernacling presence of God in their midst. John, likewise, fortified his readers with a vision of the saints who—having endured the great tribulation—now enjoy the sheltering presence of the Lamb on his throne (Rev 7:14–15). Scripture repeatedly shows that even in a polarized society, Christians' fear and love of the Lord who is with them should outweigh their fear of reprisal for proclaiming the truth of the gospel.

In an increasingly polarized society where the mere mention of Jesus' name is polemical, many Christians find it difficult to share that Jesus is the *sole* meeting place between God and humans and that outside of Christ there is no salvation. The riptide of public opinion tempts believers to soften, muffle, or abandon biblical teachings on hell and the exclusivity of Christ. The pull is relentless and many have drifted far from their theological moorings. The only acceptable option for believers, however, is faithful obedience to the one who purchased their redemption at such a great cost.

The exclusive claims of Christ are inevitably divisive. Sometimes it may help to frame them in context of the biblical narrative or to explain them with a thoughtful apologetic. Still, they may provoke insult and hostility—or perhaps, one day, outright persecution. The more Christians proclaim truth in a world that has abandoned truth, the more likely they will encounter derision or anger. Reginald Bibby observes,

> When the person with faith—complete with conviction, earnestness, and a missionary spirit—meets the person with no faith, the end result is seldom conversion. It may be martyrdom. Conversely, the person with no faith who belittles and ridicules the person with faith runs the risk of finding that such a devotee does not necessarily subscribe to the guideline of "turning the other cheek."[21]

David Wells cautions, "When rival worldviews are in play, it is not adaptation that is called for but confrontation: confrontation not of a behavioral kind which is lacking in love but of the cognitive kind which holds forth 'the truth in love' (Eph 4:15)."[22] In the face of escalating opposition, believers must not only display genuine humility but also the courage needed both to hold fast to the truth and to hold forth the truth. At all times believers need to give a defense for their hope. This combination of love and boldness may carry more weight than any apologetic or eloquent exposition of the gospel. After all, the best apologetic is a life that is transformed by the indwelling Spirit of God.

ADDRESSING THE CHALLENGE OF AN URBAN POPULATION

The City and the Mission of God

A study of the tabernacling presence of God shows that the city has a significant role in the *missio Dei*. God's redemptive plan actually culminates in a city called the New Jerusalem. Symbolic of the intimate communion God always intended to share with his people, this city is also called the Bride of Christ. As chapter 4 explains, the New Jerusalem is not streets and buildings per se but rather the vibrant community of the redeemed people of God. Purified and adorned for her husband, the city is a perfect cube, a holy-of-holies sanctuary, the dwelling place of God. This New Jerusalem radiantly reflects the glory of the unmediated presence of God, fulfilling God's purpose since the dawn of Creation.

As a result of the fall, however, the city often epitomizes the heights of human sinfulness. It seems that when humans dwell in close quarters,

21. Bibby, *Beyond the Gods*, 71.
22. Wells, "The Supremacy of Christ," 34.

the effects of sin multiply exponentially. The Tower of Babel, for example, has come to symbolize the collective arrogance of humans who attempt to glorify themselves rather than God. Likewise, the mere mention of Sodom and Gomorrah connotes the depravity of sin and the judgment of God. The extravagant descriptions of the wealth of "Babylon the Great" are matched only by the horrifying details of her total destruction in Revelation. A city without the presence of God can harbor unimaginable evil and provoke God's judgment.

Nevertheless, Scripture also yields glimpses of God's heart for the brokenness of the city. When the wickedness of Nineveh reached a tipping point, God sent the reluctant Jonah to warn them, and he spared the city when they repented. He explained, "[S]hould I not pity Nineveh, that great city, in which there are more than 120,000 persons who do not know their right hand from their left, and also much cattle?" (Jonah 4:11). When the disobedient Israelites experienced judgment themselves, the Lord instructed the exiles in Babylon: "[S]eek the welfare of the city where I have sent you into exile, and pray to the LORD on its behalf, for in its welfare you will find your welfare" (Jer 29:7). Similarly, Jesus lamented the destruction that awaited Jerusalem (Matt 23:37).

Christians in the twenty-first century need to see the nation's urban population as God does. Like all metropolitan areas, Canada's cities are filled with sin and ripe for judgment. Yet, they are also filled with broken people who need to hear the marvelous good news of a compassionate God who wants to redeem them and tabernacle in their midst. If believers want to reach the world for Christ, they will have to focus not only on the hinterlands but also on the cities because that is where the vast majority of people live. In order to penetrate these large metropolitan areas, many believers must follow the call of Christ to fulfill his mission in every place. The church needs to challenge believers to be open to the possibility of a missionary call to key urban areas. Christians who are already living in cities may need to learn to view their city through the lens of the mission of God.

The ethos of an urban population—alienation, dis-placement, and longing for community—may be a point of contact that connects with today's city dwellers. Being surrounded daily by thousands of people only exacerbates the sense of anonymity and loneliness. The preponderance of social media fails to whet the ravenous appetite for authentic relationships and authentic community. Bereft of the communion they were created for, people crave intimacy, community, and a home where they belong. As the cultural exegesis of Lavigne's song attests, this profound absence affords an excellent opportunity for the church to model and offer the communion that God intended to share with his creation. In both Testaments, it is the shared experience of the presence of God in their midst that forges the people of God into an authentic community.

A Display People and Contrast Community

The canonical survey of previous chapters reveals that God intends for humanity to be a people who display his presence. In the beginning God created humankind in his image so that they might display his glory by knowing and worshiping their Creator. He commissioned the first couple to be fruitful and multiply, thereby filling the earth with worshipers who would likewise display his glory. After the fall, God chose Abraham through whose descendants he would bless the nations of the world. God's presence and power on public display in the lives of the Israelites proclaimed both his name and his glory to the surrounding peoples.

This Almighty God condescended to take up residence in a tent in the midst of his people, filling it with his glory. He would continue to live among them only if they followed his careful instructions for animal sacrifices that covered their sin. His tabernacling presence required a holistic holiness that penetrated every aspect of their lives—not just their worship, but everything from their food and clothing to their business and sexual practices. He then set his display people on center stage before the nations in order to attract their curiosity, admiration, and eventually, their conversion. When the Israelites failed to display his glory, God displayed it himself, even as he disciplined his own.

In the New Testament, God displayed his glory through his God-tabernacled-in-flesh Son. This sinless Jesus condescended to take sinful humanity's place on the cross, thus securing the redemption of a new people for God from every nation, among whom he will dwell in the new creation. Until then, these followers of Christ are—individually and corporately—the temple of the Holy Spirit who dwells in them. Filled with the presence and power of the Spirit, believers are to display his holiness and fruit in every aspect of their lives before a watching world. Shattering any dualistic division of sacred versus secular, believers should do *everything* to the glory of God.

This study shows that the presence of a holy God requires a holy people. His followers should therefore stand out in contrast to the darkness of the world around them. Their way of life should testify to the character of God in their midst. Their answered prayers should manifest the power of the God who is with them. A reflection of their communion with God, their love for one another should identify them as followers of Christ; their unity should give credence to the gospel they proclaim (John 13:35; 17:23).

Their good works and good behavior should not only silence those who slander them, but they should also open a line of missional conversation and even draw some of their detractors into the faith (Matt 5:16; 1 Pet 3:13–17). Believers' compassion for the marginalized and concern for social justice should reflect God's concern for widows, orphans, immigrants, and the poor. Their love for a broken world should earn them the same epithet—"friend of sinners"—that described their Lord (Matt 11:19). In other words, the presence of a holy God living in the midst of his people distinguishes them from their neighbors.

The number of times that the word "should" occurs in the previous paragraph is an indicator that something is amiss in the church today. Although these descriptors admittedly refer to an ideal church, they should be present in some degree in every church. Unfortunately, however, today the stark contrast is not so much between the church and the world, but between what the church *should* be and what it often is in reality. Indeed, the temptation of Canaanization—assimilation into the surrounding culture—looms large in every generation. Surrounded by the world, believers often succumb to the world. Having adopted the spectacles of Western consumerism, many are now unable to perceive these lenses through which they view the world. For example, when Canadians who regularly attend church responded to a question regarding what church involvement adds to their lives, only one in five mentioned answers involving God and spirituality. Christians may need to remember that it is only the presence of God that constitutes a church.

When the Corinthians acted like the world around them, Paul called them back to the truth of God's tabernacling presence: "Do you not know that your body is a temple of the Holy Spirit within you, whom you have from God? You are not your own, for you were bought with a price. So glorify God in your body" (1 Cor 6:19–20). He also implored believers, "[P]resent your bodies as a living sacrifice, holy and acceptable to God which is your spiritual worship. Do not be conformed to this world, but be transformed by the renewal of your mind . . ." (Rom 12:1–2). Christians' lives should display the presence of the indwelling Holy Spirit in contrast to the spirit of the world.

Failure to live as contrast people will eventually mean a failure to be God's display people. There is a real danger of going through the motions of church minus the presence of the living God. As Jesus warned, churches that have lost their first love and refuse to repent will be removed from their place (Rev 2:5). The fact that the United Church, Canada's largest Protestant denomination, is closing churches at a rate of one per week should be a wake-up call for all Christians in Canada to consider whether or not God is present in their midst. When God threatened to withdraw his presence after the Israelites plunged headlong into idolatry, Moses protested that he would rather remain in the desert than lead God's people without God's presence: "If your presence will not go with me, do not bring us up from here. For how shall it be known that I have found favor in your sight, I and your people? Is it not in your going with us, so that we are distinct, I and your people, from every other people on the face of the earth?" (Exod 33:15–16). Christians today need to be just as desperate for the presence of God in their midst.

Witnessing Worshipers: Attractional and Missional

A survey of the tabernacling presence of God across the canon reveals that God is always the one who initiates worship. Because God is transcendent as well as immanent, human beings cannot rely on their own devices to connect with God. As the Israelites discovered time and again, the Almighty cannot be domesticated or manipulated. The Creator is inscrutable; therefore, human creatures have no right to define his identity for themselves. He has, however, revealed himself through both his written and living Word. As the only proper object of worship, God sets the parameters for proper worship. He has graciously provided a way—the only way—to enter his holy presence: the once-for-all blood-sacrifice of the sinless Lamb of God—his own Son. Amazingly, the Father still seeks those who will worship him in spirit and in truth (John 4:23).

Authentic community, therefore, firstly has an upward dimension: it begins with worship. God invites his people to dwell in his presence and to dine at his table in communion with him and in community with one another (cf. Deut 12:7; John 14:23; Rev 3:20; 21:3). Both in individuals and in the corporate body of Christ, the presence of the indwelling Spirit spills over in worship: "Be filled with the Spirit, addressing one another in psalms and hymns and spiritual songs, singing and making melody to the Lord with your heart, giving thanks always and for everything to God the Father in the name of the Lord Jesus Christ . . ." (Eph 5:18–20). True worship naturally bears witness by testifying to the reality, character, and presence of the living God.

The tabernacling presence of God on display in worship will be recognizable and attractive to those in whom the Spirit is at work. In the Old Testament, Zechariah describes this eventuality: "Thus says the LORD of hosts: In those days ten men from the nations of every tongue shall take hold of the robe of a Jew, saying, 'Let us go with you, for we have heard that God is with you'" (Zech 8:23). In the New Testament, Paul explains what can happen in worship: "[I]f all prophesy, and an unbeliever or outsider enters, he is convicted by all, he is called to account by all, the secrets of his heart are disclosed, and so, falling on his face, he will worship God and declare that God is really among you" (1 Cor 14:24–25). True worship attracts those who are being drawn to Jesus by the Spirit of Christ. Clearly, the foundation for witness is "with-ness."

An authentic Christian community secondly has an inward dimension. The nascent church in Jerusalem was just such a church. The believers in this new community were devoted to one another; they met in each other's homes and ministered to one another's needs. A community of believers filled with the presence of the Holy Spirit will inevitably attract others. As Luke records, "[T]he Lord added to their number day by day" (Acts 2:47). Paul explains that being filled with the Spirit not only overflows in worship but also includes "submitting to one another out of reverence for Christ" (Eph 5:21). The apostle then expands on this concept, sketching out what mutual submission looks like in marriage, in the family, and in the workplace (Eph 5:22–6:9). This kind of authentic community naturally attracts those who are hungry for true spirituality. People in every place deserve not only to hear the gospel communicated clearly, but also to see the gospel displayed in community. This observation points to the critical need for a commitment to planting churches that reproduce.

Authentic community thirdly has an outward dimension. Being filled with the tabernacling Spirit of God not only results in worship and fellowship but also in bold proclamation of the gospel. In the last moments that Jesus spent with his disciples before ascending to the Father, he commanded them, "But you will receive power when the Holy Spirit has come upon you, and you will be my witnesses in Jerusalem and in all Judea and Samaria, and to the end of the earth" (Acts 1:8). With the coming of the Spirit, the early church had an outward focus and a global mission. All were filled with the Spirit and proclaimed God's Word with boldness (Acts 4:31). This same commission and empowering presence of the Spirit rest on the church today. All churches should therefore be communities that are both attractional and missional.

Today's believers would do well to follow Paul's strategy in Acts 17. Although the apostle was provoked by the sin-saturated idolatry of the city, he intentionally shared the gospel with the Athenians in a contextually relevant way. He adapted the method he used depending on the specific population segment he was engaging—whether he proclaimed the Messiah in the synagogues, or "gossiped the gospel" in the marketplace, or debated the philosophers in the academy. Paul's keen cultural observations led him to connect with his audience using effective points of contact—for example, the altar to an anonymous god and lines from Greek poetry. Paul's sensitivity to culture, however, did not mean he tiptoed around truth so as not to offend. Instead, he used his knowledge of the culture to zero in on and expose misplaced religiosity. Paul proclaimed the resurrection from the dead and boldly called for repentance in view of the coming judgment. While some mocked, others were curious enough to discuss it further, and a few believed his message. Regardless of the outcome, Paul was absolutely dependent on the presence, power, and direction of the Holy Spirit for mission.

A Reflection on Today's Church

Like Paul, today's disciple-makers must depend on prayer and the indwelling Spirit for direction and insights for ministry. The unique challenges of reaching a multicultural, mostly urban population require tools and practices for sharing the gospel that were formerly considered the purview of missiologists. Missionaries in cross-cultural settings have long considered cultural exegesis, contextualization, and understanding worldviews to be indispensable skills. In light of the current cultural context in North America, Christians will find these tools just as crucial in sharing the gospel in cities where traditional worldviews are shifting and populations are increasingly pluralistic.

In a post-Christian society, believers will have to build relationships and earn trust in order to overcome negative stereotypes of Christianity. Canadians' longing for community is a natural opening for Christians to meet and engage people either by initiating affinity groups or by integrating into preexisting ones. Although Canada ranks third in the world for well-being, there is still a need to display God's compassion among the marginalized. Believers also need to be looking for opportunities to minister to people in crisis situations that shatter assumed worldviews: for example, divorce, illness, death, loss of job, disasters, etc. As the ethnographic interviews in chapter 5 attest, Canadians are more open to the gospel when the things in which they have placed their trust are shaken. While Christians need to keep in mind the power of the gospel to transform cities, they must not lose sight of Jesus' commission to make disciples in a way that actually transforms the city one person at a time. The unique thing believers have to offer the world is the one thing the world does not have but truly needs—an encounter with the one true God through Jesus who has revealed him.

The obvious erosion in church affiliation, attendance, and even belief in God has awakened many Christians to the reality of Canada's pronounced religious recession. While there is a general awareness that something is wrong, few agree on a solution. It is painfully obvious that the decision of Mainliners to alter the message in order to attract the world has failed monumentally, but today's Emergents seem to be headed down the same path. Decades of slow growth among Evangelicals suggests that simply marketing attractional ministries has likewise failed to impact the escalating lostness in Canada.

In the scramble to fix the problem, some have grasped at biblical emphases but sometimes without biblical balance. Even worse, sometimes Christians have become embroiled in arguing over which emphasis is more important. Some obsess over right doctrine (orthodoxy) and end up wrangling over theological differences that the Bible seems content to hold in tension. Others focus on right practice (orthopraxy) and single-mindedly pursue one thing above all else, whether it be social justice, community transformation, evangelism, church planting, missions, or apologetics. Still others fixate on right affections (orthopathy) and focus on charismatic demonstrations of emotion or spiritual disciplines. While right doctrine, practice, and affections are all essential, there is a danger in concentrating on these foci to the exclusion of the Lord. Author C. S. Lewis highlights the potential problem: "There have been men before . . . who got so interested in proving the existence of God that they came to care nothing for God himself . . . as if the good Lord had nothing to do but to *exist*. There have been some who were so preoccupied with spreading Christianity that they never gave a thought to Christ."[23] Barna's startling statistic that the great majority of believers do not experience the presence of God in the worship service nor do they worship God outside of weekly services indicates that there are many in church who "care nothing for God himself."

A new word might express the concept of focusing rightly on the presence of God who tabernacles in the midst of his people—perhaps "*orthosancty*." Whatever the word, the concept is absolutely crucial because the other three foci build on this foundation. God has revealed his presence in past sanctuaries: the tabernacle in the wilderness, the temple in Jerusalem, and in his uniquely Incarnate Son. Now his Spirit dwells in the "sanctuary" of individual believers and the corporate body of the church. Ultimately, he will dwell with and in his sanctuary-people at the consummation. In this interim period, Christians must not become so focused on "doing" church that they fail to commune with the God who is there. Believers need to ask the Lord to examine them and their churches to see if they are rightly related to the God who is tabernacling in their midst. What the Spirit reveals

23. Lewis, *Great Divorce*, 73–74; italics original.

will likely call for repentance, a plea for revival, and a renewed commitment to walk in the Spirit and to be on mission with God.

MISSION OF GOD

What happens when believers fail to be a display people living in a contrast community? Even then God's mission cannot be thwarted. The Israelites failed repeatedly, and still God's mission progressed. Most of the New Testament churches fell far short of the ideal described in Acts 2, and still God's mission moved forward. The fulfillment of God's mission does not depend on the success of the churches in Canada. If a church fails, the Lord may remove its lampstand, but his Spirit will move through someone else. There are indications that a shift may already be underway in the global theological center of gravity. While the lamp of the church in Europe grows dim, and the light of the church in North America begins to wane, a new day seems to be dawning in the global South.

Although it would be an unspeakable tragedy for the church in Canada to be sidelined, God will still accomplish his mission to fill the earth with the knowledge and praise of his glory. God is the primary evangelist, and the *missio Dei* moves forward at his direction, by his power, according to his plan. The Spirit dwells in believers—guiding, compelling, and empowering them to witness. The Spirit also encounters sinners—convicting, regenerating, and transforming them. Thus, the tabernacling presence of God is both the means and the ultimate goal of God's mission to redeem humanity and dwell with and in them in his redeemed creation.

—— 7 ——

Conclusion

The synthesis of the previous chapter has generated several implications for mission and gospel witness. Naturally, the missional dimensions identified in this study address more than just one aspect of the cultural context. The resulting practical reflection therefore resembles a web of implications more than a linear enumeration. For summary purposes, however, this conclusion highlights certain implications for each characteristic of the current cultural setting along with some related observations.

First, a study of the tabernacling presence of God reveals that God forges all redeemed humanity into a unified sanctuary where his Spirit dwells in their midst; a gospel witness should therefore model this transcultural unity. In light of today's increasing cultural pluralism, churches should awaken to the providential opportunity for global mission on their doorstep by celebrating cultural diversity and embracing the universality of the mission of God. At the same time, they should renew their commitment to the global scope of the commission to make disciples among every people group in every place. Believers should emphasize that their faith is not ethnocentric; rather, Jesus came to reconcile all humanity to a right relationship with the one, true, universal God. That universality, however, does not imply universalism: the uniqueness of the person and work of Christ requires that a Christian witness exalt the name of Jesus and focus on his exclusivity for salvation. A gospel witness must therefore maintain a biblical balance of both universality and particularity. As the Lord adds to his body, the church should exemplify a true multicultural mosaic.

Second, a study of the tabernacling presence of God reveals that there is a transcendent God at the center of creation and his truth is absolute; a gospel witness should therefore confront rival worldviews such as philosophical pluralism and postmodernism. Although God is immanent as well as transcendent, sinful humans cannot connect with him by relying on their own devices. The fall has so marred human reason and perception that they cannot discover God's truth, yet God has graciously revealed truth that is sufficient for salvation in his written and living Word. Relying on the indwelling Spirit for guidance, Christians should expose the inconsistencies of a worldview that is founded on relativism and religious consumerism. Because our culture is increasingly unfamiliar with the Bible, Christians should also use the biblical metanarrative to build both a biblical framework and a biblical worldview for gospel witness. Believers should take advantage of postmoderns' fondness for narrative by telling stories from the Bible as well as sharing their own and others' stories.

Third, a study of the tabernacling presence of God reveals that God's truth has always been divisive; therefore, in an increasingly polarized society, a gospel witness must proclaim biblical truth with unwavering courage. Because our culture now holds tolerance as one of the highest virtues, Christians need to be prepared to discuss those issues that provoke anger and misunderstanding in a way that demonstrates the love of Christ. They should anticipate and be ready to answer tough questions about their faith— with humility and compassion. At the same time, they must be committed to hold fast to biblical truth in the face of derision or even possible persecution. For example, although almost all people wonder about life after death, they bristle at the idea that heaven has restricted access. Believers have a marvelous message of hope to share, yet the hope of eternity in the presence of a holy God also carries a corresponding warning of hell. A gospel witness that is biblically faithful must include both. If people persist in refusing God's gracious offer of salvation, they need to know the consequences of their rejection.

Fourth, a study of the tabernacling presence of God reveals that God has created people for community with himself and with each other; a gospel witness should therefore model authentic community before a watching world. In a broken world, the shift to an urban population has resulted, ironically, not in more community, but rather in an ethos of alienation and displacement. An aching sense of absence and longings for intimacy, community, and a place that feels like home can be points of contact for sharing the gospel in terms of the indwelling presence of God. Not only do people need to hear the gospel; they also need to see it lived out before them in a church community planted in their midst. In order to reach people where they live, Christians must be willing to follow God on mission not only to remote outposts but also to metropolitan areas, seeking to bring his love and compassion to the city. The post-Christian, multicultural setting of the city also calls for the use of missiological tools, such as cultural exegesis, contextualization, and understanding worldviews.

Because Christians—individually and corporately—are the temple of the Holy Spirit, they should be a display people whose everyday lives showcase the reality and character of the God dwelling in their midst. As a contrast community, their moral and ethical behavior and their commitment to kingdom values should stand out against the surrounding darkness. The lives of Spirit-filled believers who genuinely love God will lend credence to the gospel they proclaim. Their love, joy, and concern for one another and for the world will attract notice and invite questions. As the church worships the Lord who is present in their midst, their praise, prayers, and proclamation of his Word bear witness to an authentic spirituality that answers the unmet craving of those whom the Spirit is drawing. The presence of the Spirit will also embolden, empower, and compel believers to share the great salvation God has wrought through his tabernacled-in-flesh Son. Thus, the worshiping church should be an attractional and missional community.

Finally, a study of the tabernacling presence of God also reveals that all Christians must awaken to the reality of the presence of the living God in their midst. What sets Christianity apart as unique is not only the deity of Jesus Christ but also the believer's personal relationship with this living Lord. The Christian faith is much more than a creed and a code of conduct; it is communion with the risen Lord. As Christians truly love the Lord, enjoy his nearness, meditate on his excellence, and submit to his rightful authority, they will be compelled to share him with others. When believers bear witness to the difference Christ makes in their lives, it should be natural to testify humbly to a meaningful relationship with the person of Jesus Christ. However, for Christians to share this spiritual vitality effectively, they must have first experienced it for themselves.

Because God himself is the author and source of mission, the presence of God is always missional, expanding to fill up every place with the knowledge and praise of his glory. From the dawn of creation God has determined to create a people who will reflect his glory in worship and a place that functions as a sanctuary where he may dwell in their midst. He commissioned the first humans to be fruitful and multiply and fill the earth with worshipers. Since the fall of humanity, the mission of God has been to redeem both people and place through the once-for-all sacrifice of his tabernacled-in-flesh Son. After the resurrection Jesus commissioned his followers to make disciples of all nations, who—indwelt by the Spirit—fill the earth with his praises. Both the means and the goal of this mission are the presence of God tabernacling among his people.

The grand narrative of Scripture calls for everyone in every age not just to imagine a better world, but to join those who have already tasted of the new creation and look forward in confidence to its final consummation. On the last day, when the mission is accomplished, a grateful assembly of all the redeemed of all the ages will gather around the throne of God, and myriad voices in countless languages will join the seraph-song of heaven: "Salvation belongs to our God who sits on the throne, and to the Lamb! . . . Blessing and glory and wisdom and thanksgiving and honor and power and might be to our God forever and ever! Amen" (Rev 7:10–12). The unswerving trajectory of human history thus culminates in God's dwelling in the midst of his sanctuary-people in a new heaven and earth.

As incomprehensibly marvelous as this glimpse of the future is, the redeemed people of God must awaken to the present reality that they are *already* a sanctuary-people filled with the tabernacling presence of the Holy Spirit, who empowers them to announce to a broken world the glorious news of the gospel. But what exactly does this look like in the life of an individual? Actually, it might look something like the story behind the cover photo of this book.

A couple of years ago I was on the internet, scrolling aimlessly through intriguing photos of abandoned places all over the world, from a sand-filled house in Namibia to an amusement park turned forest in Japan. When the last image rolled across my computer screen, it took my breath away. This fabulous photo seemed to capture the essence of the church's awakening to the tabernacling presence of God in their midst. On a whim I filed the link away as a possible cover photo for a future book. I forgot all about it until my editor asked for input on this book's cover design. I found the link, fast-forwarded to the last scene, clicked on the photo credit, and typed a quick email to Kevin McElheran. Thinking that he could be located anywhere in the world, I was shocked to discover that Kevin not only lives in a nearby city in the same province, but that he also grew up in the same community where we now live, on the same street, just a few houses down from our previous address! I was also fascinated to learn that the story behind this amazing photo is one of restoration.

Kevin shared with me that he had a difficult childhood. The one place he found escape was out in nature in his own backyard. Although Kevin left home before finishing high school, he found that the brokenness still followed him, affecting his relationship with his wife and children. Even though they all lived under the same roof, Kevin struggled with an inability to connect and kept them at arm's length. Twelve years ago, he was ready to give up on life. About that same time, however, he took up photography, and once again, Kevin found escape outdoors, taking pictures. But because his life was always in a place of ruin, the need to escape continually pulled him away from his family.

Repeatedly, Kevin was drawn to photograph broken, abandoned churches. When someone asked why, Kevin realized that they were, in fact, a metaphor for his own spiritual condition. Somehow he felt a sense of peace sitting inside them in the still of the night. This book cover is just such a photograph shot in 2010, in Sorrento, British Columbia. In a heavy snowfall in the middle of the night, Kevin captured the exact moment a train approached, piercing the darkness and filling the ruined church with dazzling light. Kevin said that he immediately knew the photograph was unique, and it remains his favorite image.

According to Kevin, about that same time his teenage son had the courage to confront him, saying he didn't know if he had the patience to wait for Kevin to become the father he needed him to be. In response, Kevin decided to participate in his church's three-year, Bible-based program that helps men lead lives of authentic manhood as modeled by Jesus Christ. It took the first full year for Kevin to reach the point of being able to forgive what happened in his distant past and to begin moving forward. God used these three years to reverse Kevin's sense of disconnection, and his life began to show evidence of healing and restoration.

Kevin explained that he finally recognized that the cover photo captures the moment God showed up in his life. He has also discovered that all of the abandoned church buildings he had photographed in the past have been renovated or are now undergoing restoration. They have been purchased and refurbished. No longer abandoned, they now display signs of life. For Kevin, the metaphor has come full circle.

Unprompted, the photographer volunteered to share his story in this book as a witness to God's work of restoration in his own life. He also drew my attention to a song called "Surrender" by the Christian band Nine Lashes, which he said perfectly matches both his journey and the cover photo. The songwriter expresses his deep brokenness and desperate need to know that God is with him and that he will never leave. He remembers that in the past he has heard and seen and felt the presence of the Lord. In faith the singer surrenders his broken heart to God and recalls that God's unfailing love is truly overwhelming.

One day there will be a new creation; there will be no more winter, no more night. Every tree will burst into bloom, and every voice will soar in praise. The restored heaven and earth will be filled with the knowledge of the glory of the Lord, and God himself will dwell in the midst of his redeemed people forever. But for now, God delights to tabernacle—not in church buildings—but in the surrendered hearts of his people as he takes up residence in formerly abandoned places, mending their brokenness and filling them with the life of his indwelling Spirit. Everyone who has experienced the tabernacling presence of God has a story that begs to be told in a culture that desperately needs to hear the good news of Jesus. Immanuel, God is with us.

Appendix: *Missio Dei*

FIGURE 1: THE PURPOSE OF GOD

1A) Creation
1B) Consummation

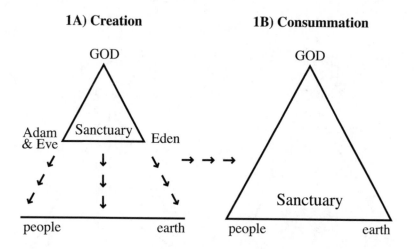

FIGURE 2: THE PLOTLINE OF THE BIBLE

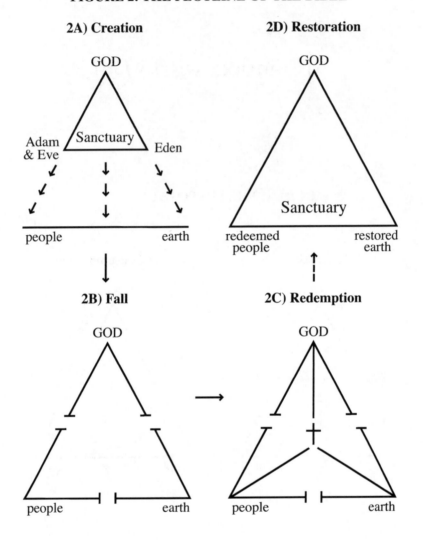

FIGURE 3: GOD'S TABERNACLING PRESENCE AND THE MISSION OF GOD

From the Fall to the Restoration

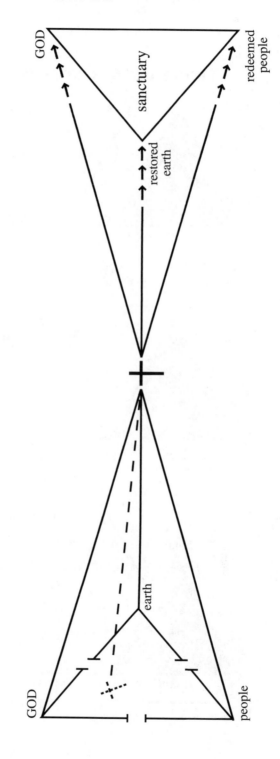

FIGURE 4: CONTRASTING WORLDVIEWS

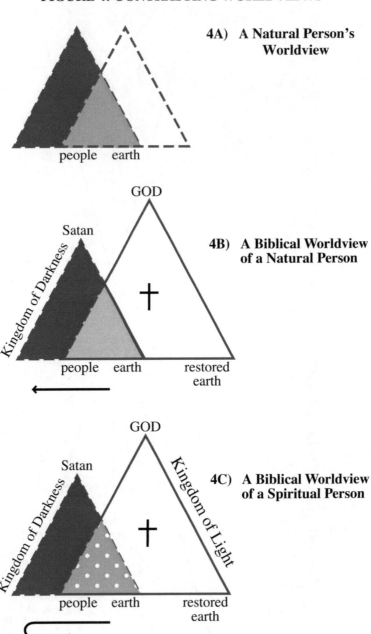

4A) A Natural Person's Worldview

4B) A Biblical Worldview of a Natural Person

4C) A Biblical Worldview of a Spiritual Person

FIGURE 5: THE GREAT DIVIDE

5A) The Division

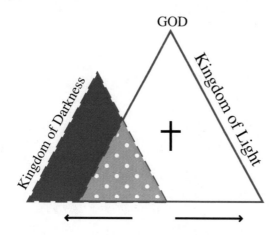

5B) The Eternal Result

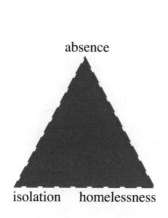

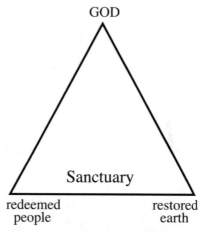

HELL   **THE KINGDOM OF HEAVEN**

Bibliography

Adams, David L. "The Present God: A Framework for Biblical Theology." *Concordia Journal* 22 (July 1996) 279–94.

Alexander, T. D. *From Paradise to the Promised Land: An Introduction to the Pentateuch.* 2nd ed. Grand Rapids: Baker Academic, 2002.

Allen, Ronald B. "Numbers." In *Genesis–Numbers*, edited by Frank E. Gaebelein, 655–1008. The Expositor's Bible Commentary 2. Grand Rapids: Zondervan, 1990.

"Americans More Morally Conservative Than Canadians and Britons." *Angus Reid* (January 31, 2013). No pages. http://www.angusreidglobal.com/wp-content/uploads/2013/01 /2013.01.31_Morality.pdf.

Angel, Andrew. "Notes and Studies Inquiring into an Inclusio—On Judgement and Love in Matthew." *Journal of Theological Studies* 60 (October 2009) 527–30. http://jts.oxfordjournals.org/content/60/2/527.full.pdf_+html?sid=f7c684ea-98d4-4c5c-a097-9ffd0d86abe2.

Armerding, Carl E. "Did I Ever Ask for a House of Cedar?" In *Heaven on Earth: The Temple in Biblical Theology*, edited by T. Desmond Alexander and Simon Gathercole, 35–47. Waynesboro, GA: Paternoster, 2004.

Ashford, Bruce Riley, ed. *Theology and Practice of Mission: God, the Church, and the Nations.* Nashville: B&H Academic, 2011.

Attridge, Harold W. *Essays on John and Hebrews.* Grand Rapids: Baker Academic, 2010.

Auld, A. Graeme. *Joshua, Judges, and Ruth.* Edited by John C. L. Gibson. The Daily Study Bible. Philadelphia: Westminster, 1984.

Averbeck, R. E. "Tabernacle." In *The Dictionary of the Old Testament: Pentateuch*, edited by T. Desmond Alexander and David W. Baker, 807–26. Downers Grove, IL: InterVarsity, 2003.

Baldwin, Joyce G. *Haggai, Zechariah, Malachi: An Introduction and Commentary.* Edited by D. J. Wiseman. Tyndale Old Testament Commentaries. Downers Grove, IL: InterVarsity, 1972.

———. *The Message of Genesis 12–50.* Edited by J. A. Motyer. The Bible Speaks Today. Downers Grove, IL: InterVarsity, 1986.

Barna, George. *Revolution: Finding Vibrant Faith beyond the Walls of the Sanctuary.* Carol Stream, IL: Tyndale, 2005.

Bartholomew, Craig G. *Where Mortals Dwell: A Christian View of Place for Today.* Grand Rapids: Baker Academic, 2011.

Bartholomew, Craig G., and Michael W. Goheen. *The Drama of Scripture: Finding Our Place in the Biblical Story*. Grand Rapids: Baker Academic, 2004.

Beale, G. K. *The Book of Revelation: A Commentary on the Greek Text*. Edited by I. Howard Marshall and Donald A. Hagner. New International Greek Testament Commentary. Grand Rapids, Eerdmans, 1999.

———. "The Descent of the Eschatological Temple in the Form of the Spirit at Pentecost." *Tyndale Bulletin* 56 (2005) 63–85.

———. "Eden, the Temple, and the Church's Mission in the New Creation." *Journal of the Evangelical Theological Society* 48 (March 2005) 5–31.

———. *A New Testament Biblical Theology: The Unfolding of the Old Testament in the New*. Grand Rapids: Baker Academic, 2011.

———. *The Temple and the Church's Mission: A Biblical Theology of the Dwelling Place of God*. Edited by D. A. Carson. New Studies in Biblical Theology 17. Downers Grove, IL: InterVarsity, 2004.

Beale, G. K., and D. A. Carson, eds. *Commentary on the New Testament Use of the Old Testament*. Grand Rapids: Baker Academic, 2007.

Beasley-Murray, George R. *John*. Edited by David A. Hubbard and Glenn W. Barker. Word Biblical Commentary 36. Waco, TX: Word, 1987.

Bedard, Stephen. "The Faith Today Interview: Leonard Sweet." *Faith Today* (July–August 2013) 22–24.

Belanger, Alain, and Eric Caron Malenfant. "Ethnocultural Diversity in Canada: Prospects for 2017." *Canadian Social Trends* 79 (Winter 2005) 19. http://www.statcan.gc.ca /pub/11–008-x/2005003/article/8968-eng.pdf.

Bergen, Robert D. *1, 2 Samuel*. Edited by E. Ray Clendenen. The New American Commentary. Nashville: Broadman & Holman, 1996.

Bethune, Brian. "Heaven Is Hot Again, and Hell Is Colder Than Ever." *Maclean's* (May 7, 2013). No pages. http://www2.macleans.ca/2013 /05/07/the-heaven-boom/.

Beyer, Peter. "Appendix: The Demographics of Christianity in Canada." In *Christianity and Ethnicity in Canada*, edited by Paul Bramadat and David Seljak, 437–40. Toronto: University of Toronto Press, 2008.

Bibby, Reginald Wayne. *Beyond the Gods and Back: Religion's Demise and Rise and Why It Matters*. Lethbridge, AB: Project Canada, 2011.

———. "Canada's Mythical Religious Mosaic: Some Census Findings." *Journal for the Scientific Study of Religion* 39 (June 2000) 235–39.

———. "Continuing the Conversation on Canada: Changing Patterns of Religious Service Attendance." *Journal for the Scientific Study of Religion* 50 (2011) 831–39.

———. *Mosaic Madness: Pluralism without a Cause*. Toronto: Stoddart, 1990.

———. *A New Day: The Resilience and Restructuring of Religion in Canada*. Lethbridge, AB: Project Canada, 2012.

———. "Project Canada 1995 Survey." Association of Religion Data Archives. No pages. http://www.thearda.com/Archive/Files/Descriptions/PC1995.asp.

———. "Why Bother with Organized Religion? A Response to Joel Thiessen." *Canadian Review of Sociology* 49 (2012) 91–101.

Blauw, Johannes. *The Missionary Nature of the Church: A Survey of the Biblical Theology of Mission*. Foundations of Christian Mission. New York: McGraw-Hill, 1962.

Blenkinsopp, Joseph. *Ezekiel*. Edited by James Luther Mays. Interpretation. Louisville: John Knox, 1990.

Block, Daniel I. *The Book of Ezekiel*. 2 vols. New International Commentary on the Old Testament. Grand Rapids: Eerdmans, 1997–1998.

———. *The Gospel according to Moses: Theological and Ethical Reflections on the Book of Deuteronomy*. Eugene, OR: Cascade, 2012.

———. *How I Love Your Torah, O LORD! Studies in the Book of Deuteronomy*. Eugene, OR: Cascade, 2011.

———. *Judges, Ruth*. Edited by E. Ray Clendenen. The New American Commentary 6. Nashville: Broadman & Holman, 1999.

———. "'What Do These Stones Mean?' The Riddle of Deuteronomy 27." *Journal of the Evangelical Theological Society* 56 (2013) 17–41.

Blomberg, Craig L. *1 Corinthians*. Edited by Terry Muck. NIV Application Commentary. Grand Rapids: Zondervan, 1994.

———. *Jesus and the Gospels: An Introduction and Survey*. 2nd ed. Nashville: B&H Academic, 2009.

———. *Matthew*. Edited by David S. Dockery. The New American Commentary 22. Nashville: Broadman, 1992.

Bock, Darrell L. *Luke*. 2 vols. Edited by Moisés Silva. Baker Exegetical Commentary on the New Testament. Grand Rapids: Baker Academic, 1994; Repr., 2006.

Boda, Mark J. *Haggai, Zechariah*. Edited by Terry Muck. The NIV Application Commentary. Grand Rapids: Zondervan, 2004.

Boring, M. Eugene. *Revelation*. Edited by James Luther Mays. Interpretation. Louisville: John Knox, 1989.

Bowen, Kurt. *Christians in a Secular World: The Canadian Experience*. Quebec City: McGill-Queen's University Press, 2004.

Bromiley, G. W. "Presence, Divine." In *Evangelical Dictionary of Theology*, edited by Walter A. Elwell, 951–52. 2nd ed. Grand Rapids: Baker Academic, 2001.

Brueggemann, Walter. *First and Second Samuel*. Edited by James Luther Mays. Interpretation. Louisville: John Knox, 1990.

———. *Genesis*. Edited by James Luther Mays. Interpretation. Atlanta: John Knox, 1982.

———. *Ichabod Toward Home: The Journey of God's Glory*. Grand Rapids: Eerdmans, 2002.

———. *Solomon: Israel's Ironic Icon of Human Achievement*. Columbia: University of South Carolina Press, 2005.

———. *To Pluck Up, To Tear Down: A Commentary of the Book of Jeremiah 1–25*. Edited by Fredrick Carlson Holmgren and George A. F. Knight. International Theological Commentary. Grand Rapids: Eerdmans, 1988.

Bryan, Steven M. "The Eschatological Temple in John 14." *Bulletin for Biblical Research* 15 (2005) 187–98.

Butler, Trent C. *Joshua*. Edited by David A. Hubbard and Glenn W. Barker. Word Biblical Commentary 7. Waco, TX: Word, 1983.

The Canada Press. "Lawyers Vote Against Christian Law School," *Maclean's* (June 10, 2014). No pages. http://www.macleans.ca/news/canada/b-c-lawyers-vote-against-trinity-western-university-amid-claims-of-gay-discrimination/.

"Canada's Changing Religious Landscape." *Pew Research: Religion and Public Life* (June 27, 2013). No pages. http://www.pewforum.org/2013/06/27/canadas-changing-religious-landscape/.

"Canadians Are Divided on the Actual Effect of Immigration." *Angus Reid* (January 31, 2012). No pages. http://www.angusreidglobal.com/polls/44322/canadians-are-divided-on-the-actual-effect-of-immigration/.

Carson, D. A. *The Gagging of God: Christianity Confronts Pluralism*. Grand Rapids: Zondervan, 1996.

———. *The Gospel according to John*. Grand Rapids: Eerdmans, 1991.

———. *The Intolerance of Tolerance*. Grand Rapids: Eerdmans, 2012.

———. "Matthew." In *Matthew, Mark, Luke*, edited by Frank E. Gaebelein, 1–599. The Expositor's Bible Commentary 8. Grand Rapids: Zondervan, 1984.

Caudill, Norah Whipple. "The Presence of God in the Exodus Narrative: Purposes, Means, and Implications." PhD diss., Fuller Theological Seminary, 2006.

"Christianity in Its Global Context, 1970–2020: Society, Religion, and Mission." Center for the Study of Global Christianity. South Hamilton, MA: Gordon-Conwell Theological Seminary, 2013. http://wwwgordonconwell.com/netcommunity/ CSGC Resources/ChristianityinitsGlobalContext.pdf.

Chui, Tina, and John Flanders. "Immigration and Ethnocultural Diversity in Canada." *Statistics Canada: National Household Survey 2011* (May 2013) 1–23. http:// www12.statcan.gc.ca/nhs-enm/2011/as-sa/99-010-x/99010-x2011001-eng.pdf.

Clark, Warren, and Susan Crompton. "Till Death Do Us Part? The Risk of First and Second Marriage Dissolution." *Canadian Social Trends* 11 (Summer 2006) 23–33. http://www.statcan.gc.ca/pub/11-008-x/2006001/pdf/9198-eng.pdf.

Clemenger, Bruce J. "Organizations Free to Maintain Religious Identity: Reflections on TWU v. Nova Scotia Barristers' Society." *Evangelical Fellowship of Canada* (February 4, 2015). No pages. http://www.evangelicalfellowship.ca/NSBS2015.

Clowney, Edmund P. "The Final Temple." *Westminster Theological Journal* 35 (1973) 156–89.

Coloe, Mary L. *God Dwells with Us: Temple Symbolism in the Fourth Gospel*. Collegeville, MN: Liturgical, 2001.

Conseco, Mario. "Canadians Are Divided on the Actual Effect of Immigration." *Angus Reid Strategies* (January 31, 2012). No pages. http://www.angusreidglobal.com/ wp-content/uploads/2012/01/2012.01.31_Immigration_CAN.pdf.

"Country Comparison: Population." *The World Factbook*. No pages. https://www.cia. gov/library/publications/the-world-factbook/rankorder/2119rank.html.

Craig, William Lane. *Reasonable Faith: Christian Truth and Apologetics*. 3rd ed. Wheaton, IL: Crossway, 2008.

Craigie, Peter C. *The Book of Deuteronomy*. Edited by R. K. Harrison. The New International Commentary on the Old Testament. Grand Rapids: Eerdmans, 1976.

Danker, Frederick W., et al. *A Greek-English Lexicon of the New Testament and Other Early Christian Literature*. 3rd ed. Chicago: University of Chicago Press, 2000.

De Ridder, Richard R. *Discipling the Nations*. Grand Rapids: Baker, 1971.

Derrida, Jacques. *Limited Inc*. Translated by Samuel Weber. Evanston, IL: Northwestern University Press, 1988.

DeVries, Simon J. *1 Kings*. Word Biblical Commentary 12. Waco, TX: Word, 1985.

Dods, Marcus. *The Book of Genesis*. 8th ed. London: Hodder & Stoughton, 1895.

Donaghy, Henry. "Holy Scripture: God with Us." *Worship* 31 (1957) 276–84.

Dueck, Lorna. "Trinity Western Affair a Trial of Canadian Civility and Tolerance." *The Globe and Mail* (December 11, 2014). No pages. http://www.theglobeandmail.com/

globe-debate/trinity-western-affair-a-trial-of-canadian-civility-and-tolerance/article 22041303/?cmpid=rss1&utm_source=twitterfeed&utm_medium=twitter.

Dumbrell, William J. *The End of the Beginning: Revelation 21–22 and the Old Testament*. Moore Theological College Lecture Series. Grand Rapids: Baker, 1985.

Durham, John I. *Exodus*. Edited by David A. Hubbard and Glenn W. Barker. Word Biblical Commentary 3. Waco, TX: Word, 1987.

Epp, Aaron. "Hellbound: Should We Be Worried?" *Christian Week* 26 (October 2012) 24.

Evans, Craig A. "From 'House of Prayer' to 'Cave of Robbers': Jesus' Prophetic Criticism of the Temple Establishment." In *The Quest for Context and Meaning: Studies in Biblical Intertextuality in Honor of James A. Sanders*, edited by Craig A. Evans and Shemaryahu Talmon, 417–42. Leiden: Brill, 1997.

———. *Luke*. Edited by W. Ward Gasque. New International Biblical Commentary. Peabody, MA: Hendrickson, 1990.

Fee, Gordon D. *The First Epistle to the Corinthians*. Edited by Ned B. Stonehouse et al. The New International Commentary of the New Testament. Grand Rapids: Eerdmans, 1987.

———. *God's Empowering Presence: The Holy Spirit in the Letters of Paul*. Peabody, MA: Hendrickson, 1994.

———. *Revelation: A New Covenant Community*. Edited by Michael F. Bird and Craig Keener. New Covenant Commentary 18. Eugene, OR: Cascade, 2011.

Feinberg, Charles L. "Jeremiah." In *Isaiah–Ezekiel*, edited by Frank E. Gaebelein, 355–691. The Expositor's Bible Commentary 6. Grand Rapids: Zondervan, 1986.

Ferrer, Ana M., et al. "New Directions in Immigration Policy: Canada's Evolving Approach to Immigration Selection." Canadian Labour Market and Skills Researcher Network: Working Paper No. 107 (November 2012) 1–36.

France, R. T. *The Gospel of Matthew*. Edited by Ned B. Stonehouse et al. The New International Commentary on the New Testament. Grand Rapids: Eerdmans, 2007.

Fretheim, Terence E. *Exodus*. Edited by James Luther Mays. Interpretation. Louisville: John Knox, 1991.

———. *First and Second Kings*. Edited by Patrick D. Miller and David L. Bartlett. Westminster Bible Companion. Louisville: Westminster John Knox, 1999.

———. *The Suffering of God: An Old Testament Perspective*. Edited by Walter Brueggemann and John R. Donahue. Overtures to Biblical Theology 14. Philadelphia: Fortress, 1984.

Friberg, Timothy, et al. *Analytical Lexicon of the Greek New Testament*. Grand Rapids: Baker, 2000.

Fuchs, Cynthia. "A Chick with Edge." *PopMatters* (January 29, 2003). No pages. http://www.popmatters.com/music/videos/l/lavigneavril-imwithyou.shtml.

Fyall, Robert. "A Curious Silence: The Temple in 1 and 2 Kings." In *Heaven on Earth: The Temple in Biblical Theology*, edited by T. Desmond Alexander and Simon Gathercole, 50–58. Waynesboro, GA: Paternoster, 2004.

Garrett, James Leo. *Systematic Theology: Biblical, Historical, and Evangelical*. Vol. 1. Grand Rapids: Eerdmans, 1990.

Glasser, Arthur F. *Announcing the Kingdom: The Story of God's Mission in the Bible*. Grand Rapids: Baker Academic, 2003.

Goheen, Michael W. *A Light to the Nations: The Missional Church and the Biblical Story.* Grand Rapids: Baker Academic, 2011.

Goheen, Michael W., and Craig G. Bartholomew. *Living at the Crossroads: An Introduction to Christian Worldview.* Grand Rapids: Baker Academic, 2008.

Goldsmith, Martin. *Matthew and Mission: The Gospel through Jewish Eyes.* Waynesboro, GA: Paternoster, 2001.

Gordon, Robert P. *I and II Samuel: A Commentary.* Grand Rapids: Regency Reference Library, 1986.

Gowan, Donald E. *Eschatology in the Old Testament.* Philadelphia: Fortress, 1986.

Greene, Joseph R. "The Spirit in the Temple: Bridging the Gap between Old Testament Absence and New Testament Assumption." *Journal of the Evangelical Theological Society* 55 (2012) 717–42.

Greidanus, Sidney. *Preaching Christ from Genesis: Foundations for Expository Sermons.* Grand Rapids: Eerdmans, 2007.

———. *Preaching Christ from the Old Testament: A Contemporary Hermeneutical Method.* Grand Rapids: Eerdmans, 1999.

Grenz, Stanley J. *A Primer on Postmodernism.* Grand Rapids: Eerdmans, 1996.

Guenther, Bruce L. "Ethnicity and Evangelical Protestants in Canada." In *Christianity and Ethnicity in Canada*, edited by Paul Bramadat and David Seljak, 365–414. Toronto: University of Toronto Press, 2008.

Gundry, Robert H. "The New Jerusalem: People as Place, Not Place for People." *Novum Testamentum* 29 (1987) 254–64.

Gupta, Nijay K. "Which Body Is a Temple (1 Corinthians 6:19)? Paul Beyond the Individual/Communal Divide." *The Catholic Biblical Quarterly* 72 (2010) 518–36.

Guthrie, George H. *Hebrews.* NIV Application. Grand Rapids: Zondervan, 1998.

Hamilton, Victor P. "שָׁכַן (shākan)," In *Theological Wordbook of the Old Testament*, edited by R. Laird Harris et al., 1:925–26. 2 vols. Chicago: Moody, 1980.

Harris, Murray J. *The Second Epistle to the Corinthians.* Edited by I. Howard Marshall and Donald A. Hagner. The New International Greek Testament Commentary. Grand Rapids: Eerdmans, 2005.

Haskell, David M. *Through a Lens Darkly: How the News Media Perceive and Portray Evangelicals.* Toronto: Clements, 2009.

"Having Enough Time to Do What They Want Is Key for Canadians." *Angus Reid* (June 9, 2008). No pages. https://www.angusreidforum.com/Admin/mediaserver/3/documents/2008%2006%2009_Life.pdf.

Hays, J. Daniel. "Just How Glorious Was Solomon's Temple? A Narrative and Theological Comparison of Solomon's Approach to Building the Temple with Moses' Approach to Building the Tabernacle." Paper delivered at the annual meeting of the Evangelical Theological Society, San Francisco, November 16, 2011.

Hays, Richard B. "The Conversion of the Imagination: Scripture and Eschatology in 1 Corinthians." *New Testament Studies* 45 (1999) 391–412.

Hendry, George S. *The Holy Spirit in Christian Theology.* Philadelphia: Westminster, 1956.

Hess, Richard S. *Joshua: An Introduction and Commentary.* Edited by D. J. Wiseman. Tyndale Old Testament Commentaries 6. Downers Grove, IL: InterVarsity, 1996.

Hiemstra, Rick. "Confidence, Conversation and Community: Bible Engagement in Canada, 2013." Toronto: Faith Today, 2014. http://www.bibleengagementstudy.ca/.

————. "Counting Canadian Evangelicals." *Church and Faith Trends* 1 (October 2007) 1–10. http://files.efc-canada.net/min/rc/cft/V01I01/Counting_Canadian_Evangelicals .pdf.

Hiller, Harry H. *Urban Canada*. 2nd ed. Don Mills, ON: Oxford University Press, 2010.

Hobbs, T. R. *2 Kings*. Edited by David A. Hubbard and Glenn W. Barker. Word Biblical Commentary 13. Waco, TX: Word, 1985.

Homan, Michael M. "The Divine Warrior in His Tent: A Military Model for Yahweh's Tent." *Bible Review* 16 (2000) 22–27.

House, Paul R. *1 and 2 Kings*. Edited by E. Ray Clendenen. The New American Commentary 8. Nashville: Broadman & Holman, 1995.

Howard, David M., Jr. *Joshua*. Edited by E. Ray Clendenen. The New American Commentary 5. Nashville: Broadman & Holman, 1998.

Ibbitson, John. *The Polite Revolution: Perfecting the Canadian Dream*. Toronto: McClelland and Stewart, 2006.

International Social Survey Programme. "Religion III." February 2010. Collected by Carleton University and the Montreal-based Association of Canadian Studies.

Johnson, Dennis E. *Him We Proclaim: Preaching Christ from All the Scriptures*. Phillipsburg, NJ: P&R, 2007.

Kaiser, Walter C., Jr. "Exodus." In *Genesis–Numbers*, edited by Frank E. Gaebelein, 285–497. The Expositor's Bible Commentary 2. Grand Rapids: Zondervan, 1990.

————. *Mission in the Old Testament: Israel as a Light to the Nations*. 2nd ed. Grand Rapids: Baker Academic, 2012.

Keener, Craig S. *The Gospel of John: A Commentary*. 2 vols. Peabody, MA: Hendrickson, 2003.

————. *Revelation*. Edited by Terry Muck. The NIV Application Commentary. Grand Rapids: Zondervan, 2000.

————. *The Spirit in the Gospels and in Acts: Divine Purity and Power*. Peabody, MA: Hendrickson, 1997.

Keller, Timothy. "The Gospel and the Supremacy of Christ in a Postmodern World." In *The Supremacy of Christ in a Postmodern World*, edited by John Piper and Justin Taylor, 103–23. Wheaton, IL: Crossway, 2007.

Kidner, Derek. *Genesis: An Introduction and Commentary*. Tyndale OT Commentaries. London: Tyndale, 1967.

Kistemaker, Simon J. "The Temple in the Apocalypse." *Journal of the Evangelical Theological Society* 43 (September 2000) 433–41.

Kitchen, K. A. "The Desert Tabernacle." *Bible Review* 16 (2000) 14–21.

Kline, Meredith G. *Images of the Spirit*. Eugene, OR: Wipf & Stock, 1998.

Koester, Craig R. *The Dwelling of God: The Tabernacle in the Old Testament, Intertestamental Jewish Literature, and the New Testament*. Edited by Robert J. Karris. Catholic Biblical Quarterly Monograph 22. Washington, DC: Catholic Biblical Association of America, 1989.

Köstenberger, Andreas J. *John*. Edited by Robert Yarbrough and Robert H. Stein. Baker Exegetical Commentary on the New Testament. Grand Rapids: Baker, 2004.

————. *A Theology of John's Gospel and Letters*. Biblical Theology of the New Testament. Grand Rapids: Zondervan, 2009.

————. "What Does It Mean to Be Filled with the Spirit? A Biblical Investigation." *Journal of the Evangelical Theological Society* 40 (June 1997) 229–40.

Köstenberger, Andreas, and Peter O'Brien. *Salvation to the Ends of the Earth: A Biblical Theology of Mission.* Edited by D. A. Carson. New Studies in Biblical Theology 11. Downers Grove, IL: InterVarsity, 2001.

Lane, William L. *Hebrews: A Call to Commitment.* Peabody, MA: Hendrickson, 1985.

Larkin, William J., Jr. *Acts.* Edited by Grant R. Osborne. IVP New Testament Commentary. Downers Grove, IL: InterVarsity, 1995.

Lavigne, Avril. "I'm with You." From the album: *Let Go.* Arista Records, 2002. Music video directed by David LaChapelle. http://www.youtube.com/watch?v=dGR65RWwzg8.

Legrand, Lucien. *Unity and Plurality: Mission in the Bible.* Translated by Robert R. Barr. Maryknoll, NY: Orbis, 1990.

Levy, David M. *The Tabernacle: Shadows of the Messiah: Its Sacrifices, Services, and Priesthood.* Grand Rapids: Kregel, 2003.

Lewis, C. S. *The Great Divorce.* New York: HarperCollins, 1946. Repr., 2001.

Liederbach, Mark, and Alvin Reid. *The Convergent Church: Missional Worshippers in an Emerging Culture.* Grand Rapids: Kregel, 2009.

Lioy, Dan. *Axis of Glory: A Biblical and Theological Analysis of the Temple Motif in Scripture.* Edited by Hemchand Gossai. Studies in Biblical Literature 138. New York: Peter Lang, 2010.

Lister, John Ryan. "'The Lord Your God Is in Your Midst': The Presence of God and the Means and End of Redemptive History." PhD diss., The Southern Baptist Theological Seminary, 2010.

Longman, Tremper, III. *How to Read Exodus.* Downers Grove, IL: IVP Academic, 2009.

———. *Immanuel in Our Place: Seeing Christ in Israel's Worship.* Edited by Tremper Longman III and J. Alan Groves. The Gospel according to the Old Testament. Phillipsburg, NJ: P&R, 2001.

Lyotard, Jean François. *The Postmodern Condition: A Report on Knowledge.* Translated by Geoff Bennington and Brian Massumi. Minneapolis: University of Minnesota Press, 1984.

Mann, Thomas W. "The Pillar of Cloud in the Reed Sea Narrative." *Journal of Biblical Literature* 90 (1971) 15–30.

Marshall, I. Howard. *Acts of the Apostles: An Introduction and Commentary.* Edited by R. V. G. Tasker. Tyndale New Testament Commentary 5. Grand Rapids: Eerdmans, 1980. Repr., 1989.

———. "Church and Temple in the New Testament." *Tyndale Bulletin* 40 (1989) 203–22.

Martel, Laurent, and Jonathan Chagnon. "The Canadian Population in 2011: Population Counts and Growth." *Statistics Canada* (February 2012) 1–26. http://www12.statcan.gc.ca/census-recensement/2011/as-sa/98-310-x/98-310-x2011003_1-eng.cfm.

Martens Elmer A. "Jeremiah and Lamentations." In *Isaiah, Jeremiah, and Lamentations,* edited by Philip W. Comfort, 293–593. Cornerstone Biblical Commentary 8. Wheaton, IL: Tyndale, 2005.

Martin-Achard, Robert. *A Light to the Nations: A Study of the Old Testament Conception of Israel's Mission to the World.* Translated by John Penney Smith. London: Oliver and Boyd, 1962.

McCaffrey, James. *The House with Many Rooms: The Temple Theme of Jn. 14, 2–3.* Analecta Biblica 114. Rome: Editrice Pontificio Istituto Biblico, 1988.

McConville, J. Gordon. "God's 'Name' and God's 'Glory.'" *Tyndale Bulletin* 30 (1979) 149–63.

McKelvey, R. J. *The New Temple: The Church in the New Testament*. Edited by H. Chadwick et al. Oxford Theological Monographs 3. London: Oxford University Press, 1969.

Meyers, Carol L., and Eric M. Meyers. *Haggai, Zechariah 1–8*. The Anchor Bible 25B. Garden City, NY: Doubleday, 1987.

Middleton, J. Richard. *The Liberating Image: The Imago Dei in Genesis 1*. Grand Rapids: Brazos, 2005.

Miner, John. "Predeceased by Their Churches." *The London Free Press* (May 21, 2010). No pages. http://www.lfpress.com/news/london/2010/05/18/13993046.html.

Morris, Leon. *1 Corinthians*. Edited by Leon Morris. Tyndale New Testament Commentaries 7. Grand Rapids: Eerdmans, 1985. Repr., 2001.

———. *The Gospel according to St. Luke*. Edited by R. V. G. Tasker. Tyndale New Testament Commentaries. Grand Rapids: Eerdmans, 1974. Repr., 1984.

———. *Jesus Is the Christ: Studies in the Theology of John*. Grand Rapids: Eerdmans, 1989.

Motyer, J. Alec. *The Prophecy of Isaiah: An Introduction and Commentary*. Downers Grove, IL: InterVarsity, 1993.

Mounce, Robert H. *The Book of Revelation*. 2nd ed. The New International Commentary on the New Testament. Grand Rapids: Eerdmans, 1998.

Newman, Randy. *Questioning Evangelism: Engaging People's Hearts the Way Jesus Did*. Grand Rapids: Kregel, 2004.

Noll, Mark A. "What Happened to Christian Canada?" *Church History* 75 (June 2006) 245–73.

———. *What Happened to Christian Canada?* Vancouver, BC: Regent College Publishing, 2007.

"OECD Better Life Index: Country Reports." Organization for Economic Cooperation and Development (May 28, 2013) 1–110. http://www.oecd.org/newsroom/BLI2013-Country-Notes.pdf.

Osborne, Grant R. *Revelation*. Edited by Moisés Silva. Baker Exegetical Commentary on the New Testament. Grand Rapids: Baker Academic, 2002. Repr., 2009.

Oswalt, John N. *The Book of Isaiah Chapters 1–39*. Edited by R. K. Harrison. The New International Commentary on the Old Testament. Grand Rapids: Eerdmans, 1991.

Patrick, Dale. *Old Testament Law*. Atlanta: John Knox, 1984.

Penner, James, et al. *Hemorrhaging Faith: Why and When Canadian Young Adults Are Leaving, Staying, and Returning to the Church*. 2012. http://hemorrhagingfaith.com/product/hemorrhaging-faith-single-download/.

Penner, Myron Bradley. *The End of Apologetics: Christian Witness in a Postmodern Context*. Grand Rapids: Baker Academic, 2013.

Perrin, Nicholas. *Jesus the Temple*. Grand Rapids: Baker Academic, 2010.

Petersen, David L. *Haggai and Zechariah 1–8*. Edited by Peter Ackroyd et al. The Old Testament Library. Philadelphia: Westminster, 1984.

Piper, John. *Let the Nations Be Glad: The Supremacy of God in Missions*. 3rd ed. Grand Rapids: Baker Academic, 2010.

Rad, Gerhard von. *Genesis: A Commentary*. Translated by John H. Marks. Old Testament Library. Philadelphia: Westminster, 1959.

Reimer, Sam. "Does Religion Matter? Canadian Traditions and Attitudes toward Diversity." In *Religion and Diversity in Canada*, edited by Lori G. Beaman and Peter Beyer, 105–25. Religion and the Social Order 16. Leiden: Brill, 2008.

Reimer, Sam, and Michael Wilkinson. "A Demographic Look at Evangelical Congregations." *Church and Faith Trends* 3 (August 2010) 1–21. http://files.efc-canada.net/min/rc/cft/V03I02/Demographic_Look_Evangelical_Congregations-CECS.pdf.

Ridderbos, Herman. *The Gospel according to John: A Theological Commentary.* Translated by John Vriend. Grand Rapids: Eerdmans, 1991.

———. *Matthew.* Translated by Ray Togtman. Bible Student's Commentary. Grand Rapids: Regency Reference Library, 1987.

Roberts, Lance. *Recent Social Trends in Canada, 1960–2000.* Montreal: McGill-Queens University Press, 2005.

Robinson, Bernard P. "Moses and the Burning Bush." *Journal for the Study of the Old Testament* 75 (1997) 107–22.

Ross, Allen P. *Creation and Blessing: A Guide to the Study and Exposition of Genesis.* Grand Rapids: Baker Academic, 1998.

———. *Holiness to the Lord: A Guide to the Exposition of the Book of Leviticus.* Grand Rapids: Baker Academic, 2002.

———. *Recalling the Hope of Glory: Biblical Worship from the Garden to the New Creation.* Grand Rapids: Kregel, 2006.

Ryan, Andrew. "Avril Lavigne Gives Breathless Account of Chateau Wedding." *The Globe and Mail* (July 8, 2013). No pages. http://www.theglobeandmail.com/life/the-hot-button/avril-lavigne-gives-breathless-account-of-chateau-wedding/article13060355/.

Sailhamer, John H. "Genesis." In *Genesis–Numbers*, edited by Frank E. Gaebelein, 1–284. Expositor's Bible Commentary 2. Grand Rapids: Zondervan, 1990.

Schaeffer, Francis A. *The God Who Is There.* In *Francis A. Schaeffer Trilogy: The Essential Books in One Volume*, 1–205. Westchester, IL: Crossway, 1990.

Schnabel, Eckhard J. *Paul the Missionary: Realities, Strategies, and Methods.* Downers Grove, IL: IVP Academic, 2008.

Smalley, Stephen S. *The Revelation to John: A Commentary on the Greek Text of the Apocalypse.* Downers Grove, IL: InterVarsity, 2005.

Smith, Christian, and Melinda Lundquist Denton. *Soul Searching: The Religious and Spiritual Lives of American Teenagers.* New York: Oxford University Press, 2005.

Smith, Glenn. "Canadian Urban Ministry: Proposals for New Initiatives." In *Discipling Our Nation: Equipping the Canadian Church for Its Mission*, edited by Murray Moerman, 77–95. Delta, BC: Church Leadership Library, 2005.

Smith, James K. A. *Who's Afraid of Postmodernism: Taking Derrida, Lyotard, and Foucault to Church.* The Church and Postmodern Culture. Grand Rapids: Baker Academic, 2006.

Smith, Robert H. *Matthew.* Edited by Roy A. Harrisville et al. Augsburg Commentary on the New Testament. Minneapolis: Augsburg, 1989.

Spatafora, Andrea. *From the "Temple of God" to God as the Temple: A Biblical Theological Study of the Temple in the Book of Revelation.* Serie Teologia 27. Rome: Gregorian University Press, 1997.

Stackhouse, John G., Jr. *Humble Apologetics: Defending the Faith Today.* New York: Oxford University Press, 2002.

Stahl, William A. "Is Anyone in Canada Secular?" In *Secularism and Secularity: Contemporary International Perspectives*, edited by Barry Alexander Kosmin and Ariela Keysar, 59–72. Hartford, CT: Institute for the Study of Secularism in Society and Culture, 2007.

Statistics Canada. "2011 Census of Population: Families, Households, Marital Status, Structural Type of Dwelling, Collectives." *The Daily* (September 19, 2012) 1–4. http://www.statcan.gc.ca/dailyquotidien/120919/dq120919a-eng.pdf.

———. "2011 National Household Survey: Immigration, Place of Birth, Citizenship, Ethnic Origin, Visible Minorities, Language and Religion." *The Daily* (May 8, 2013) 1–4. http://www.statcan.gc.ca/daily-quotidien/130508/dq130508b-eng.pdf.

———. "Fifty Years of Families in Canada: 1961 to 2011." *Census in Brief* (2012) 1–7. http://www12.statcan.gc.ca/census-recensement/2011/as-sa/98-312-x/98-312-x2011003_1-eng.pdf.

Stek, John H. "What Says the Scripture?" In *Portraits of Creation: Biblical and Scientific Perspectives on the World's Formation*, edited by Howard J. Van Till et al., 203–65. Grand Rapids: Eerdmans, 1990.

Stott, John R. W. *The Message of Acts*. Edited by John R. W. Stott. The Bible Speaks Today. Downers Grove, IL: InterVarsity, 1990.

———. *The Message of Ephesians: God's New Society*. Edited by John R. W. Stott. The Bible Speaks Today. Downers Grove, IL: InterVarsity, 1979. Repr., 1986.

Taylor, Justin. "Conversations with the Contributors." In *The Supremacy of Christ in a Postmodern World*, edited by John Piper and Justin Taylor, 149–79. Wheaton, IL: Crossway, 2007.

Terrien, Samuel. *The Elusive Presence: Toward a New Biblical Theology*. Edited by Ruth Nanda Anshen. Religious Perspectives 26. San Francisco: Harper & Row, 1978.

Thiselton, Anthony C. *The First Epistle to the Corinthians*. Edited by I. Howard Marshall and Donald A. Hagner. The New International Greek Testament Commentary. Grand Rapids: Eerdmans, 2000.

Toon, Peter. *Our Triune God: A Biblical Portrayal of the Trinity*. Wheaton, IL: BridgePoint, 1996.

"Trinity Western Law School: B.C. Advanced Education Minister Revokes Approval." *CBC News* (December 11, 2014). No pages. http://www.cbc.ca/news/canada/british-columbia/trinity-western-law-school-b-c-advanced-education-minister-revokes-approval-1.2870640.

Vanhoozer, Kevin J. *Everyday Theology: How to Read Cultural Texts and Interpret Trends*. Grand Rapids: Baker Academic, 2007.

Veith, Gene Edward, Jr. *Postmodern Times: A Christian Guide to Contemporary Thought and Culture*. Wheaton, IL: Crossway, 1994.

Walker, Peter W. L. *Jesus and the Holy City: New Testament Perspectives on Jerusalem*. Grand Rapids: Eerdmans, 1996.

Walsh, Jerome T. *1 Kings*. Edited by David W. Cotter. Berit Olam. Collegeville, MN: Liturgical, 1996.

Waltke, Bruce K., and Cathi J. Fredericks. *Genesis: A Commentary*. Grand Rapids: Zondervan, 2001.

Walton, John H. *Ancient Near Eastern Thought and the Old Testament: Introducing the Conceptual World of the Hebrew Bible*. Grand Rapids: Baker Academic, 2006.

———. *The Lost World of Genesis One: Ancient Cosmology and the Origins Debate*. Downers Grove, IL: IVP Academic, 2009.

Wells, David F. *The Courage to Be Protestant: Truth-lovers, Marketers, and Emergents in the Postmodern World.* Grand Rapids: Eerdmans, 2008.

———. "The Supremacy of Christ in a Postmodern World." In *The Supremacy of Christ in a Postmodern World,* edited by John Piper and Justin Taylor, 21–49. Wheaton, IL: Crossway, 2007.

Wenham, Gordon J. *The Book of Leviticus.* Edited by R. K. Harrison. The New International Commentary on the Old Testament. Grand Rapids: Eerdmans, 1979.

———. *Genesis 1–15.* Edited by David A. Hubbard and Glenn W. Barker. Word Biblical Commentary 1. Waco, TX: Word, 1987.

———. *Numbers: An Introduction and Commentary.* Edited by D. J. Wiseman. The Tyndale Old Testament Commentaries. Downers Grove, IL: InterVarsity, 1981.

———. "Sanctuary Symbolism in the Garden of Eden Story." In *I Studied Inscriptions from Before the Flood: Ancient Near Eastern, Literary, and Linguistic Approaches to Genesis 1–11,* edited by Richard S. Hess and David Toshio Tsumura, 400–403. Winona Lake, IN: Eisenbrauns, 1994.

"Who We Are." *The Canadian Atlas Online.* Canadian Geographic. No pages. http://www.canadiangeographic.ca/atlas/themes.aspx?id=whoweare&sub=whoweare_demographics_birth&lang=En.

Wilke, Jon D. "Churchgoers Believe in Sharing Faith, Most Never Do." August 13, 2012. No pages. http://www.lifeway.com/article/research-survey-sharing-christ-2012.

Woudstra, Marten H. *The Book of Joshua.* Edited by R. K. Harrison. The New International Commentary on the Old Testament. Grand Rapids: Eerdmans, 1982.

Wright, Christopher J. H. *The Message of Ezekiel: A New Heart and a New Spirit.* Edited by J. A. Motyer. Downers Grove, IL: InterVarsity, 2001.

———. "Mission as a Matrix for Hermeneutics and Biblical Theology." In *Out of Egypt: Biblical Theology and Biblical Interpretation,* edited by Craig Bartholomew et al., 102–43. Scripture and Hermeneutics. Grand Rapids: Zondervan, 2004.

———. *The Mission of God: Unlocking the Bible's Grand Narrative.* Downers Grove, IL: IVP Academic, 2006.

Wright, N. T. "Jerusalem in the New Testament." In *Jerusalem: Past and Present in the Purposes of God,* edited by P. W. L. Walker, 53–77. Cambridge: Tyndale, 1992.

———. "Opportunities for the Church-in-Mission." Lecture delivered at Newbigin House of Studies, San Francisco. November 17, 2011. http://newbiginhouse.org/media/.

———. *Surprised by Hope: Rethinking Heaven, the Resurrection, and the Mission of the Church.* New York: HarperOne, 2008.

Young, Pamela Dickey. "Two by Two: Religion, Sexuality and Diversity." In *Religion and Diversity in Canada,* edited by Lori G. Beaman and Peter Beyer, 85–101. Religion and the Social Order 16. Leiden: Brill, 2008.

Youngblood, Ronald F. "1, 2 Samuel." In *Deuteronomy, Joshua, Judges, Ruth, 1 and 2 Samuel,* edited by Frank E. Gaebelein, 552–1104. Expositor's Bible Commentary 3. Grand Rapids: Zondervan, 1992.

Index of Scripture References